STILLWATER
BOOKS

D1202628

RETURNING FROM AFAR

A MEMOIR

Benson Bobrick

STILLWATER BOOKS

Brattleboro, Vermont

STILLWATER BOOKS
P. O. Box 2218
Brattleboro, VT 05303

Designed by Helen Merena
Cover and page iv (image cropped and reversed)
Thomas Fearnley, *Landscape with a Wanderer*, 1830,
National Museum of Art Architecture and Design, Oslo

Manufactured in the United States of America

First Printing August 2019

Library of Congress Control Number: 2019910795
Bobrick, Benson, date.
Returning From Afar: a memoir/
Benson Bobrick
p. cm.
Includes bibliographical references in endnotes (p.)
1. Memoir

ISBN 978-0-578-52642-3

For Hilary,

& THE MEMBERS OF MY FAMILY,

LIVING & DEAD,

EACH ONE

CONTENTS

EVERNESS

One thing does not exist: Oblivion.
God saves the metal and he saves the dross,
And his prophetic memory guards from loss
The moons to come, and those of evenings gone.
Everything *is*: the shadows in the glass
Which, in between the day's two twilights, you
Have scattered by the thousands, or shall strew
Henceforward in the mirrors that you pass.
And everything is part of that diverse
Crystalline memory, the universe;
Whoever through its endless mazes wanders
Hears door on door click shut behind his stride,
And only from the sunset's farther side
Shall view at last the Archetypes and the Splendors.

—Jorge Luis Borges
(Trans. Richard Wilbur)

Part One

❦

"Everyone should live his life twice,
for the first attempt is always blind."

—Edwin Muir,
The Story and the Fable

CHAPTER ONE

✻

If the unexamined life is not worth living, it is also not worth writing about.

In 1972, the year my father earned his place on President Nixon's "Enemies List,"* I was humbled with astonished pride. My father had been a kind of Goliath to me in my youth, looming over me with his gigantic, red-faced rages. And the turbulent environment in which I had been raised had darkened my view of him, in so far as I could view him, from my limited stance. Yet in time he had also emerged as a Biblical David, confronting the corrupt and powerful, including the mighty ogre in our public sphere. He had recently founded the "National Committee for the Impeachment of the President" that had run a two-page ad in *The New York Times*. That ad—and this enthralled me, too—had been covertly funded by Alexander Calder, the great sculptor, and his wife, Louisa, the grand-niece of Henry James. It was the first public call, prior to the Watergate Scandal, for Nixon's impeachment, and charged him with conducting an illegal war in Vietnam. It created a national sensation and roused Nixon's ire. Seventeen days later, the Watergate Break-In occurred, a crime that the ad, acting as a leavening yeast to Nixon's gloomy fears, may have helped precipitate—so some would surmise.

*Confidential White House Memo, Joanne Gordon to John Dean, June 2, 1972.

Yet it was also about this time that I had begun to see my father, as well as others, in a more complex light. That new understanding was part of a process of deep reassessment that would come to illuminate every aspect of my world.

*

The most interesting part of life is the growth of the soul. The rest, in the main, is theater—names, dates, adventures, masquerades, escapes. A memoir can be—as I hope this is—not only a record of events, but of the stages of an evolution, in so far as that can be grasped. The light that sheds on the life means more than any cavalcade of facts. "What use is the right fact," as a character remarks in a story by P.L. Travers, "when the point of view is wrong?"

The process of self-discovery makes living worthwhile.

Sometime in my mid to late 30s, I read *Lost in the Cosmos* by Walker Percy and was deeply affected by his distinction between an organism in an environment, governed entirely by natural appetites and needs, and a Self in the world that can only be satisfied by contact with the mythic and divine. In time, I came to understand that God can not always save you from evil—from "the slings and arrows of outrageous fortune," which are rampant—but from being evil. And by not being evil, you—and those around you—may be spared many evil things. In the words of St. John of the Cross: "I am made and unmade not by the things that happen to me, but by my reactions to them." And so we forge our souls.

In the parable of the Prodigal Son in *The Gospel According to St. Luke*, the son "comes to himself"—that is, he wakes up. Sleep is a far away state. When you return to yourself, it is always as if you were returning from afar. There is no middling distance for the soul.

When Pegasus, the faithful, mortal winged horse of Zeus, was transformed into a constellation, a single feather from one of his wings fell to earth where the town of Tarsus arose. When I was a child, I was fascinated by a colored illustration in a family Bible of St. Paul as a boy standing on the wharves of Tarsus looking out to sea. That legend of the feather is congenial to my soul, for it links my unworthy life with a delicate lightness to St. Paul. In my horoscope, Markab, a troublous bright star in Pegasus where the shoulder joins the wing, was conjunct my Sun at birth. Its name is often derived from the Arab word for "ship" or "saddle" (meaning anything ridden or steered), though some take it from the Hebrew "merhak," meanng "returning from afar."

The deepest meanings in our lives converge.

*

I am amazed at how little of my early childhood I recall. While it lasted it seemed to go on forever; now it comes back to me in intermittent flashes—a revolving beam of light from a distant coast. My mother died when I was eight, and the trauma of her loss seems to have eclipsed almost every memory I have of my life before that time.

Recently I was reminded of some things I hadn't thought of in sixty years. I remember a tree-house my parents built for my brothers in the yard; a grape arbor and a patch of rhubarb in the back; trying to dig to China under the latticed porch; my mother tending flowers in the front; the tall milkweed in a patch of nearby forest, which we called "train woods"; the great corrugated section of rusting water pipe that I hid in when the train went by; catching my shoe once on the track and tumbling down the embankment just in time; an abandoned chicken coop that I imagined as my outlaw hideout; and a black boy who stayed overnight with me from time to time in first grade.

The beam of light revolves. I recall now, too, our large orange cat named "Lucinda" and her orange successor, Tangerine; being madly in love in the second grade with a girl named Carey Ford; kissing her wildly behind the apartment building where she lived; being told in the first or second grade I might be held back; asking adults at street intersections to "cross me"; fishing in two large ponds we called twin lakes (now Huguenot Lake) near the local high school; a knife fight between two teen-age boys, one black, one white, on a school athletic field—their blades taped toward the tip to allow for slashing but not deep, plunging wounds; wandering through a fenced-in electric power station one day on my way home from school; being apprehended; a policeman coming that night to the door; at which my father took me upstairs in a fury and struck me so hard it left a scar on one side of my head; and feeling hopeless, as if in a desert, in a parched and blighted world.

*

Of my mother, three clear, precious memories remain. In the first, I am emerging from Sunday School (I must have been about five) at St. John's Methodist Church in New Rochelle. I am clinging to my mother's skirt and my eyes are at about the level of the steps as they descend to the street. I notice—I can see it still—some couples descending together in perfect time. I look up at her and ask: "What does it mean when people are in step?" She looks down at me and says, "That means they're in love."

In the second, she is teaching me to spell; or rather, we are playing a spelling game. We are in a little flower garden in front of our house (again, I must have been about six), and I am arbitrarily stringing letters together to make words. Each time I do this, I ask her: "What does that spell?" Most of the time, she says, "It doesn't spell anything, dear." But now and then, it does. When that happens, it gives me a tremendous sense of power—a God-like power, really, like the power of the Word.

In the third, we engage in an antiphonal exchange of bedtime endearments—a ritual response. It must never vary. "Good night," I say.

"Good night."

"Sweet dreams."

"Same to you."

As long as this exchange is complete, I feel secure. But once or twice my mother forgets her part. I become terribly upset and can't settle down until the right words are said.

These mingled images, suffused with a kind of tender sorrow, compose for me the essential picture of my earliest years. They strike their own resounding themes; and in the weight they carried in the life I lived, supersede, perhaps, all other facts, whatever they might be.

*

"In my end is my beginning"—is this not true? I was born on the morning of March 15, 1947 at 190 Waverly Place in Greenwich Village, New York. By the time and place of our advent, the celestial clock is set, and our lives described by dialogues of light in the constant revolutions of the sky.

My father was a lawyer; my mother, at the time of my birth, a housewife. I was the youngest of three sons, and perhaps because I was expected to be the last child, christened with three family names—Benson-Baker-Bobrick—imposing (it seems to me now) upon my fragile frame the heaviest branches of our family tree. A month later, on April 13, I was baptized at the family apartment by my maternal grandfather, a Methodist Bishop. The certificate is quaintly adorned by two watercolor angels praying over a sleeping child. Between them is a hopeful little rhyme:

> The day they christened me, the angels
> Sat among the clouds
> And though I can't be sure of it,
> I think their heads were bowed.
> We couldn't really hear them
> But I think they said a prayer,
> That God would guide me as I grew
> And keep me in his care.

Not long after I was born, we moved to the suburb of New Rochelle, which my Huguenot forbears had helped to found in 1688. The Old Drake Homestead, which was said to be their original dwelling, was still standing then. Our own modest home at 87 Fifth Avenue was on a lower-to middle-income suburban street.

*

I am proud to be an ethnic mix. On my father's side—Russian, Polish, Jewish; on my Mother's—English, French Huguenot, Swedish, Dutch. Genetic testing tells me that I am 49% Jewish (Ashkenazi), 40% Anglo-Saxon, and 11% Viking (Swedish, Varangian/Slav). My mother's side of the family is pretty well mapped. My father's, obscure. When I was growing up, my father had almost nothing to say about his roots. When pressed, he would wave away the question with his hand. Once he joked that some forebears might have been "horse thieves." His sister, Sylvia, claimed that one had been "a violinist to the Tsar." Either may or may not be true. In any case, my father had a healthy disregard for pedigree. Once, when someone at a party began to boast about his line, he exclaimed, "As a Jew, I'm related to the Prophets!" which stilled all other claims. But there were no family stories of shtetls or pogroms, or of the marginalized if defiant world in which most Jews were forced to live. All that my brothers and I really knew was that my father's father, Paul, had been born in Smolensk; fled to Warsaw, Poland, as a young man to escape the Tsar's draft; and there met and married Anna Lindner, a red-haired corseteer. Their first child was my father, born in 1902 on Christmas Day.

In 1904, the family emigrated to the United States; changed or simplified their last name (from Bobrovnikov, perhaps); and settled in Brooklyn, where Paul opened a grocery store. He had business acumen; did well; and managed to secure the American Sugar Refinery franchise for Boro Park, as I understand it, so that anyone wanting sugar had to obtain it from him. All four children (my father, his brother, and two sisters) helped in managing the stock. My Aunt Sylvia told me that even in her old age she could guess to the ounce the precise weight of any bag of sugar she picked up. The store prospered, at least into the 1930s, but Paul subsequently lost much of what he had in a bad real estate deal. For the rest of their lives my father's parents lived quite modestly in a little building at 81 Tehama Street in the Flatbush section of Brooklyn. I don't remember them at all, for they both died when I was about five. Anna, who was said to be warm and kind, used to take the subway from Brooklyn to Greenwich Village, where I was born, and climb three flights of stairs with homemade soup.

If my father's family linked me to the Old World of Eastern Europe, my mother's tied me to the New. Her colonial forebears had come early, tilled the land, and fought and died on both sides of the Revolutionary War. The English, stem and branch, were the "Bakers"; the Dutch and Swedish, the "Bensons"; the French Huguenot, the "Valleaus." As I remarked in the Preface to *Angel in the Whirlwind*, my book on the American Revolution (from which the following is drawn), "some had been in America since 1649, settled New Amsterdam and New Rochelle, served for three quarters of a century in the king's American wars; but when the Revolution came were divided among themselves. The Bakers were all staunch patriots. But within the Benson and Valleau families, brother stood against brother, father against son. At least two served in the Continental Army, three in Loyalist (pro-British) troops. One of the patriots, Isaiah Valleau, was captured by the British, and succumbed in prison to starvation and disease. His younger brother Peter remained a Loyalist to the end. One of the Loyalists (Matthew Benson, an officer in the King's Orange Rangers) had his property expropriated by his brother, John, who became a patriot judge. Matthew's eldest son was killed by patriots in battle; John's son witnessed the execution of Major John Andre (Benedict Arnold's co-conspirator) on October 2, 1780 at Tappan."

A story handed down for generations had it that on the day Matthew's son was killed, his mother, sitting by a window, saw him ride by. Overjoyed at the sight of her boy, she ran and called her husband, only to learn later that he had fallen in battle far from home at the time his apparition appeared.

At the end of the war, Matthew Benson and Peter Valleau were both exiled with many others to the Cataraqui area of Western Canada, north of Lake Ontario. Matthew sailed on July 4, 1783, with his wife and surviving children from New York City on the British transport Hope, wintered with some four hundred other refugees in canvas tents at Sorel northeast of Montreal, and in the spring of 1784 proceeded by bateaux up the St. Lawrence River, dragging the boats by hand up numerous rapids to Adolphustown on the Bay of Quinte, where they arrived on June 16, 1784. In the beginning, Matthew worked as a mill hand and during the 'Hungry Years' (1793–94) survived in part on flour dust swept up from the floor.

Peter Valleau also settled in the same region and there in 1801 his daughter married Matthew's son. Eventually both families prospered, thanks in part to generous land-grants from the Crown. In the civic life of Prince Edward County, they played a vital role. In the historic White Chapel graveyard outside Picton, Ontario, every third or fourth headstone bears the Benson family name. Meanwhile, the Bakers had remained in the States, were eventually joined by marriage to the Valleau-Benson line (a reconciliation in my blood) and came down squarely on the same side of the other great American divide—the Civil War.

*

By and large, the Bensons were blacksmiths, wheelwrights, and farmers; the Valleaus (who had come from the Isle de Re on the west coast of France) assessors, surveyors, and town supervisors in the civic life of New York. Meanwhile, in the 1700s, several branches of the Baker family had also settled in Connecticut, New York, and Vermont. By the fourth generation, some had moved to the Midwest, and eventually to Coles County, Illinois. I know little about them, except that some of their lives must have been hard, as shown by their severe and weathered faces, unsexed by toil to a neutrality of features, deeply furrowed like the fields they plowed. Aside from land records, real estate transactions, deeds of purchase, sale, marriage certificates and the like, none of the Bensons, Bakers, or Valleaus left much of a personal story, until we come to my great-grandfather, Benjamin W. ("Webb") Baker, on my mother's side. He was a substantial man, and left a substantial record, which deserves to be recalled.

Born on Thanksgiving Day, 1841 in Hutton Township, Coles

County, Illinois, Webb grew up on a farm. His father taught school part time, but most of his immediate relatives were farmers— though an Episcopal Rector, a Methodist Circuit Rider, and a Baptist Minister were among them, too. There was also a touch of ancestral glory in his blood. His mother was the granddaughter of Elijah Adams, a soldier of the Revolution and, according to family tradition, a cousin of John Adams, second President of the United States. But in Webb's eyes, Elijah gave glory enough. As a soldier of the Continental line, he had reenlisted twice, and fought Indians and Tories from the Mohawk Valley to Lake Champlain. On Lake Champlain, he had served in a row-galley under Benedict Arnold, when Arnold was still loyal. After the war, he was granted an annual pension of $79.95 a year. He lived to be 89 and died on December 12, 1844, when Webb was three.

By then, Webb's parents had bought a forty-acre spread and had begun to farm the land. Though the land was high, dry, and rich, the work was hard, and in the mechanics of it hadn't changed much since "Ruth had gleaned in the fields of Boaz." A good spot for a cabin was found on a knoll near a spring, but the cabin itself was spare, with four rooms built around a central stone chimney, and clapboards laid on joists to form a loft. There was a large barn with fenced-in stalls for livestock, a root cellar for summer storage, and a smokehouse for the winter preservation of meats.

By all accounts—as I recounted in *Testament*, a little book about his life—Webb "lived the life of the ordinary farm boy of the period, attending school briefly during the winter months where he learned to 'read, rite and cipher to the rule of three.' He learned to spell out of Noah Webster's *American Spelling Book*, to read from McGuffey's reader, and was taught facts about the world around him from a book called *The Science of Common Things*. In helping to manage the farm, he was proficient at his tasks, and had to learn them all quite early, in fact, for in 1845 his father suddenly died. In time he grew into a strong, able, self-reliant (if somewhat headstrong) young man, stout but fit, tall, fair complexioned, with dark hair and hazel eyes."

Inevitably, he got caught up in the ferment that preceded the Civil War. At the age of sixteen, he stood in the audience of one of the Lincoln-Douglas debates, and when the war began, answered Abraham Lincoln's first call for volunteers. In early August 1865, he entrained for St. Louis, Missouri; and on the 9th was mustered into service for three years at the Arsenal Park. His company (Company E of the 25th Illinois Regiment of Volunteer Infantry) was composed almost entirely of Coles County men and included a number of friends, two cousins, and a stepbrother, too.

Webb fought almost the whole war through. In the course of it, he wrote some ninety remarkable letters home—in aggregate, among the most compelling the war produced. If some men saw the war as an adventure. Webb was fired by patriotic pride. His grandfather had staunchly opposed his going, but once at St. Louis, Webb promptly wrote to explain: "I ask forgiveness for going contrary to your wishes. But I feel I have only discharged a duty which as a good citizen I owe to my country, to my friends & to liberty itself. So now I ask your blessing, as with my face to the enemy's land I go forward. As long as this arm has strength to wield a sword or handle a rifle; as long as these feet can carry me & these eyes can see to direct my steps, I expect to march forward unless they [the Rebels] submit to the Constitution & laws."

At St. Louis, Webb adapted to the doleful realities of camp life—poor shelter, moldy rations, fever, and disease—and as he waited to be tested, pondered his hopes and fears: "I almost feel anxious to be in a battle," he confided to his mother, who hung on every word, "& yet I am almost afraid. I feel very brave sometimes & think if I should be in an engagement, I never would leave the field alive unless the stars & stripes floated triumphant. I do not know how it may be. If there is a battle & I should fall, tell with pride & not with grief that I fell in defense of liberty. Pray that I may be a true soldier."

In time, he calmly embraced his fate. After four months of service, he wrote to a cousin: "I have seen some pretty hard times, went hungry a good many days, slept many a night on the ground with a stone for a pillow & went some nights without sleep. But that is nothing for a soldier . . . .We don't look for easy times here." He also sought, in more than stoic fashion, to turn it to account. "It is true there are a great many hardships to be endured, but those I expected to find, & in them I find pleasure in the tendency they have to develop the unselfish in one's character." Before long, he embarked on a program of self-improvement that he would never forsake. He took up mathematics (for which he had a gift); was tutored by his staff sergeant in grammar, using *Bullion's Grammar* as a guide; and tried to read as much history as he could—books on Napoleon Bonaparte and ancient Greece, for example—even as his unit fought its way through the South and West. He marched through snow and freezing rain from central Missouri southward across the Ozark Mountains; up into the cane brakes of Kentucky; down into the blistering heat of Mississippi; and across the mountains and valleys of Georgia and Tennessee. In the course of it all, he covered some 3,000 miles on foot and another 1,700 or so by boat and rail; took part in numerous major battles (including Stones River, Tennessee and Chickamauga, Georgia, among the bloodiest of the war); was wounded three times, once severely; lost friends and relations; and (a sorrow that would never heal) buried his only, beloved brother, John—after the Battle of Perryville, Kentucky—on the field.

On August 1, 1864, with his regiment before Atlanta, his service expired and on September 5, 1864, he was mustered out at Camp Butler, Springfield, Illinois.

Webb emerged with his left arm partly disabled, a chunk of flesh missing from his back, and "an ounce of Rebel lead" in one shoulder for the rest of his life. "Though wearied and saddened by the war, he believed," as I wrote in *Testament*, "it had been fought to good purpose. He had thought so at the beginning; and he thought so at the end. But he had no taste for war itself. He would later write: 'The tendency of war is to disorganize society, to arrest the wheels of civilization, to drag men down in the scale of manhood and to add to the sum of human misery.' He had seen enough of that."

Webb went home to his farm, where he persevered for a few years, then gave it up and returned to school. A student by inclination, "he was intellectually hungry, and lost—and found—himself in history." The story of modern science intrigued him, but it was political and religious history that held him most in thrall. "With Protestant pride," as I wrote, "he rejoiced in the fate of the Spanish Armada; was repelled by the Inquisition; and scornful of the presumptions of a Renaissance pope who pretended to divide the discoverable world between the two great Catholic powers of Portugal and Spain . . . He also wondered if the fate of French imperial ambitions in the New World had ultimately suffered because 'there was upon them the unavenged blood of St. Bartholomew's Day.'" Webb, in truth, had something of the Puritan soldier in him, and like one of Cromwell's "Ironsides," had gone into battle with a copy of the "Soldier's Pocket Bible" in his boots.

It was the Puritan settlers, indeed, he most admired. "You can more easily prove the perseverance of the saints by these men than by the Bible," he wrote. "When they husked their first harvest of twenty acres of corn they met and thanked God and sung Psalms, and offered prayers. Then they built a church and beside it a school-house, and then a college while they yet lived in log houses covered with clapboard roofs. The God who nourished Jacob when he was small, and Israel on the breast of Egypt, took this great country in His arms and carried it."

There was a natural eloquence in him that had begun to shine.

The more Webb thought about the Civil War, the more he understood it in terms of the larger contest between tyranny and freedom—both in the world of his own day, and reaching back in time. In his view, the "same love of human rights that had sustained the patriotic band on the plains of Marathon [when the ancient Greeks defeated the Persians], had prompted the French Revolution, commanded at Yorktown, emancipated the Russian serfs, and directed the course of the Civil War."

Webb set his heart on teaching and in 1866 applied for admission to Illinois State Normal University, a teachers' college founded a decade before near Bloomington. He wrote an essay on the Battle of Marathon to demonstrate what he could do; was accepted; and enrolled that fall. At the time, "the university consisted of one handsomely-domed three-story building built on a hill between a cornfield and an abandoned spur of track. Its president was Richard Edwards, a learned man of Calvinist bent, who believed in the operation of a Divine Intelligence in the control of human affairs. In addition to his other duties, Edwards gave a series of lectures on 'The Heritage of Culture' that traced 'the achievements of history through the character and precepts of great men.'" Under his direction, Webb embarked on an ambitious, five-year course of study that, in breadth and scope, might be favorably compared to the best college curriculums today. He must have excelled overall, for upon his graduation in 1870, he was immediately taken into the faculty as Principal of the Practice School. Meanwhile, he had met a young woman, Martha Frances Henry, at the college and when she didn't come back to school one year, Webb sent word that he was building a house and was coming to get her at Christmas. He did and they were married and started a family of their own. In subsequent years, he pursued his advanced studies at nearby Illinois Wesleyan, from which he eventually earned a doctorate in history.

If education was a passion for him, "the ministry," as I wrote, "was in his blood. Both of his grandparents had been preachers— one Methodist, the other Baptist—and the first two churches in Hutton Township had been built by their hands. Webb himself had been raised in a moderately religious fashion, and during the war had regularly attended service in camp. But he seems not to have thought of the ministry until 1874, when he suddenly felt the call. He was admitted on trial to the Central Illinois Conference of the Methodist Church, assigned to various towns, and in all of his early pastorates organized Chautauqua reading circles, evidently believing with John Wesley that he should 'press reading upon the people. They cannot grow in grace otherwise.'" His own family life was marked by "daily morning prayers and a once a week joyous singing of hymns." Meanwhile, the government, having judged him "disabled from obtaining his subsistence by manual labor," had granted him a pension of $12 a month.

Webb rose in the Church, was a pastor in Denver, Colorado, where he built St. James Church; made a Presiding Elder of the Illinois Streator District in 1885, and over the next fifteen years distinguished himself in the administration of Methodist schools: first, as the Financial Secretary of Illinois Wesleyan; then, as the President of two colleges—Chaddock, in Quincy, Illinois; and Missouri Wesleyan, in Cameron, Missouri.

He had come a long way from the young soldier who had tried to learn some grammar on the march.

Moreover, as a man of some local prominence, he was often called upon to make speeches on public occasions—on the 4th of July, for example, or Memorial Day. In one July 4th address, delivered in 1896, he touchingly recalled his roots, as he tied the day's observance to the land. "It seems providential," he said, "that this festive day should come at this season of the year . . . when the smaller cereals are ripening and being harvested, when a good estimate of what our prosperity is for the year can be made, at the time when men have an hour for rest between the finished cultivation and the gathering of small grain." In speaking of the war, he had no taste for platitudes. One Memorial Day, he told a large crowd: "Especially today we commemorate the dead. And yet I would also have you remember the sacrifices of those soldiers living . . . Many say we ought to forget the past; we ought not to stir up bad blood by services which keep alive the memory of our great fratricidal strife. What? Shall I tell my children that their father gave the three best years of his life to a foolish war? Shall I tell them, 'Your father had an only brother, John, possessed of almost every human virtue, who foolishly threw his life away? Or, worse still, that Papa found his mangled form foremost in the front, where he had fallen, in battle, for nothing? God forbid! . . . Let us teach [our children] that the men who stayed at home and got rich on the spoils of war, while they talked loud about patriotism . . . are not to be compared in point of true manhood with the men whom they were willing to sacrifice."

From a non-Abolitionist Unionist Webb had also developed

into an ardent apostle of Emancipation, opposing discrimination of any kind. Toward the end of his life, he even stood in the forefront of the woman's suffrage movement, for (as he wrote) he could find no argument to justify the vote for men that wouldn't apply to women, too.

Though he had a rough exterior, roughened by life, Webb was known for his manifold acts of kindness which revealed a tenderness and delicacy underneath. In his personal and professional life, he also showed great fortitude. He lost three of his six children, yet kept to almost all of his official commitments without pausing. How many secret tears he must have shed! His income was ever modest, despite his selfless toil, and at Missouri Wesleyan, in addition to his administrative tasks, he taught seven classes a day. He also gave three sermons on Sundays, and often traveled at night in connection with his pastoral cares.

Meanwhile, his wife, Martha, who suffered from asthma, had undergone "static electricity treatments," which failed to give relief. These were succeeded by medicated cigarettes laced with stramonium, then promoted as the latest cure. Derived from the thorn-apple or "witches' weed," stramonium was an antispasmodic rich in belladonna alkaloids that eased bronchoconstriction. However, it also had hallucinogenic properties that produced night terrors and other neurasthenic ills.

In the fall of 1906, Webb and his wife went south to Defuniak Springs, Florida in search of a therapeutic clime. En route, on his 65th birthday, Webb stopped at Chattanooga, Tennessee and walked the National Cemetery where 15,000 Union soldiers were interred. It seemed to him then, as he thought about his faith, family, and friends, that he had had a blessed life. Yet he felt that in God's service he might have done more. He told his eldest son, James: "I expect you to be better and do more for the income of the Kingdom than your father has." Meanwhile, Webb's own health had begun to fail and he was diagnosed with acute nephritis, known then as "Bright's Disease." In November of 1908, he suffered a crippling stroke and seven months later, on June 20, 1909, he died.

He is buried in Oakwood Cemetery in Metamora, Illinois.

In a eulogy delivered at his funeral, a longtime friend and fellow pastor, declared: "Dr. Baker impressed himself on the community in which he labored as a man who had a message in which he absolutely believed ... His personal character was uncompromisingly honest, and . . . he went straight to the mark he had set, always higher up. He had that in his character which compelled men to believe in him ... He was a most lovable, noble and manly man." He also had a fine sense of humor about himself. The story goes, as I wrote in *Testament*, that when he first began to court his future wife, he was a bit self-conscious about his weight, having always been a large man physically, even as a soldier in the ranks. But she deftly put him at his ease. One day, when they were at a student social together, the girls were asked to write a rhymed description of their escorts. She wrote of him:

> All flesh is grass—so doth the good Book say—
> And grass, when mown, is turned to hay.
> When Father Time his scythe to you doth take,
> My! What a haystack you will make.

The homely wit and agrarian grandeur of these lines seem fit for his epitaph.

CHAPTER TWO

~

My maternal grandfather, James Chamberlain Baker, was Webb's eldest son. And he fulfilled his father's hopes. I remember him now as a kindly, learned man, remote from me in time and space (he was 68 when I was born, though he lived to be 90) who made his home in California, three thousand miles away. Yet he was a constant, mighty, and benevolent presence in my life. A man of some eminence, as the leading bishop of the largest Protestant denomination in the United States, he was once described by my father as "the Pope of the Methodist Church." For a time, if any one could claim that title, he could. Certainly, he was an ecumenical leader and churchman of great standing, especially in the development of American Methodism into the huge, mainstream denomination it became.

From first to last, he lived a very intentional life. Born on June 2, 1879, in Sheldon, Illinois, he was an accelerated student; graduated from college at 19; taught English Literature and Greek at Missouri Wesleyan for four years; married, in 1901, the school's Preceptor of Studies, Lena Sarah Benson; entered the ministry; and in 1902 enrolled in the Boston University School of Theology. He held a series of pastorates from 1902 to 1928 (first in Ashland, Massachusetts, then in McLean and Urbana, Illinois); served as

Bishop for Korea, Manchuria, and Japan from 1928 to 1932; afterwards in California; was Chairman of the International Missionary Council from 1941 to 1947; a founding member of the World Council of Churches in 1948; President of the Council of Bishops of the Methodist Church from 1948 to 1949; and an advisor to the U.S. Delegation at the founding of the United Nations.

Yet with all his public honors, for much of his life he was known primarily as the "Father of the Wesley Foundation," a church-based student center founded in 1913 in Champaign-Urbana at the University of Illinois. It became the model for student ministries of all faiths at tax-supported institutions of higher learning, and at my grandfather's urging, the Catholic Church created the analogous Columbus Foundation (later the Newman Society) in 1920, and the university's resident Rabbi the first Hillel Foundation in 1923. Hillel was later adopted by B'nai Brith and has since grown into the largest Jewish youth organization in the world. Not surprisingly, my grandfather came to enjoy an honored place in the modern chronicles of both faiths.

His upbringing strongly shaped his life. His parents, he wrote, had "great character and integrity," enjoyed mutual love and respect, and "established their home on a high level" with books, music, and "worthy causes," all anchored in religious observance, including morning prayers. He revered his father as "a notable character—rugged, vigorous, keen minded—a great human person," "very positive" and given to "gigantic laughter"; and his mother for her tender lovingkindness and daily fortitude. He also acquired from her "an interest in great characters; concern for world missions; and a life-long hatred of the deadly ravages of alcohol." When he read the short chapter in J.M. Barrie's little book about his mother titled "How My Mother Got Her Soft Face," it brought his own to mind. Barrie wrote: "When you looked into my mother's eyes you knew, as if He had told you, why God sent her into the world—it was to open the minds of all who looked to beautiful thoughts. And that is the beginning and end of literature. Those eyes . . . have guided me through life, and I pray God they may remain my only earthly judge to the last."

Though my grandfather's early reading was steeped in the classics, he drew his own kind of sustenance from Christian guidebooks, too, such as *How To Get On In the World*, or *A Ladder to Practical Success*, published by *The Christian Herald* in 1895. He read this book when he was sixteen and embraced its emphasis on "The Need for Constant Effort," "Duty as the end and aim of the highest life," "Perseverance against discouragements," the virtues of strict temperance, and so on. Above all, it advised, "In all your transactions remember the final account." He carefully underlined the sentence: "Character is crystallized habit, the result of training and conviction" and I'm sure he worked to developed good habits early in his life. Some of the guidebook's homilies were melodramatic and warned in droll terms of the fate of yielding to any temptation, but it also leavened its maxims with apt quotations from Shakespeare, Milton, George Herbert, Erasmus, Cicero, Vergil, Horace, and others, and on the whole was an edifying work. Notably, it praised "a good book" as "the urn of a life, enshrining the best thoughts of which that life was capable" and commended biographies "of those whom it is well to imitate"—an idea my grandfather sought to pass on to me.

As a young teacher, he explored the leading lights of contemporary thought and became so enamored of the New England Transcendentalists that for a time his father feared his faith might be beguiled. On August 1, 1899, Webb wrote to him: "Have a good time and get all the good you can but don't make a mistake in your heroes. Lowell and Holmes and Longfellow may be great and are but they are not the Man who made the world. There is hardly a poor of the poorest Methodist preachers who has been faithful to his work abiding in the love of the Infinite Precious Christ and keeping his commandments who has not done more for the world than either or all of the[se] men. I do not disparage them but do not put them first in the redemption of the world."

My grandfather's response was possibly guarded, for in the following year Webb pressed the point home. In a remarkable letter, made up almost entirely of a single, long, unpunctuated sentence, he wrote: "Hang on to the old Methodist standards and the doctrine of the Divinity of Jesus and the vicarious sacrifice and instantaneous conversion and salvation by faith and the witness of the spirit and the resurrection of the body and the fall of Adam, and the iniquity—depravity—of the human heart and the hourly need of God's help and the inspiration of the Scriptures—the Old Testament Scriptures from Genesis to Malachi, including the story of the Garden of Eden—the snake story—the story of Job and the story of Jonah and the story of Noah and the story of Joseph and the story of Moses and of the Red Sea and all of the Old Testament—as a book not of cunningly devised fables nor old wives tales, but a sure word of inspiration spoken by holy men of old as they were moved by the Holy Ghost—men who know more than [academic theologians] and whose word shall abide in the present form to be preached to the world as God's Word after these gentlemen with all their wisdom shall be forgotten—the very places that know them now as mighty theological chieftains having forgotten them."

My grandfather's thirst for general knowledge was not to be constrained. At Boston University's School of Theology, he was introduced to Biblical textual criticism and new theological trends, and his "take-home quizzes" evolved into substantial essays, fifty pages or more, on such topics as "Empiricism and Rationalism," "Personal Idealism," and "Ethics," which he expounded with clarity and depth. The leading light of the faculty then was Borden Parker Bowne, a Christian philosopher and Methodist theologian who once described his own views as a kind of "Transcendental Empiricism" combining the thought of Berkeley and Kant. His mature doctrine of "Personalism"—that the human person is the supreme reality of Creation—later reverberated through the thought of Martin Luther King, Jr., whom one of Bowne's pupils taught.

Webb was happy enough for his son to develop his intellectual powers—for, after all, as a young man he had done the same. But on November 8, 2003, he once more warned against the pretensions of "higher criticism" in matters of faith: "Religion is an actual experience, a reality, and entity, a certainty, as much demonstrated to one who has it as the theorem that the square of the hypotenuse of a right triangle is equal to the sum of the squares of the other two sides." As for Bowne himself: "I ... know that he is a philosopher, very eminent, but he is of the Porch and the head, with little that reaches the heart ... I want you to know his Philosophy, but don't take it for religion for it is not and his kind will not save the world, nor hardly touch the masses. I want you to know all knowledge and then bring it to the masses as Jesus did, as Paul did, as Wesley did ... The Gospel is the Power of God unto salvation to every one that believeth, to Jew and Gentile, to Peasant and Philosopher and there is no other." A week later, he added: "The hope of philosophy is the hope of Bolingbroke and Hobbes, mighty philosophers but leaping into the dark ... The Word is the power of God unto salvation to every one that complies with the condition, whether he knows any philosophy or not. How I love you and long for you to be a gospel preacher who counts the Word of authority and the church of supernatural origin."

In the end, my grandfather emerged close to where his father stood. Though he often liked to quote Matthew Arnold's ecumenical description of God as "a [divine] power, not ourselves, that makes for righteousness," yet he subscribed to the fundamental Methodist doctrine that all men can be saved because God wants to save them, and that God works to do so through their will. Each person, endowed with free will, can accept grace by repentance, which leads to an inner assurance of salvation—"an inner consciousness of sins having been forgiven, joy, and acceptance by God." At his student pastorate in Ashland, Massachusetts, "a small, old shoe town" from which he commuted to Boston each day, he began to preach himself and develop his own rhetorical gifts. Once more his father advised: "Give them the simple Gospel and leave out all theory, and God will do his part."

In 1905, he returned to Illinois to become the pastor of a tiny church in McLean, where the parsonage was a shack. Two years later, he was appointed to Urbana's Trinity Church and went to his task "with a compelling conviction and a profound sense of mission, as though I were literally being sent." He thrived in his new pastorate, with a congregation that grew under his care, and impressed others (as one admirer wrote) as "a deep and broad student not only of books but of men." For a university pastor, he was also the right man. He was at home with the advancements of science, up to date with current events, and alert to contemporary trends. "We have got to know our time," he wrote, "the currents of thought and feeling. How can we preach to a time that we do not know?"

For him, religion and education were entwined. He was convinced that "the most ominous defect of modern civilization" was "the divorce of the intellectual from the spiritual," and that "a pagan theory of human life" had emerged in that divide to exalt "personal gain by day and passionate indulgence by night." In so far as the culture subscribed to this "unchanneled turmoil of instinct and passion," it formed "a piteous chronicle of diseased frivolity and tainted appetite. We know," he eloquently declared, "something of what it brings in its train—lust and pride, the unspeakable customs of the world's shame, dishonor of the home, the injustice and cruelty that live in the industrial order, . . . the ghastly smile that covers the loveless heart." His antidote was "irresistible good will"—"not," as he explained, "the sickly sentimental thing that some people imagine—a kindly spirit, . . . an easy tolerance; or general good temper"—but a positive, energetic force that "comes from God." God worked through the righteous to fulfill His aims: "God wants to turn humanity right side up, but he needs a fulcrum. Every saved soul is a fixed point on which God can set up his lever . . . and every inspired man is a channel through which the spirit of God can enter humanity." Such a man had "miraculous power . . . A mind set free by God and energized by a great purpose is an incomputable force."

Aside from inaugurating the first Wesley Foundation, he had also begun to establish his reputation as a man who could bridge religious divides. In his own ecumenical heart, he believed in a

Universal Church with kinship in the Fatherhood of God; and in February 1927, he joined with a Catholic priest (Father John A. O'Brien) and a Rabbi (Benjamin Frankel), both of Urbana, in composing an ecumenical prayer—unique for its time:

> Almighty God—We, who are members of different races and faiths, desire together Thy fatherhood and our kinship with each other. In our difference we find that many of our hopes, our fears, our aspirations are one. Thou art Our Father and we are Thy children.
>
> We are heartily sorry for the mists of fear, envy, hatred, suspicion and greed which have blinded our eyes and thrust us asunder. May the light that comes from Thee scatter these mists, cleanse our hearts and give health to our spirits, teach us to put away all bitterness and walk together in the ways of human friendship.
>
> Open our eyes to see that as nature ends in variation, so differences in human beings make for richness in the common life. May we give honor where honor is due—regardless of race, color or circumstance. Deepen our respect for unlikeness and our eagerness to understand one another. Through the deeper unities of the spirit in sympathy, insight and cooperation may we gladly share with each other our best gifts and together seek for a human world fashioned in good under Thy guidance. Amen.

Throughout these years, my grandfather was so engaged in his student work that his first nomination as a bishop in 1924 came as an unwelcome surprise. He declined the honor promptly, but four years later accepted the call. In 1928, he was therefore assigned to the Far East, though he had never been abroad and in fact knew nothing about the Orient first-hand. However, at Urbana he had met each Friday evening with a group of Oriental students to discuss Eastern as well as Western religious thought. That must have played a part. After seeing my mother (then twenty) off on her own first trip abroad in September 1928 to France, my grandparents (both in their early 50s) returned to Urbana where they relinquished their home and drove to the West Coast. At Seattle, they made their final arrangements and on September 8, embarked for Yokohama on the steamship President Cleveland as "ropes of bright colored paper extended from boat to shore." Their voyage across was rough through tur-bulent seas, made all the more so because the ship carried a load of rattan furniture—poor ballast in such waves. For the most part they kept to their cabin and read books on China, Korea, and Japan. My grandfather also had a compact, onion-skin edition of *Milton's Complete Poems* at hand. They reached Yokohama on the morning of September 21st, proceeded to Tokyo, where my grandfather called on Viscount Saito Makoto,* then Governor-General of Korea; boarded a train for the coast; and embarked for the Korean port city of Fusan.

My grandmother, who kept a diary, was dismayed to see so many human beings "used as beasts of burden. The coolie straining at his cart—the rickshaw men panting in the hills—the mothers and young children bent with the burden of babies strapped to their backs." And she was surprised at how casual the customs for sleeping-car travel were, the aisles full of men in all stages of undress "calmly disrobing to the 'uttermost' with absolutely no concern." From Fusan they traveled to Seoul. Korea struck them as "more rugged" than Japan, from what they had seen, "with a wilder beauty," and they were charmed by the terraced rice fields high up in the mountains; the pine and poplar forests, with their varied hues of blue and green; the slow moving oxcarts with sleepy drivers making their way over "surprisingly good roads"; and the yangban or scholarly officials striding haughtily along in

---

*Viscount Saito Makoto was the son of a Samurai of the Mizusawa Clan. An admiral in the Imperial Japanese Navy before becoming Governor-General of Korea, he would later, from May 26, 1932 to July 8, 1934, serve as Prime Minister of Japan. An enlightened man, he was subsequently assassinated on February 26, 1936 by militarists at his Tokyo home.

tall hats and flowing white robes. As they drew near to Seoul, various delegations came to meet them and my grandmother was "reminded," rather over grandly, "of Paul on the Appian Way."

A few days later they left for the Japanese island of Kyushu, where they presided over the dedication of a new chapel for a Methodist school. As it happened, it was the Coronation Year and Kyushu had been selected by divination—based on the directional markings on a cracked tortoise shell—as the site of the sacred rice field that would feed the royal family and its guests. For the ceremonial planting, choice maidens, ritualistically cleansed, had carried individual grains of rice with consecrated chopsticks to the places where they were sown. As harvest time approached, days of sacred dancing, singing, and worship were followed by the visit of an official who presented a sample of the rice for approval to a goddess who dwelt in a nearby shrine.

My grandparents visited many sites. At Peng Yang, they saw the ancient walled city with its six massive gates, and one evening walked out among the ancient imperial tombs that dotted the hills. At Nagasaki, where Christianity had been introduced to Japan, they found a memorial to the first Christian martyrs crucified outside the gates. The island had also been the scene of Madame Butterfly's tragic love. As my grandmother, who took an interest in this heartbreaking tale, noted: "The story is a true one. Nagasaki was formerly—before ships began burning oil—a great coaling center and there were always many foreign ships in port. An English officer on one of these ships was the Japanese girl's lover. From a hill at the entrance of the beautiful harbor, she used to look out over the sea on which her lover had sailed away. As she gazed, she also dreamed—as she sings in the opera—'Some bright day he will come.'" From Hiroshima, they traveled north to the old royal city of Hirosaki where the castle grounds had been converted into a public park. In a hamlet outside Sapporo, they beheld the pitiable Ainu (an outcast subclass of Japan) in their degraded and squalid state.

At Sapporo, my grandfather met with Baron Shosuke Sato, a Methodist convert, who had been a friend and classmate of

Woodrow Wilson's at John Hopkins University. When Wilson was elected President, he had invited the Baron to the White House where he gave him the proof sheets of his own dissertation on Congressional Government. At the recent coronation, the Baron had also been honored by the Emperor, who presented him with a solid silver sake cup engraved with the royal crest. He showed it to my grandparents, along with an old ancestral Samurai sword with a small dagger in the handle of its sheath. In his youth, he told them, as part of his Samurai training, he had learned to throw the dagger with deadly skill.

My grandfather's task in the Far East was to supervise the Methodist missions. In the following four years, his bags were seldom unpacked and he became familiar with most of the national ships in the Pacific as well as those that sailed round the world. With my grandmother by his side, he shuttled back and forth between Japan and Korea, and on numerous occasions went to China, Malaysia, Indonesia, and the Philippines. In all, he covered some 125,000 miles.

He returned to the States in 1932, and as a bishop assigned to California merged his churchly duties with the drive for social reform. He had a strong social conscience; was appalled by injustice, materialistic determinism, and prejudice of any kind. In opposing "crass pagan philosophies of life," including that of unbridled capitalism, he supported the progressive Social Creed that had been set forth for his Church in 1912. As such, he was involved with the Methodist Federation for Social Service, a radical organization founded by Harry F. Ward.

Though not a Communist, or even a Socialist (as my father was in his youth), my grandfather believed that humanity has a prior right over property, and supported the right of labor to strike. At the same time, he was not a Pacifist and believed that some wars (the American Revolution and the Civil War being two) were just. He had served as military chaplain at Fort Benjamin Harrison in Indiana during World War I; and as a member of the War-Work Council of the Y.M.C.A., raised money for buildings, supplies and other help for enlisted men. More broadly, however, he viewed militarism itself as "one of the sins at the root of Christ's crucifixion," and as a member of the National Committee of the American Civil Liberties Union (from 1946 to 1952) opposed compulsory military training at state schools. He also came to the defense of conscientious objectors during World War II, and in January 1943, along with other churchmen—Henry Sloane Coffin, Harry Emerson Fosdick, Reinhold Niebuhr, Rt. Rev. Msgr. John A. Ryan, and Rabbi Abba Hillel Silver—signed a statement that condemned the war-time persecution of Jehovah's Witnesses who refused to salute the flag.

Meanwhile, as relations between the United States and Japan deteriorated, he traveled to Japan early in 1941 and recommended that all American missionaries be withdrawn. When the internment of Japanese Americans began, he condemned it; testified on behalf of their rights before Congress; and on July 2, 1942 held an all-Japanese Methodist Conference at the Santa Anita, California Assembly Center (a pre-internment camp) with armed soldiers guarding the gates.

On June 27, 1945, *The Los Angeles Times* in an editorial attacked him and other church leaders for speaking out on current affairs. It charged that at a recent conference they had committed the church to the abolition of private property and to disclosing the American terms of surrender in advance to the Japanese. "Leave these matters to the experts," the paper said. In his letter of rebuttal, my grandfather noted that the churchmen had merely endorsed a statement by the Cleveland Conference of Protestant churches (chaired, not incidentally, by John Foster Dulles, later Eisenhower's Secretary of State) that: "The right of private property is not an absolute right but a right qualified by the public interest." As for openly announcing the surrender terms, it was thought the Japanese might accept them, thus saving lives.

His reputation remained untarnished. In the spring of 1945, he served as one of three church consultants accredited by the State Department to the founding Conference of the United Nations at San Francisco; and a few months later, on October 21,1945, he embarked with the blessing of President Truman on a goodwill mission to Japan. He represented both the United Methodist Episcopal Church and the International Missionary Council, of which he was then chairman, and with three Protestant colleagues landed at Atsugi Air Field outside Tokyo on the 24th. There he was received by General Douglas MacArthur; flown over Hiroshima and Nagasaki; conferred with Japanese leaders; was granted an interview with Emperor Hirohito; and studied the relief and rehabilitation needs of the people before returning to the States. On the eve of his departure, he was also taken on a tour of Tokyo's formidable harbor defenses to show him how costly it would have been to have taken the city by assault.

During his stay, he saw much of the country's devastation first hand. Seventy of Japan's largest cities lay in ruins and Kyoto, the ancient capital, was "the only city of any size which had not been almost entirely destroyed." The Emperor, in their interview, had seemed to welcome Christian missions, and MacArthur was almost evangelical about the role they might play. The Japanese were desperate to shed their militaristic past, and in Christianity many saw, or seemed to see, "a free and noble way of living" and the foundation of a democratic way of life. One prince of the Imperial House, Prince Naruhiko Higashikuni, had even taken up the study of Christianity with Toyohiko Kagawa, "the St. Francis of Japan."

Before the war, there had been hundreds of Christian schools. Many had been destroyed. At a Presbyterian school in Osaka one morning my grandfather came upon 600 girls at worship on a hillside beyond the ruins of their dorms. Later he made a sentimental journey to Tokyo's Aoyama Gakuin University where he had lived years before. Little remained, he wrote, yet "things were there which cannot be burned and never will be burned," as he communed with his memories and the dead. He also found two occasions to preach—in Tokyo's ruined, roofless Ginza Church, and in a brick church in Kobe surrounded by cinder piles. Two American silk parachutes lay by the pulpit on the floor. His text was: "One in Christ." In a Congregational Church in Tokyo, he also celebrated communion with bread from a ration kit. Two months later, at Christmas, one hundred American soldiers would join with two hundred Japanese in singing Handel's "Messiah" on that very spot.

When MacArthur saw the churchmen off, he said: "You don't know what this has meant, both to the American forces and the Japanese."

*

Over time, my grandfather wrote a number of articles, a little book on *The First Wesley Foundation*, and a booklet entitled *The Church In a World in Ferment*. His public writing had a conventional ring to it but now and then the tone was raised. Some of his unpublished sermons are inspired. His public standing also spanned administrations. Eight years after his mission to Japan, President Eisenhower wrote to thank him—through Sherman Adams, his Chief of Staff—for supporting his message in 1953 to the National Conference of Christians and Jews.

In his person, my grandfather was a relatively tall man, of medium build, with blue eyes and wisps of brown hair swept across a bald crown. He had a ready laugh, a wonderful smile, and a natural dignity that inspired respect. In his general demeanor he proved that to be serious you don't have to be solemn, however devout you are. After my book on the English Bible was published, I received a letter from Paul Woudenberg, the last elder he ordained: "Bishop Baker . . . defined 'bishop' for me," he wrote. "He was held in awe by all of us—majestic yet kindly. The year I was ordained, 1952, he was in a nostalgic mood and everyone was eager to pay tribute to this great man." In another letter, Woudenberg recalled: "Presiding at Conference, [he] was always calming and gracious, . . . His piety and obvious Christian charity gave him an authority that was unmatched." Though down-to-earth in some ways, he was also open—beyond strict doctrine—to other worlds. With Shakespeare's Hamlet, he believed that "There are more things in heaven and earth than are dreamt of" in philosophy, and did not discount psychic experience or insight, occult learning, or other means of accessing invisible realms.

When my grandparents married, he was 22 and she was 25. By all accounts, including their own, their marriage was a happy one. More than 800 people attended their Golden wedding anniversary in June 1951 at the home of a friend where huge baskets of gladiolas adorned the halls. My grandmother reportedly wore a lovely gown of gold brocade made from a Japanese obe. Evidently, I stood in the reception line with my mother and two brothers, though I don't remember a thing. A year or two before, my grandfather's portrait had also been painted twice: for the Methodist headquarters building in Los Angeles, and for the First Wesley Foundation at the University of Illinois.

Throughout his life, my grandfather read widely, knew most of the great novelists and poets, including some of the moderns, and when he preached quoted richly from their work. For diversion, both he and my grandmother liked Westerns, especially those by Ernest Haycox and Luke Short. To keep up with current events, he read periodicals like The *Nation* and *The New Republic*; while books by John Dewey, Charles A. Beard, Alfred North Whitehead, and others kept him abreast of contemporary thought. He prized the theological works of William E. Hocking (in particular, *The Meaning of God in Human Experience* and *The Self, the Body, and Freedom*) and William Newton Clarke. Clarke's *An Outline of Christian Theology* began: "Theology is preceded by religion as botany by the life of plants. Religion is the reality of which theology is the study." My grandfather thought that exact. When it came to public morality, he liked to quote a wry remark by Oliver Wendell Holmes: "Most people are willing to take the Sermon on the Mount as a flag to sail under, but few will use it as a rudder by which to steer."

I wouldn't begin to know him as he was until almost the end of his life.

CHAPTER THREE

॰॰॰

In the world of my childhood, there was one other figure of near-legendary stature—my great uncle Charles G. Howard, who married my grandmother's sister, Susan.

As with my grandfather, I wish I had known him better than I did.

Born in 1892 in Oakwood, Illinois, he had run away from home in his teens (to escape an abusive parent); joined a railroad section gang; thereafter made his way; enlisted in the army; and in 1916 became one of the first motorcycle dispatch riders with the American forces under General John J. Pershing, who was then chasing Pancho Villa on the Mexican frontier. His motorcycle was one of Pershing's "motorized scouts," which had an air-cooled Maxim machine gun, fitted on a steel frame on the handlebars, with a small armored shield. Instead of a passenger seat it had a cache of cartridge boxes with an ammunition belt.

Pancho Villa, the Mexican Revolutionary general and national hero, had attacked a detachment of the 13th Cavalry Regiment at Columbus, New Mexico, killed ten civilians and eight soldiers, burned the town, and seized horses, guns, ammunition, and supplies. In response, President Woodrow Wilson sent 5,000 soldiers under Pershing into Mexico to track him down. The chase went on for nine months, but despite the pioneering use of aircraft and trucks, Villa eluded his grasp. During this campaign, prostitutes often followed the American camp; and to control the rate of venereal disease, Pershing dispensed condoms to his troops and established the women in a regulated brothel behind a stockade with medics on hand. Elsewhere, things weren't so controlled. My great uncle once showed my eldest brother, Jim, a shocking picture of a little shack in the middle of the wilderness with a long line of soldiers in pairs snaking off into the distant hills. "That there, Jamie," he said, poking a warning finger at the shack, "is a whorehouse."

After his army service (which included a supervisory role in a World War I training camp), Charles attended the University of Illinois at Urbana; graduated in 1922; earned his law degree in 1927; and thereafter taught at the University of Oregon Law School, where he was Editor-in-Chief of the Law Review for thirty years.

He was a celebrated teacher, taught in the Socratic fashion, and was known for his "colorful and stimulating" style." He swore a good deal and scowled; gestured often with his hands; and brought to life judicial figures like Benjamin Cardoza, Oliver Wendell Holmes, and Learned Hand. When questioned once about his tendency to "pepper his lectures with profanity," he replied that he had "a private understanding about that with God." His students "sweated under his assignments . . . but loved him," it was said, for he instilled in them his own love of the law. There were no easy answers in his class. He told one student, yearning for the right answer in a case, "Son, there is nothing more certain than the uncertainty of the law." His office door was always open, and he was known to help students not only in their studies, but with crises in their lives. It seems he even loaned money to a few on occasion, and once posted bail for a student in jail. In every way, he "put into day-to-day practice what he continually tried to impress upon his students," one colleague said, "that a member of the legal profession should devote a substantial portion of his time and effort to the discharge of his duties as a good citizen."

A scholarship at the Law School was later established in his name.

In politics, he was a liberal champion of civil liberties "who, in plain terms, didn't like people who push other people around"; on Constitutional matters, the strict constructionists drew his scorn. In a 1967 address on "The Bill of Rights and the Supreme Court," he noted that the Founders had declined to enumerate all of our inalienable rights on the grounds the list would never end. It would, for example, have required clauses asserting one's right "to fish in good weather," or a man's right to "sleep on his left side, turning on his back when tired from sleeping on his right."

His eminently thorough and judicial discussion of court rulings with respect to the 1st and 6th amendments displayed the kind of invincible reasoning one would hope for in a Justice on the Supreme Court. He never sat on a court, but an attempt was once made to entice him to run for the U.S. Senate as a Democrat. Had he done so and been elected, I suspect his impact would have been great: he had a Lincolnesque charisma; strong, deep civic and religious community ties; and a reputation for unimpeachable integrity that was wholly deserved. "Nobody could dislike him," wrote a friend, "even when he made you mad. Sometimes, the madder you got at him, the more you liked him." From time to time, he once admitted, "I really liked to stir things up."

In his religious convictions, Charles was devout. He had been a Methodist delegate to the World Council of Churches; head of the university's Wesley Foundation; and a Sunday-school teacher through the years. Due to his efforts, a Department of Religion was established at the school. Eventually, a university chapel was also named after him. Like my grandfather, he hated alcohol "in all its forms and quantities and at all times and could deliver a temperance lecture," it was said, "that shook the rafters."

In the fall of 1943, he took a leave of absence from teaching and, with the rank of Major, served as a legal officer in the European theater until 1946. His role, as I understand it, was to help set up military governments in areas from which the Germans had been expelled. At some point during this time he acquired Erwin Rommel's riding crop, dress-up suit, and sword.

Upon his return, he taught at the law school for another decade, until his retirement in 1957. At a banquet held in his honor, he was presented with a handsomely bound volume containing 200 letters from former students along with a comic poem written for him by Ernest G. Moll, the Australian naturalist and poet, who was also a colleague and friend. The poem, now lost, evidently imagined the conversations he might have had with Homer, Chaucer, Edmund Spenser, and other literary lights.

Aside from teaching, Charles was a forest ranger, and during the summer months oversaw a large area in the Oregon mountains where other rangers were posted in towers to look for fires. Every now and then, because of the isolation of the job, a ranger would go a little mad. One day one of them called him to say he'd just seen some elephants. "Charles," he said, "maybe I'm crazy, but I see elephants." "Ok," said Charles. "Just hold on. I'll be up there in a while." When he arrived, it turned out to be true. A circus train had derailed and some elephants, having escaped, were trying to pick their way over the sharp lava butte.

All in all, Charles had a remarkable life. As a young man, he had been struck by lightning while standing by a tree. The flash knocked him out, and when he came to, he discovered burns on his feet that followed the exact pattern of the hobnails on his boots. On another occasion, when camping with a companion in the hills, he woke to find a rattlesnake curled up for warmth against his neck. He heard his companion say, "Keep still." Then, with an exactly aimed blow, his friend beheaded the snake with an axe.

I remember my great uncle as a rough-and-ready character with a long, craggy face; a no-nonsense demeanor; and a punitive glower. But like Webb there was great kindness and consideration underneath. When my mother was dying, I began to abscond with things from school—beautiful things, like semi-precious stones—from a glass case. I can't be sure of my motive, but I think I was trying to console myself with objects of value—though of course they were really ordinary geological specimens on display for a second-grade class. I recall showing one or two of my "finds" to my grandparents, with whom we were staying, and to my great uncle, too, who was there. "Look what I found!" I said. My great uncle examined the stone. "Where did you find this?" "I dug it up!" I said. He held my gaze. A light seemed to flicker behind his eyes. I knew he knew I was lying. But I also knew he somehow "understood." In a gentle voice, he asked me if I had any other finds like it. Then he took them, returned them to the school, and I never heard anything about it again.

That was in 1955, when I was eight. Four years before, in 1951, after we had visited my grandparents on their 50th wedding anniversary, my parents, brothers, and I had gone to Oregon, where we stayed with my great uncle and aunt at their summer cabin on Odell Lake. On this excursion, I saw part of the Pacific Northwest—according to my scrapbook, Mt. Rainier, as viewed from Tipsoo Lake at Chinook Pass in Washington State; giant Douglas Fir trees; Crater Lake; and trucks on the highway bearing huge logs with a diameter of 12 feet. I was captivated by a National Park Service flyer warning of bears, and intrigued by the fish ladders of the Bonneville Dam.

My memories of this time are those of a child of four. At Odell Lake, I was fascinated by chipmunks; dressed up as an Indian; carried a walking stick; and found the water too cold. But my outings in my great uncle's outboard motorboat were thrilling, as I huddled in my life-jacket against the spray. My chief memory, however, was an unhappy one, when I was forced to eat my cereal with evaporated milk. I'm sure that up in the mountains, cans of evaporated milk were a practical supply. But I found the taste so unpalatable I couldn't take it and one morning sat for hours refusing to eat. I think my great aunt and uncle finally relented, but the experience was so sour it almost erased the rest.

In Eugene, Oregon, where he lived for most of the year, Charles had a woodworking shop behind his house. He could build just about anything, and at Odell Lake, six miles long near

Willamette Pass in the Pacific Cascades—an area now encircled by developed campgrounds with two private resorts—he had built his summer cabin himself in a fairly isolated spot. Next to the cabin, he rigged up a wheel smeared with scraps of food and fat that was kept spinning with the feeding antics of chipmunks, birds, and squirrels.

One day we all went out for a ride in his motorboat, which he had also built, and toward dusk were stranded near an abandoned cabin at the far end of the lake. In those days, the shoreline was nearly empty with only a few cabins on its fringe. While the rest of us waited for help, Charles and my brother, Jim, climbed up an embankment to a single line of track—the Cascade Summit siding—which they followed for miles to a general store. Charles knew the store's owner—a man named Perky Pyle—who sent a boat to pick us up.

Upon his retirement from the Law School, Charles went into private practice for five years. In comparing his new vocation to his old, he remarked: "Practice of the law requires quick decisions on fixed facts. A teacher can control the facts, change them to suit a theory, and take time for discussion. When the client is before you, either you know the law or you don't. If you know the law you can speak it and collect your fee. If you don't, you can tell the client his case has never been adjudicated, it is new and novel, and politely ask him to return the next day."

Charles co-wrote two books: *The Principles of Business Law,* a 900 page compendium, written with Essel R. Dillavou, which went through eight editions and was long standard; and *The Law: Its Nature, Functions, and Limits,* written with Robert S. Summers, which is a useful, entertaining guide. In 1962, he moved to Claremont, California (to the same retirement community my grandparents had joined), and on March 15, 1971, just after his 79th birthday, had a stroke. Two days later, he died. His wife, Susan, whom he adored, lived another eight years. They had one son, Peter Benson Howard, who had been a prodigy of sorts, with a vocabulary of a thousand words by the age of two. By the age of four, he could identify over 100 famous works of art. By then, he had also learned the elements of sign language, which somehow intrigued him. Later, as a student at the University of Oregon, he excelled. In his senior year, however, he was diagnosed with leukemia and died at nineteen. One need hardly say they never got over his loss. Their three, simple gravestones lie together at the Rest-Haven Memorial Park in Eugene, Oregon. In an incredibly poignant triptych of family unity and grief, each is inscribed with one word—"Father," "Mother," "Son."

*

All this, as I have described it, might seem like a familial heritage of irresistible power. But its world of positive energy and confident faith was not mine growing up, for I was cut off from it early on. I attended private Quaker and Episcopal schools; went to chapel; sang hymns, and so on, but the home my brothers and I inhabited was secular, skeptical, discouraged, if idealistic, decidedly worldly, and Eastern European in the tenor of its left-wing beliefs. It was a rich inheritance, but it would have been richer (I think now) had Hebrew Scripture been part of our daily bread. In effect, I was more the child and grandchild of unaffiliated Jewish émigré Ashkenazis than the scion of Anglo-Methodist stock. Though my grandfather touched my consciousness now and then from afar, I thought of myself as neither Jewish nor Christian, but as a kind of wandering soul—much in keeping with the books and films to which I was drawn. My father's preoccupation with social justice was not incompatible with religious belief, but its band-width was social engineering, so that it lacked the depth and dimension of a life tuned to the divine.

My own faith, which developed rather slowly, had little in common with the simple goodness my grandfather seemed to know but was more geared to the tormented, paradoxical world of Good and Evil as depicted in the novels of Graham Greene. The deadly duel between the anti-clerical but dignified police Lieutenant in *The Power and the Glory* and his besotted, dedicated counterpart in the "whiskey-priest," seemed truer to life's cleaved halves both within me and without. At least, that is how I tended to think of things once I began to reflect on where I stood.

CHAPTER FOUR

࿇

I know something of the world of my mother, but she is a mystery to me still. As best I could, I have tried to assemble her life from gathered fragments: objects, documents, pictures, anecdotes, reports: a silver napkin ring inscribed with a nursery rhyme—"Little Miss Muffet, Sat on a Tuffet, Eating her Curds and Whey"; pictures of her wielding a shovel at the groundbreaking of the first Wesley Foundation; her various diplomas; a college yearbook; her Phi Beta Kappa pin from the University of Illinois; her two passports; a handful of letters; a silver cigarette case acquired in China and embossed with roses, dragons, and bats; her gold wedding band, inscribed Bob and Lois, 1941—though my parents had married the year before; a delicate silver filigree necklace with beveled settings of polished carnelian stones; an inlaid turquoise silver pill box; and so on. There are my own few memories, too, of course, as well as those of others, though they are likewise meager; and the awful, substantial fact of her absence, which implies all that was subtracted from my life.

Born Lois Benson Baker on October 8, 1908 in Urbana, Illinois, she had been named for one of her father's sisters, Lois, who had died at the age of fifteen. When my mother was seven, she had a sister, briefly, too: Elizabeth Benson Baker, who died within the year. As a child, she attended Trinity Methodist Episcopal Church, where my grandfather preached; and was described by one who knew her then as a "sturdy little girl, quiet and reserved, apparently shy and rather pretty, with very blue eyes and blonde braids of hair." At times, her hair flowed in waves down to her waist. Later, in her teens, she favored a pageboy cut. She also had an occasional stutter, which my eldest brother and I both acquired.

My great uncle Charles was fond of her, and in March 1917, during World War I, when she was eight, he wrote her a long letter from an Army Training post at Fort Riley, Kansas. He apologized for not writing sooner but explained, "I have been busy doing a great many things. Last week I had to dig trenches, this way," and he drew a stick figure swinging a pick-axe. "We dig holes in the ground and live in them like beavers....Last night all the soldier boys went out and played a big game of hide and seek. I found a nice place to hide down in a valley behind a big tree. No one found me but I found five others....We march 10 to 18 miles every day and carry 45 pounds on our backs."

When my mother was fifteen, she spent part of a summer with her family and friends in Estes Park, Colorado, where she reveled in the great outdoors. Her love of mountain climbing (which friends later liked to recall) perhaps began at this time. She kept a meticulously neat scrapbook from the trip and in the pictures she looks ruggedly happy in a girl-scout uniform and hiking gear. Often she is smiling, with children and other companions, including a donkey and a dog. She is also shown sitting comfortably astride a horse named "Sam." She loved flowers and in her album she carefully pasted in a Wild Rose from Horseshoe Falls; Spanish Moss from Fern Lake; Canterbury Bells and Columbine from Odessa Lake; and an Indian Paint Brush from the Continental Divide. Near a photo of my grandfather playing a little golf, she attached a slightly off-color joke: "Golf Professional—'Now before we begin, I'd like to know just how much you know about golf?' Wealthy Lady—'Oh I don't know a thing! I wouldn't even know which end of the caddy to take a hold of.'"

My mother did well at the University of Illinois; presided over her sorority house (the Omicron chapter of Gamma Phi Beta—"noted for the academic success of its members and its promotion of women's issues on campus"); wrote for the student newspaper, the *Daily Illini*; belonged to the Alethenai Literary Society, a women's group "founded for the purpose of stimulating forensic eloquence"; and joined the Women's Athletic Association, as a member (I believe) of the swimming and field hockey teams. Even though her parents' home adjoined the campus, she preferred to live in a dorm. She also spent part of one undergraduate year at Barnard College in New York. When she left home for the first time, my grandfather noted some verses in her Bible as a guide: Psalms 23, 91, 121; Isaiah 40; 1 Corinthians 13; and Philippians 4:8. Years later, when my eldest brother, Jim, left home for the first time, too, she inscribed those references in his.

Only a handful of my mother's college papers—all brief stories or descriptions from her freshman year—survive. Though slight, they show a certain artistic determination to get the sound and sense of something right. My whimsical favorite, which also suggests her independent streak, is "The Joys of Thievery." It begins:

> Sally and I are jolly reprobates, confirmed, old bums. And what is our favorite line of misdemeanor? Thievery! Stealing money out of gymnasium lockers (the annoying pastime of some)? No. Hooking tulips from under a professor's back fence? No indeed. Swiping apples from an honor apple stand? Certainly not. We steal time!
>
> When we steal time, we steal something precious, I tell you. So precious it is, that every hour of the twenty-four and about a dozen more imaginary hours are packed as full of duties and 'responsibilities' as a sardine box is full of sardines. In the beginning Sally and I were conscientious young freshmen. But after a few frantic attempts to complete that thirty-six hours work in twenty-four, we degenerated and turned thieves. We stole time, quantities of it, just to play with and enjoy."

> For instance, yesterday we appropriated that lazy hazy hour
> after lunch and went gaily forth in search of adventure . . . .

They discover a little fairy cottage—"White-painted it was, a slender crescent-moon cut in the corner of each green shutter, with grassy terraces leading up to the broad door-step, and purple lilacs blooming all around. A brass dragon's head knocker shone in the sun." Their theft of time, however, takes up the time they need to prepare for an algebra quiz, which they fail. Yet the piece concludes, gaily: "Oh, well. They say that all thieves come to a day of reckoning. Sally and I are afraid that ours is coming—about May 29. But we are going to smile philosophically and remark (like the old fellow in *Alice in Wonderland*), "Be good and you'll be happy, but you won't have any fun."

My mother, while finding time to have fun, must have been good and happy too, for she graduated with high honors in June of 1928. At the time, she was committed to a year of service in the Methodist Social Center at Chateau Thierry, France. Athough my grandfather had just been elected bishop, she saw no reason to change her plans. In late June, my grandparents drove her to New York; and on the 21st, she sailed. "I can never forget the desolation which swept over us," my grandmother later recalled, "as we stood on the wharf waving farewell to our daughter standing alone on the deck of the receding ship."

Chateau-Thierry had been heavily damaged by fighting during World War I and a Methodist Mission and Social Center had been established there to aid in the relief of returning refugees. A decade after the war, its work was still urgent, and in striving to repair the enormous damage done to the local social fabric, thirty-two villages had been entrusted to its care. A maternity clinic had been organized, with a day nursery for infants and children from indigent homes; Scout troupe outings for those in their teens; a free circulating library and reading room; and classes in shorthand, typewriting, hat-making, sewing, drawing, housekeeping, and gymnastics.

In volunteering, my mother brought with her a number of

skills, including a gift for teaching children; a calm, patient, firm but gentle nature; and a fluent knowledge of French. At Chateau Thierry, she stayed with Julian and Marie Wadsworth, who ran the Mission, and on her 20th birthday they gave her a leather-bound pocket edition of the New Testament and Psalms in French.

At the end of her service, she traveled east to the Orient to meet up with my grandparents in Seoul. Her journey took her through Europe to Moscow, where she boarded the Trans-Siberian Railway that rumbled over the Urals and across the whole of northern Asia, to the Russian naval port of Vladivostok. She was twenty-one at the time and traveled alone. A friend later recalled, "Lois was always fearless, so far as I could discover, of any elements of nature or of any possible ill that might come her way." Later, in the company of her parents, she spent some time in China, Korea, and Japan.

After she returned from abroad, she worked for a year or two as a journalist at *The New York Morning World*. When the paper closed in 1931, Walter Lippmann, then editor of the Editorial Page, offered her his typewriter as a keepsake. She also worked for *The American Scholar* and *The Brooklyn Eagle*, where she occasionally wrote charming little features for their Sunday magazine. One piece, for example, published on May 31, 1931, was about a fifteen-year-old coloratura boy soprano named Duncan Peckham at St. Paul's Episcopal Church who had won New York's Gold Medal in a singing contest. According to the organist and choir director, however, little Duncan had only a year left to sing before his voice would change. My mother evoked him rather sweetly, describing his range of interests, young enterprise, and simple fortitude.

As a free-lance journalist, however, she found it hard to make ends meet and sometime in the mid-1930s she became the private secretary to Henry Pitney Van Dusen, then Dean, later President, of the Union Theological Seminary in New York. Years later, after she died, he would write that she was about as fine a person as he had ever known. It is one of those luminous fragments of a delineated profile, in lieu of a complete portrait, I prize.

In 1938–1939, my mother traveled abroad again—to England, France, North Africa, and Southeast Asia. Her photographs tell me something of her interests, at least by inference, from what caught her eye. In Paris, she admired the Church of St. Germaine des Pres, with its starry-spangled vault (which years later became an object of wonder for me, too), the Rue de Beaux Arts, the Café Des Deux Maggots, and the Hotel d'Alsace—on the whole, cosmopolitan haunts. In Arles, she visited the ancient Roman necropolis with its trail of crypts, encasements, and open tombs, and the imposing Coliseum-like Roman amphitheater nearby, with its thirty-three tiers of stone steps, oval arena, galleries and arcades.

After a stopover in Marseilles, she went on to Carthage (now a suburb of Tunis), viewed the Suez Canal, explored the old Arab quarter of Port Said, and at the Red Sea port of Aden paused to view the enormous, ancient rainwater cisterns of Tawila carved out of volcanic rock. From there she made her way down into India; paused at Darjeeling, in West Bengal, in the foothills of the Himalayas; went on to Delhi, where she took numerous pictures of the famed Red Fort complex with its white marble "Pearl Mosque." She he also lingered at the Anglican Church of St. James, where British viceroys had worshipped, near the double-arched Kashmiri Gate. In Agra, she visited the Taj Mahal; recorded the simple festivities of a Hindu wedding; and traveled down the Ganges River, where she encountered Hindu beggar-pilgrims and other mendicant ascetics with painted faces and marked brows. At Benares, she noted the holy "burning ghats" or wide cremation steps by the river, where all true Hindus hope to be cleansed and burned. In Calcutta, she attended the equestrian maneuvers of some Punjabi Lancers; was intrigued by a street barber, standing ready on a curb with shears in hand; saw the palatial memorial to Queen Victoria, built of white Makrana marble; and took a number of pictures of the lavish adornments of a Jain Temple as well as those of a Hindu shrine.

Elsewhere, my mother was obviously moved by the pitiable spectacle of a tethered bullock treading in endless circles as it ground cement. At Fatehpur Sikri, a city in northern India west of

Agra, a dancing bear was featured in the market place; in Bombay, a snake charmer, squatting with his mongoose and cobra, as the latter uncoiled from a basket on the street.

She took in all these things; and so I take them in, too, with my mind's eye. Her passport tells me (but no photographs record) that she also spent time afterwards in Singapore, Shanghai, Hong Kong, and Saigon. In the summer of 1939, she returned to Europe, stopping in Geneva on her way to Cherbourg. From Cherbourg, on May 31, she sailed on the Queen Mary for New York, arriving July 5th.

*

I cannot say how my parents met. It may have been at a summer course at the University of Wisconsin, as my brother, Jim, suspects; or (as I think) in Greenwich Village, where my father used to frequent Socialist gatherings, and where both of them lived. My mother was at 12 Bank Street; my father at 261 West 11th Street, a few blocks away. They were married on her thirty-second birthday by a Justice of the Peace in Hoboken, New Jersey, my father then just shy of thirty-eight. Before or after their marriage, my parents may have moved in together, at his place or hers. By the fall of 1942 they had found a nearby studio apartment with a coveted skylight at 190 Waverly Place. There my two brothers and I were born. My father fenced in part of the roof as a play-pen, but the apartment was already crowded and they considered applying for a cooperative housing venture—designed by Frank Lloyd Wright as single-story units near White Plains—known as Usonian Homes. In 1947, they found a house in the suburbs at 87 Fifth Avenue in New Rochelle.

Meanwhile, in 1942 the United States had entered World War II. My father was then forty years old, and his draft registration card, dated February 15, 1942, described him as 5'7" and 180 lbs. Due to his age and family status, he received deferments through the war.

As our little family grew, there are touching pictures of my parents with Jim as an infant, then a toddler, at Waverly Place; and a letter my mother wrote to my grandfather on Good Friday, 1944, is full of good cheer. She addressed him as "Dearest Dad"; expressed love and admiration for all his doings; talked about Jim's antics, as well as family outings; spoke of her recent reading, which included George Santayana's *Persons and Places*, John Hersey's *A Bell for Adano*, Betty Smith's *A Tree Grows in Brooklyn*, and Richard Wright's *Native Son*; and promised in another letter soon to touch on politics. Though she enjoyed her parents' approval, she was also living on her own terms. She had discreetly rebelled perhaps by marrying outside the Christian church (though she later served as head of the Primary School at St. John's Methodist Episcopal Church in New Rochelle); enjoyed outings with my father to parties and clubs; smoked; and liked an occasional drink. Unfortunately, she felt obliged to conceal this from her parents, and on at least one occasion, when she paid them a visit, hid Scotch in bottles of perfume.

The weight of family feeling on the matter must have been a strain. My great-grandmother, Martha, had belonged to the Temperance League and my grandfather completely embraced her views. In 1914, he got involved in a heated dispute with the Chattanooga Medicine Company and one of its directors, John A. Patten (a philanthropist and influential church layman) over a potion it made called the "Wine of Cardui." The potion was marketed as a cure for women's ills and consisted of Black Haw, Goldenseal and Blessed Thistle dissolved in alcohol. It was a plausible compound, since Black Haw was a folk remedy for menstrual cramps; Goldenseal aids digestion; and Blessed Thistle helps with lactation. But the medical community doubted its virtues, and my grandfather saw it as marketing liquor under a medicinal veil.

CHAPTER FIVE

❦

On the face of it, my parents were oddly matched. She was delicate and slender, quiet if not retiring, sparing of speech; he was short, stocky, boisterous, even verbose. In a larger sense, they belonged to worlds that often collide. Born on Christmas Day in Warsaw, Poland, in 1902, he was an ethnic, but not religious, Jew (though his parents kept a kosher home); had come to the States in 1904; grew up in Brooklyn; graduated from the City College of New York; and studied law at the Brooklyn Law School, St. Lawrence University, where he earned his LL.B. in 1925 and his Master of Laws in 1940.

His passion was social justice, and he had a tempestuous hatred of capitalism in its more mercenary forms. A founding member of the Workers Defense League and the National Lawyers Guild, he was long active in the Socialist Party of Eugene V. Debs and ran for several offices—State Assemblyman, Alderman, Judge, and so on—on the Party line. Then, in 1937, two years before he met my mother, he was the Socialist Party candidate against Thomas E. Dewey for District Attorney of New York. In response to a questionnaire from the Citizen's Union at the time, he wrote: "I re-affirm the basic philosophy of Socialism, that not until we have production for use in contradistinction to production for profit, will we make any real progress towards having an honest and efficient government, a world of plenty, peace, security, and happiness." The National Lawyers Guild ranked him as "qualified and preferred," but in all his campaigns he won only a fraction of the vote. Later in the 1950s, when the Liberal Party was a force in New York, he was an active member and hoped for a judgeship through Party ties.

Meanwhile, in the 1930s he had traveled abroad to Cuba, with his lifelong friend and colleague Marion Severn, a noted patent attorney; and in the summer of 1934 to the Soviet Union, on an itinerary that took him through Poland to Vladikavkas, at the foothills of the Caucasus Mountains. There he climbed Mount Kasbek, went on to Tbilisi and Batumi in Georgia on the Black Sea; took a steamer to Tuapse, on the sea's northeast shore; then traveled by train to Moscow and Leningrad, before returning home on September 13, 1934. He brought back a handful of souvenirs, including a set of Soviet playing cards, that ridiculed the perceived hypocrisies of bankers and priests; and a Soviet sports medal, bestowed upon him in thanks by a man to whom he had given his overcoat. Three years later, on August 24, 1937, he sailed for Paris on the M.S. Batory where he took in the International Exposition of Art and Technology in Modern Life.

His other, early movements have been hard to track. In 1934, he had an apartment at 9 Gramercy Park, upstairs (as I recall) from an abortionist. From there, he moved to Greenwich Village. At some point (in or after law school, according to a confidence once blurted out by an aunt) he was briefly involved romantically with the daughter of someone in the crime family of Al Capone.

His law practice went through various incarnations. I have been unable to determine where his first office was, but in 1931 his stationery read: "Robert Landor Bobrick, Counsellor at Law, 320 Broadway, New York." The "Landor" was his invention, to give his name a stately sound, and he often wrote his middle initial— and indeed, his whole signature—with a flourish, with swirls and arabesques. Around 1938 his law practice became a partnership, as "Herzog, Brown and Bobrick, 220 Broadway," only to emerge two years later as "Boochever, Cameron, and Bobrick, 90 Broad Street, with Law Offices in New York, Washington, Paris." This projected a magnitude and stature his practice never enjoyed. "Cameron" remains as elusive to me as "Herzog" and "Brown," despite much searching; but George Behr Boochever was a known expert in international and aviation law, and sometime General Counsel to the New York Board of Trade. As a political operative, he had also served as the Brooklyn campaign manager for Mayor Fiorella La Guardia in 1933. He was a firm believer in what he called "Preventive Law," convinced that most matters could be handled by arbitration, but his main interest seems to have been in promoting business ventures between Czechoslovakia and the United States. He helped establish the Anglo-Czech and Prague Credit Bank of New York, and received the Order of the White Lion—previously awarded to Nicolai Tesla—from the Czechoslovakian government in 1938.

My father admired him; kept his portrait; and prized a Samurai brush painting Boochever had given him as a gift. However, their partnership dissolved (apparently with no ill-will) in 1946, and thereafter my father was on his own. He established himself first at 30 Broad Street, which he described as a "good address"; then in 1963 at 165 Broadway. Meanwhile, he had been admitted to the Bar of the Supreme Court of the United States.

*

During my childhood, our family circle was small. My mother had various cousins, most of them remote; my father had a brother and two sisters who figured somewhat in our lives. His brother, Mack, had been an aspiring borscht circuit comedian, whose wife, Minn, taught school. They had no children of their own but had adopted her sister's illegitimate son. My father's sister, Sylvia, worked for most of her life as a saleswoman in Lord & Taylor's famous Fifth Avenue department store. She was a wonderfully warm and gregarious person and, with her husband Sam, became our occasional surrogate parents during our teenage years. My

father's youngest sister, Frieda, was equally caring but led a dis-
advantaged life. Born with a birthmark on her face, she had been
terribly deformed by radiation treatments meant to erase it that
instead gave her a blotched and reddened complexion (always
heavily covered in make-up) and an oversized tongue. It lolled
part way out of her mouth like Quasimodo's in Charles Laughton's
film portrayal of the hunchback of Notre Dame. Nevertheless, no
bitterness subdued her, and she was a sweet, tender soul. I believe
she worked as a bookkeeper for most of her life. Our nearest cousin
(about the only one we ever saw) was Sylvia's daughter, Joan, who
looked rather like Elizabeth Taylor and married a handsome,
charismatic man by the name of Arthur Cohen, who had driven a
tank in North Africa during World War II. Arthur had great business savvy and prospered as a regional sales manager for Bulova
Watches before becoming the head of Pulsar Watches in Japan.

*

My mother must have been ill for much of the brief time I knew her.
She had her first operation for colon cancer in November 1952, when
I was five; and her diagnosis must have followed months of feeling
ill. She recovered, or seemed to, as the cancer "went into remission";
before it returned, she had to cope with troubling signs of her uncer-
tain health. I was surely aware, intuitively or otherwise, of her ordeal,
and sensed her sadness, which may explain why the world seemed
such a desert to me then. Later, it helped me to understand my father's
strained state and how wrought up he had been with angst when he
had struck me a child.

   In the spring and summer of 1955, my mother was once
more treated for cancer at the Huntington Memorial Hospital in
California, not far from where my grandparents lived. My father
spent time in both California and New York, as he tried to keep
his practice going; my brothers and I stayed with my grandparents
and attended California schools. I remember the tropical climate
and the general beauty of San Marino and Pasadena, with palm
trees lining the streets. Even more distinctly, I remember that I

was absolutely terrified by a tarantula displayed in a glass case at school. I began to imagine I saw these spiders everywhere, and sometimes, as I rode my bike home, took elaborate detours if I so much as saw the stirring of a leaf.

*

My grandparents' home in San Marino had a Spanish pantile roof and was beautifully furnished with elegant items acquired in the Far East. There was a spiral staircase to the right of the entrance; a dining room, kitchen, pantry, and guest room on the ground floor. At the rear of the house was an oval backyard enclosed by a stucco wall edged round with flowers and plants. The living room had a grand piano and was adorned with oriental carpets, brass-fixtured chests, tapestries, and lacquered screens; in the back was a screened-in porch level with the yard, along with another above where my brothers and I slept. Bookcases lined an upstairs landing, where my grandfather had his study; next to it was the room where my grandparents slept. In his study was a bust of Dante, along with piles of books. Correspondence and other papers were strewn across a desk. There was also a small, alcove-like room that had a radio and T.V. in it, and when summer came, that was my retreat. Hit songs played on the radio all day long, and among them I remember clearly "Earth Angel," "Let Me Go Lover," "Unchained Melody," and "Only You." All of them moved me, but none more so than "The Yellow Rose of Texas," which had an almost mystical effect upon my imagination inspired by the line—"her eyes are bright as diamonds, they sparkle like the dew"—that seemed to mingle the divinely human with Nature itself.

My mother faced death bravely, even as she tried to keep my father's spirits up. In a letter begun on April 22nd and continued on the 25th, she assured him that her appetite and strength were improving, recounted a get-together at the local school and a trip into the mountains with her parents to see a famous huge old wisteria vine. Though burdened with the notion that she could hardly expect to recover when others at least as deserving had not, she woke one night "with a sudden great sense of peace," she told him, "that it wasn't up to me or within my power to determine what I 'deserved.'" That gave her a kind of hope—almost a conviction—that she might get well after all. In the meantime, she was grateful for the improvement she felt. Her mind then returned to practical concerns—for example, whether she was "entitled to any more hospitalization benefits. And if so, how we go about it"; wondered if my father had seen an Edward R. Murrow broadcast—"Some of Our Books Are Missing"—about right-wing attempts to suppress liberal books and magazines; and promised to write him "some kind of decent letter" the next day about the upkeep of the house. In closing, she said: "I am concerned about you all the time with all my heart."

Handwriting often reflects a person's emotional state. In her letter, my mother's well-formed script moved evenly and clearly in straight lines across the page.

She was just as steady as she seemed.

Despite the tremendous strain everyone was under, I can't remember a single intemperate word—with the exception of a brief exchange my father and grandfather had one day when we were driving to the hospital in my grandfather's car. My father was understandably subdued, and when my grandfather asked him a question and he failed to reply promptly, my grandfather said, "Speak up, Bob, like a good lawyer should!" The tone seemed uncalled for; and my father, blushing deeply, said something sharp in return. In the awful silence that followed, I was mortified. My world was coming to an end; and to ensure its absolute destruction, these two remaining pillars of my life had clashed.

About a month before my mother died, my father took us to nearby Lacey Park in the San Rafael Hills. Ostensibly, we were there to play a little baseball. Beforehand, however, we had a long family conference around a table under a magnolia tree. "Geneva," my father wrote afterwards in a letter to his friend, Marion Severn, "was not conducted with more decorum and patient deliberation and protocol." We all wanted to return to New Rochelle, he wrote, but agreed we shouldn't until our mother was well. Of course, my father knew what the future held.

On August 1, 1955, he wrote to Marion again: "Forgive me if I do not write much, for truly I have no desire to do so. Lois is putting up a gallant fight. As courageous as she was in life, she is more so in her sickness and I know will be equally so to the end. There has been no substantial change. However, she is helpless and is attended by nurses throughout the day & night. Her mind is crystal clear, lucid—her memory excellent. She smokes a few cigarettes & chats with me about home—I should not forget to send the carpets out for a cleaning, to get this or that—talks a lot about the garden, etc.—Imagine that!"

Three weeks later, she died at the age of 46, on August 24, 1955. My great Uncle Charles brought us the news. The day before, I had been working on a little gift for her—one of those symmetrical patterns you make when you cut along the edge of a folded paper sheet—and among my other dreadful memories of that day was a feeling of irremediable sadness, even guilt, that I had failed to finish it in time.

My father was overwhelmed by her loss and kept repeating, through his tears, "She didn't deserve to die."

Two days later there was a memorial service at my grandparents' home. The tributes she received united in describing her as "intelligent, thoughtful, quick," "patient and courageous," and a woman of "lovely, resolute character," radiant to the core. "Her poise and dignity was mingled with that kindliness which could win assent and keep open the channels of sympathy and understanding. Even to the end, she was cheerful and unselfish, never complaining, always thoughtful of the family and friends who surrounded her with love and prayer."

According to my father, in all their time together, he had "never heard her say a harsh or unkind word about anyone." If true—and I have no reason to disbelieve it—that would set her apart from anyone I've ever known.

The memorial closed with John Masefield's "Easter Hymn," which celebrates perpetual Easter and resurrection through the year. When my grandfather was near 90, he was interviewed as part of an oral history project, and chose to recite this poem-hymn—from among all the poems he knew—beautifully by heart.

We returned that fall from California a permanently unhappy family. We ought to have kept together. But my father was in debt, with a neglected practice to repair, a house to keep up (though he would shortly sell it), and three young children (thirteen, ten, and eight) to raise. So we were dispersed, on scholarship, to private schools.

My father was deeply dejected by the whole turn of events, and for the rest of his life inordinately anxious about money and sometimes seethed with rage.

CHAPTER SIX

My eldest brother, Jim, was enrolled in Webb School in California, which allowed him to stay with my grandparents on weekends; my brother, Pete, and I at Mohonk School north of New Paltz, New York. Located in the wing of a famous hotel resort near the summit of one of the Shawangunk Mountains, its location was dramatic, beautiful, idyllic, and pristine. However, the school was strictly run by Quakers, and there now began for me what seemed an interminable journey through private institutions that would not cease for ten years. It was a world for which I was hardly prepared. I was already withdrawn and shy, due in part to an inherited stutter. Now, in my mother's place, I was given a series of "house mothers"—and later dorm masters—who were often emotionally removed. Our lives at Mohonk, in fact, were regulated with such precision that one might have thought it a reform school. Our outgoing mail was screened for complaints, and we were even told on which side to sleep when we took our mandatory afternoon nap. I later summed up the whole punitive experience (as it felt) in an epigram:

> A sin each year was punished in me when
> I went away to boarding school for ten.

That made the Decalogue. Before I came
To sinning as a man, I knew the shame.

Mohonk was a small school, with only about thirty students, and taught boys from the third grade through the sixth. Its headmaster, Edward Lafferty, was a well-meaning but rigid disciplinarian, and I will never forget the short speech he gave to our assembly in the "Common Room" on the first day I was there. He looked us over with a kind of wry distaste, signed for quiet, and began: "I've heard it said that boys will be boys. *But I say boys will be pigs if you let 'em!*" This harsh, impersonal verdict—levied from on high—was scarcely the welcome I had hoped for. And I was in no shape to adapt. Drained by grief and pale as a ghost, I was told I had "iron deficiency anemia" and kept for days in the infirmary by the resident nurse, who plied me with Geritol. I think my sensibility was also deeply marred, for well beyond my teens I favored books of futile and foredoomed longing, like *Wuthering Heights*, or mournful Welsh ballads like "The Ash Grove," which seemed to me to capture the world as it was. A poem I conceived (but failed to finish) in my thirties began:

My soul lives in a city I have seen
In post-war newsreels, in black and white.
In one interchangeably repeated frieze
The buildings are in rubble. Refugees
Hurry without hope across the screen,
While something harshly blanched about the light
Betrays the day's decline in every scene.

In a gray doorway somewhere, or a room,
Two desperate lovers have been trying to meet.
It doesn't matter since their love is doomed—
Either by some arbitrary act of the police.....

And there my inspiration flagged.

I remained at Mohonk for four years. For the first year or so (while I retained some semblance of religious habit), I knelt in prayer to my mother each night beside my bed.

The Mohonk hotel complex was a grand Victorian structure that resembled a Swiss chalet. The main building, or Mountain House, was beautifully paneled throughout, had a dining room with vaulted ceilings and clerestory windows, and a stone tower modeled on the Campanile of the Basilica of St. Mark's. It was fronted by a mystical black water lake—known to local Native Americans as the "Lake of the Sky"—surrounded by a pine, chestnut, and hemlock forest with sheer conglomerate cliffs. The Quaker family that owned and managed the hotel had great reverence for Nature and over time had developed their vast property of 7,500 acres into a wildlife reserve. There was a magical otherworldliness to its solitude and quiet; and viewed from the stately porch of the hotel, particularly through the mist, the cliffs beyond were a vision of Shangri La.

Over the years, a hundred miles of broad carriage roads, with planked bridges and beds of crushed slate, had been built on winding courses up the slopes. These were furnished with timber rest-stops at scenic overlooks bearing evocative names like Eagle Cliff, the Great Crevice, Pine Bluff, Cope's Lookout, and the Gate of the Winds. In a number of places, huge talus piles of fallen boulders, seamed with crevices and caverns, made for a rock-climber's dream. At the top of the mountain stood a stone tower, known as "Sky Top," with a commanding view of the terrain. From its observation deck, on a clear day, one could see the far away hills of five adjacent states. The tower was reached by a winding road—or, for the more daring, by a "Labyrinth Path" that began on the far side of the lake and wound its way through caverns and fissures, and over boulders and gaps, to a slender, vertical crevice 150 feet high that had to be scaled by ladder to the Tower's base.

Nearby, the old quarry for the tower stone had been turned

into a reservoir, known as "Paul Bunyan's Footprint" from its shape.

My health in time rebounded from daily mountain walks, rock-climbing, caving, skiing, sledding and the like, as my constitution gained strength. In my outings, I sometimes followed trails that had once been traced by the Lenape or Delaware Indians and accumulated a little collection of stone arrowheads, as well as quartz crystals from the Oneida Conglomerate that gleamed like jewels along the paths. I learned to skate, and during the late winter afternoons often glided across the lake to the lyrical strains of Viennese waltzes that were piped, for the benefit of hotel guests, from the hotel.

I have little specific memory now of what I was taught, beyond the usual reading, writing, geography and math. But I read much, often beyond my years (not always to my good); was said to be studious; and while technically a third grader, was taught with those in the fourth. I was captivated by James Fennimore Cooper's books, especially *The Last of the Mohicans* (with its fantastically vivid illustrations by N.C. Wyeth); haunted by a Poe story, "The Murders in the Rue Morgue;" and earned my first fountain pen for learning script. I considered it a thing of great value, along with the right it gave me to write with flowing ink.

My first roommate was a boy named Alex Tze—the son of an opera singer, I believe—who had a talent for drawing bridges with exactly rendered detail. He taught me how to depict the Tappan Zee Bridge with convincing trusswork, and I was enthralled by my newfound skill.

As students, we were very well fed, for the hotel's great kitchen served us, but the medical care was lax. One day one of my skates caught in the space between two boards on the dock and I fell forward against a snowplow and broke my two front teeth. They weren't repaired correctly, which caused me distress in later years.

Other memories are fond. In 1957, we were allowed to watch the World Series, and I saw Don Larson of the Yankees pitch his perfect game. Every Christmas, we were served snow cones with vanilla as the students joined together in raising a towering pine tree fresh from the woods. As we gathered round later that evening to sing carols and hymns, we all held hands, and I experienced a tremendous sense of fellowship that I have seldom felt since.

After the shock of my new situation wore off, my insurgent nature appeared. I was inclined to break rules I did not agree with; smuggled in forbidden sweets (all sweets were forbidden); objected when my reading (and outgoing mail) was censored; and the way our nap-times were regimented by the nurse. She had an untenable theory (perhaps common then) that it was healthier for children to nap on their left sides rather than their right. Incredibly, we were punished for doing otherwise. In the hall of my lower-class (3rd-4th grade) dorm, I set up a system of mirrors at the corners of the doors, so we could spot the nurse advancing on our rooms. One day, when I was in the 5th grade, the headmaster confiscated my copy of Hemingway's *To Have and Have Not*, which I had borrowed from by brother, Jim. Admittedly, it had a lurid cover; but Jim had read it, so why shouldn't I? "My brother read it!" I exclaimed. "Well, I have to question whether he should have been allowed to, either," the headmaster said. Which seemed to me absurd.

The Hotel—known in part for its early Conferences on International Arbitration, which helped inspire the League of Nations—occasionally hosted ecumenical religious groups, and one day I found myself summoned to meet Rabbi Louis Finkelstein, then head of the Jewish Theological Seminary of America. He was also my grandfather's friend. I think of him now as a towering man with a kindly face, twinkling eyes, and a rabbinical beard, who reached down deeply, almost bowing, to grasp my hand. Given how small I was, it was perhaps his formidable presence that made him seem so grand. Long after, when I became interested in Biblical studies, I learned that he was a Talmud scholar of great standing. In my brief encounter with him, he said, "Your grandfather told me you were a student here and I wanted to say hello." It was such a thoughtful thing to do. A little over a decade later, when I entered Columbia University, my grandfather also arranged for me to have lunch with John C. Bennett, the new President of the Union Theological Seminary in New York. But I was then an angry, bohemian student, full of my generation's distinctive angst, distrusting authority of any kind, and I probably missed a chance to have a good talk.

In my fourth year at Mohonk (that is, in 1958), the school moved to the Cragsmoor Inn in nearby Ellenville, New York. There I spent my sixth grade year. The year seemed aimless, and in academic terms was possibly a waste. My grandfather paid me a visit, but all I remember about it now is that he chided the headmaster for praising me in my presence, thinking it might go to my head. By then, my brother, Pete, had gone on to Cheshire Academy in Connecticut. We hadn't spent much time together at Mohonk, despite the smallness of the school, and that under-lying disconnect set the pattern for our lives.

*

After Mohonk, I spent two years at Tuxedo Park School, a "pre-prep school" set within a gated community in the Ramapo Mountains. Founded in 1885 by Pierre Lorillard, the wealthy tobacco magnate, the Park was forty miles north of New York City and resplendent with turn-of-the century mansions that reflected the wealth its denizens enjoyed. The term "tuxedo" had been coined there for men's formal dinner-wear after a resident was introduced to the short-tailed dinner jacket by the Prince of Wales. Many of the residents indulged in a country-club life-style, centered around the Park's lovely lake, boathouse, golf course, swimming pool, tennis, raquet, and squash courts. The community was also known for its "coming out" parties for debutantes and autumn Balls.

The year I entered, Samuel Hazard—a brilliant, lean, sharp-featured, handsome man, with close set, concentrated eyes—became the new headmaster. He was stern in his way, with an alert, vigilant air; introduced reforms that improved the school's standing;

established its art department and new library; converted the basement into a gym; and was dedicated to high educational ideals. He also taught eighth grade English with insight and literary flair.

The curriculum at the school was demanding and at first I was overwhelmed, especially by having to take Latin and French at the same time. Like everyone else in my class, I was also obliged to take the first year of Algebra over after the "New Math" came in, with its novel, more abstract way of presenting equations. Our former grades were erased and the very same problems I had solved before with ease now baffled my best efforts. By the end of the term I had managed to convince myself that I had no aptitude for math at all. That stayed with me through school. Later, when I wrote a book that required some knowledge of the mathematics of engineering, I found that whenever I brought my mind to bear upon a subject, I could bring it within my grasp.

Most of the pupils at the school were day students, lived in the Park, and came from wealth. Their parents were investment bankers, advertising executives, corporate lawyers, judges, members of the New York Stock Exchange, and so on. Few of the pupils put on airs, but I was acutely aware of where I stood in the social scale. At one memorable birthday party for a classmate, for example, I was astonished to find myself partaking of a "money cake" embedded with envelopes containing $50 bills.

There were relatively few boarders like myself, but their backgrounds were more diverse. Among them, I remember the son of the actor Sidney Blackmer (who made his debut with Edward G. Robinson in "Little Caesar" in 1931); Kate Aldrich, the adopted daughter of Larry Aldrich, the fashion designer; Peter Raiziss, the son of an Italian poet, Sonia Raiziss, who championed the early work of Umberto Eco, Grace Paley, Raymond Carver and Sylvia Plath; and Maria and Judith Maleter, daughters of Colonel Pal Maleter, whom the Soviets had shot for his role in the Hungarian Revolution of 1956. With their mother and brother, Paul, they had just barely escaped to freedom in a hay cart across the Hungarian frontier. Maria told me, in fact, that a guard, searching the cart, had discovered them, but in an act of great mercy let them pass.

As it happened, I had read all about the Hungarian Revolution before I met them and knew of their father's fate. When the Revolution was crushed, my brothers and I had all been "wrought up about it" (in my father's words); and after one protest march in front of the Soviet Delegation to the United Nations a picture of my brother, Jim—holding a sign that read "Stop the Bloodshed in Hungary"—had appeared in the August 1, 1958 issue of *U.S. News and World Report*. We also joined ACEN (the Assembly of Captive European Nations), a coalition of representatives from nine Central and Eastern Europe states under Soviet control.

I was eleven years old at the time.

*

At Tuxedo Park, none of my friendships were governed by class. At that age, other things count more, and we are more likely to see each other as we are. Unfortunately, that doesn't last long, and it generally isn't until we are well on in life that a democratic clarity of insight is restored. Though self-conscious about my stutter, I was considered "bright," did well in my studies, well enough at sports—football, softball, track; wrestled and boxed; won (but didn't deserve) the Music Prize for a poem about music; competed each year for honors in English; had small parts in the seventh grade in the "Mikado" and the "H.M.S. Pinafore"; and the lead (as Mr. Metcalf, the policeman in disguise) in Agatha Christie's *The Mouse Trap* in the eighth. Given my speech impediment, my casting was an act of faith. Yet I somehow managed (as others have) to find my voice on stage. The school put on only two performances for alumni and parents, but by the end of the second I was so enraptured by my newfound thespian skills, I was ready "to take it on the road."

These were also the years when I was first forced to compare myself in an academic way with others, since the standardized system of scholastic aptitude, I.Q., and other tests were taking hold.

My scores varied wildly (depending, it seemed, on how anxious I was at each testing), but from the start Hazard pressed me to excel.

I was inspired by his faith in my abilities and fell afoul of him only once.

In the boarding wing of the school, the girls' and boys' quarters were separated by a few empty rooms. I had a crush on my fellow student, Kate Aldrich, in the seventh grade, and the dorm master caught us one night in one of the empty rooms making out. The next day, Hazard called me into his office, seized me by the shoulders, and pushed me up against the wall. By the look on his face, I thought I would be expelled. "As a scholarship student," he said, "you have to walk on eggshells here!" Worst of all, I felt I had betrayed his trust.

My situation at the school was an anomalous one. On weekends, most of the boarding students went home. That left me virtually alone. My Latin teacher, Colin Newey, an Englishman—who at the time was studying to be an Anglican priest—intervened in angelic fashion and volunteered to act as my surrogate parent on some weekend days. With or without Hazard's consent, he used to drive me to New York for day trips with his girlfriend (a member of the school staff); treated me like an adult; allowed me to smoke; and took me to dinner, museums, and films—including Michael Todd's *The Scent of Mystery*, the first unsuccessful experiment in "Smell-O-Vision" cinema, on Times Square. I vividly remember the various scents—of flowers, perfume, tobacco, oranges, baked bread, lavender, peppermint, and port wine—that were piped through plastic tubing to our seats. It was immensely kind of them, and showed an incredible amount of trust.

Once, noticing a hole in one of my shoes, Colin bought me a new black pair in a smart Italian style. He also replaced an ill-fitting hand-me-down jacket I had that was laughably too large. So far as I know, he paid for all of this out of pocket, yet did so with such tact and discretion that his charity was concealed. To an outside eye, his broad indulgence might almost seem corrupting, especially with respect to a minor. But the opposite was true. On those remarkable days, I enjoyed a rare reprieve from an institutional life of strict regulation, breathed deeply and afresh, and felt connected to a wider world. In all else, he was absolutely conventional and proper, corrected me in old-world fashion, and never favored me in class.

That summer I attended a course at *La Maison Francaise* in New York to improve my French, and otherwise helped out at my father's short-lived Madison Avenue art gallery—the "Benson Baker Gallery," as it was called, because my father thought it had a Madison Avenue ring. Unfortunately, most of the work shown was second rate, "done in the style of," and the venture failed within the year. Meanwhile, in late August I received a long letter from Colin, who had since returned to England. Dated August 21st, 1960, it was written on the stationery of "Father C.J. Gardner, Pembroke House, Pembroke College Mission," and began: "Dear Barry [this was the familiar name I was known by, growing up], I should really be writing this letter within the walls of some Victorian mock-Gothic theological college, refreshed by invigorating cocoa and rock buns, but unfortunately I have been having what Anglicans politely call 'doubts' but which should more honestly be called 'cold feet,' so that I am still pacing up and down the College Mission, driving Father Gardner mad, and hurling abuse at Cockney children who peer in through the windows." He remarked that he had recently gone to a party at Haileybury School in Southampton ("a vast pile designed in the classical style in the early 19th century to turn out splendid chaps to 'run' India") and "there gracing the proceedings as the guest of honour was Peter Sellers whom we last laughed at as the Trade Union Leader in 'I'm All Right Jack.'"

He urged me to make the most of the coming year and "to try hard" for a prep school scholarship, which he thought I could obtain.

On December 22, he wrote again: "Dear Barry, I am staying with my eldest sister and her husband in Yorkshire—about five miles from Huddersfield, a grimy manufacturing town in the heart of "Room at the Top" country. From where we are we can look out across the hills towards the smoking factory chimneys of Huddersfield and Dewsbury which ... blanket the fields in a layer of coal-dust and grime. But in its own way the countryside is lovely—a series of dales and valleys, secluded and self-sufficient. Unlike the States you don't have to travel very far in England to move from one world to another." He went on to explain that while he remained unsure of the priesthood, he had decided to teach Latin and French at a Roman Catholic Prep School in Lancashire. The students, he said, far surpassed those he had taught in the States, and even though their average age was thirteen, "they have already done four years of both Latin & French, so you can imagine how advanced they are." That delighted him as a teacher, though he couldn't "quite get used to the idea of such young pupils translating Caesar, Ovid, or Virgil with consummate ease." Meanwhile, his health had been poor ("three bouts of bronchitis in less than six months") and he had returned home to spend time with his younger brother, who was then reading *The Once and Future King.* "I see," he added, "that it has been transformed into an indifferent Broadway musical under the title of *Camelot.*" As he looked back in amazement at the "extraordinary band" of Tuxedo Park students he had taught, he wondered if he had dreamed them up? "Every so often I have to check my passport and the year book to remind myself—like the man questioned by Robert Browning in his advanced years, 'And did you see Shelley plain?'"

I wonder if I replied to this splendid letter—written, with such open generosity, as to one beyond my years? I hope so. But I don't know. How careless we can be when we are young with the affections an elder bestows!

Meanwhile, Hazard had decided, as an economy measure, that boarding students would no longer be allowed to remain on weekends. Every other boarder arranged to go home, but for some logistical reason, which my father raised, it was apparently out of the question that I could. So I had to find a family to take me in. The divorced mother of a classmate, Gaines Gwathmey, agreed, and though her son was not exactly a friend—big for his age, he had once knocked me out in a snow-ball fight with an ice-ball thrown at close range—she was welcoming, informal, rather open, generous, and kind. I think Colin was behind this arrangement, for he had commended her as one to approach. Now and then, another classmate, Kurt Graetzer (who was almost as big as Gaines) had me over on weekends to watch episodes of "The Twilight Zone."

Gaines went on to head the Environmental Protection Unit of the U.S. Attorney's Office for the Southern District of New York; Kurt became an advertising executive who developed the enormously successful "Got milk" commercials that were featured for some time in almost every American magazine.

*

Upon graduating I received the Headmaster's Cup for overall achievement (which was meant to console me for missing out on the English Prize), and beside my picture in the year book, Hazard set down his farewell impressions, as he did for other members of the class. "An honor student—almost; a postponed trip to the barber shop; a scholarly nature; a class philosopher; an occasional afternoon tutor; a boarder down the road; a budding poet laureate; and then the certain knowledge of a successful career."

I wouldn't have thought so; but the fact that he seemed to gave me heart.

Hazard himself soon left Tuxedo Park to make his mark as an educator at other schools. Colin Newey disappeared. I would like to know what became of him. Unfortunately, all my searching turned up only his doppelganger opposite—a notorious London killer of the same name.

CHAPTER SEVEN

✿

It seems to me now—though perhaps this is special pleading—
that after my mother's death I received little conventional guidance.
Either my father was unable to provide it, or expected the schools
to perform that role. In the meantime, he had sold our house in
New Rochelle, and in 1957 we moved to a small, one bedroom
apartment on Beverly Road in the Flatbush section of Brooklyn,
not far from where his brother and two sisters lived. My father
and I occupied twin beds in the bedroom proper; my brothers
"camped out" in the living room on cots.

We were adrift in the summer months, without companions,
since our friends weren't local but had been made at boarding
school. We played stickball together in schoolyards, read, smoked,
listened to music, and went to films. The Beverly Theater on
Church Avenue was our regular haunt, and we saw movies there
almost every week. My reading was edgy: Mickey Spillane thrillers
(*Kiss Me Deadly, My Gun Is Quick*), Calder Willingham's *End As
A Man*, Hubert Selby's *Last Exit to Brooklyn*, Willi Heinrich's *The
Cross of Iron*, Eugene Burdick's *The Ninth Wave*. Science fiction
and westerns were part of the mix too, along with a good deal of
Somerset Maugham.

Once a year on average, my grandfather would come east

for a visit, and my brothers and I would meet him at Brooklyn's famed St. George's Hotel. We would all have lunch together and he would ask us about our lives. The hotel occupied an entire city block in Brooklyn Heights and had a large, Olympic-size salt water pool with a waterfall at one end. I was too shy to say much, and hardly remember what was said. On one occasion, my great uncle Charles and his wife, Susan, had also come east for a visit to Mohonk. That would have been in the Spring of 1957. I only remember it because that June my grandfather spent a day or two with us in Brooklyn and took us to a Dodgers game. The Dodgers were playing the Milwaukee Braves, and it was particularly memorable because a big fight broke out between the two teams. I put together a scrapbook of newspaper clippings about it the next day.

Later that summer, I went off to St. George's Episcopal Camp in Saugerties, New York, and my grandfather jokingly predicted I would come back "an Episcopalian." But no religious observances were part of the routine. Moreover, the whole thing got off to a terrible start when I arrived to find that thousands of ants had invaded the steamer trunk of my belongings sent forward in advance. After I settled in, I enjoyed the various sports and games and received a badge for swimming the Hudson River where it was a mile and a quarter wide. My brothers remained at home, which I'm sure was their preference, but at the end of August we all spent five days at "Camp Three Arrows," a cooperative summer colony founded in 1936 by young progressives at Shrub Oak, New York. At some point, I also attended a day camp at Coney Island. That time is a blank for me now, except that I remember sitting on the bus with others singing, a bit mournfully, "Que sera, sera," a hit song that year.

In the summer of 1959, we had a more meaningful excursion to Provincetown, Massachusetts, where I was captivated by the ocean, dunes, and sky. I eavesdropped on rehearsals at the Provincetown Playhouse for Eugene O'Neill's *The Emperor Jones*; did a few elementary drawings of the landscape with pastels; saw Ingmar Bergman's *Wild Strawberries*; and read *The White Company* and other books by Sir Arthur Conan Doyle. I was also infatuated that summer with the daughter of an artist we knew, and the very air I breathed was like nitrous oxide to my blood.

During these years, my father and grandfather exchanged a number of letters. These reveal that while my grandfather was mainly concerned about our upbringing, my father was obsessed by his struggle to make ends meet. Throughout my adolescence I had the impression we were on the verge of destitution, and if any of us so much as asked for a nickel, he made a thundering poor-house speech. It was like something out of Eugene O'Neill's *Long Day's Journey into Night*.

My father, in truth, was an unsettling mix—naïve yet shrewd, rational, strategic, often astute, yet so emotional he let his feelings overwhelm his common sense. With others, he was affable, sociable, often good-humored. But as a father he was hard to talk to; prone to sudden, explosive, rages; much speechifying; and even in response to simple statements, could assume a belligerent stance. Sometimes, he would declaim at you with a fierce emphasis, even if you agreed with him, as if you did not. When entertaining guests, he also had the mortifying habit of trotting us out as exhibits, while proclaiming our achievements. His pride in us (such as we were) was no doubt real, but on the whole we felt unequal to his claims; and so these attempts to bolster our self-confidence had the opposite effect.

Meanwhile, in March 1957 my father had drafted a Will that made my grandparents our guardians, should anything happen to him.

Yet now and then in their letters another note stole in. On April 4, 1958, my grandfather wrote: "We are in the Easter Season—a very precious household period for us. It has always been a high season in our home—holding all the faith and hope of life in the Courts of Light. So we think of Dear Lois—and life can go on. We trust that the same faith and hope may be yours. Blessings on you—and great wisdom in caring for the Boys."

My father did his best. He was a proud man of sorely injured pride, and a good and devoted parent—more so than I could know at the time. Though dazed by misfortune, he was responsible, conscientious, never neglected his work, upheld his ideals, and in time managed to recover from his loss. I know now, too, that for a long time we were, in fact, living on the edge. Certainly I forgive him for any hurt he caused me, and regret having clung to certain grievances so long.

Thanks to his example, moreover, I was uncorrupted by anything like racial hatred growing up. Indeed, though New Rochelle was the scene of the first court-ordered desegregation case in the North (in 1962), my parents had already desegregated our former neighborhood by selling our house to a black family a decade before. Our new home, at 15 Parcot Avenue, was adjacent to the local High School; below it and across the road were the small "Twin Lakes" of Huguenot Park where we used to catch sunfish with bait on a string. Near the causeway leading to the High School from North Avenue stood a white marble statue erected to the memory of fifteen local marines killed in World War II.

Late one afternoon, after school had ended, I climbed a fence and went down onto the athletic field where I saw a crowd of people surrounding two teenage boys, one white, one black, in a fight. Both were bleeding and had pocket knives taped up toward the tip, so they could hurt each other by slashing, but (in theory) not inflict a mortal wound. I was aghast. Then a year or so later, when I was ten, I read an item in *Time* Magazine about an Alabama black man who had been talking to his girlfriend on a street corner when he was abducted by several hooded members of the Ku Klux Klan. They took him to a deserted shack, beat him, castrated him with a razor, and poured turpentine on the wound. I was so shocked by the brutality of it that I couldn't get it out of my mind. A year after that, when we moved to the Flatbush section of Brooklyn, I got another lesson in what random ethnic hatred means.

A friend of my father's had gone to Israel on holiday and brought back an Arab keffiyeh or headdress for me as a gift. We lived in a very Jewish part of Brooklyn; but without any thought of it, I donned the keffiyeh and began walking over to the apartment where an aunt and uncle lived. I was maybe eleven at the time and wanted to show off my gift. Before I had gotten far, however, I heard shouting; then (to my astonishment) I heard myself being cursed. Someone screamed me, "Filthy Arab!" Another, that I should be hanged.

Perhaps the same thing might have happened in reverse if I had appeared with a yarmulke in an Arab neighborhood in Cairo. But in 1958 in Brooklyn it had happened to me.

*

My father had a handful of old friends, whom we saw occasionally but never got to know—among them: Fay and Roland Watts, Jacob L. Holtzmann, and a man we called "Doc" Davidoff. Roland had belonged to the Workers Defense League and was later a legal director for the A.C.L.U. His wife, Fay, also did civil liberties work, and during the Kennedy and Johnson administrations belonged to the National Committee on Rural Development for the Department of Agriculture. Holtzmann, from a different realm, was an Austrian born lawyer and philanthropist who in 1912 had helped organize the National Progressive Party of Theodore Roosevelt. He was involved in Jewish charitable causes, and in his later years emerged as a power in Republican politics. For a while, I believe, he was president of the Electoral College and a Republican elector for New York State. As for Morris "Doc" Davidoff, he was a shadowy figure who had evidently lent my father money during hard times.

Meanwhile, whatever my father's law practice had once been, it had taken a quixotic turn. From the mid-1950s on it was marked by hopeless ventures against large corporations as he jousted from his tiny office with financial titans who commanded huge law firms with multi-story suites. His scant legal means made these contests seem surreal, yet (given my father's innate skill and determination) their various stays, reversals, and appeals went on for years. Now and then his fortunes even trembled on the cusp of success. Toward the end of his life, he once admitted to me, in a rare personal aside: "I was a good lawyer, but a terrible businessman."

One of the windmills he tilted against was the Alleghany Corporation, a holding company with ten million shares that controlled various large entities including the New York Central Railroad. When a struggle developed for control at the helm, my father rounded up some 200 incidental stockholders to form a "Stockholders' Committee" to negotiate a truce. In theory, its role was to heal the breach between Allan P. Kirby, heir to the Woolworth five-and-dime store chain, and the Murchison brothers (John and Clint) who owned the Dallas Cowboys. At stake was a $6.7 billion financial empire. Years of in-fighting ensued in the largest proxy fight in American history. The theatrical magnitude of it led one appeals court judge to describe it as "a modern War of the Roses." Eventually, Kirby prevailed and placed Charles T. Ireland Jr., a former secretary of the New York Central Railroad, at the helm.

What was my father, who could barely afford our lower middle class apartment, doing in the middle of all this? With his customary insight, after Kirby's triumph, he had uncovered an insider trading scheme, orchestrated by the victors. On behalf of two small stockholders, he therefore filed suit in the United States Court of Appeals for the Second Circuit for redress. Kirby and Ireland summoned to their defense three large law firms: Donovan, Leisure, Newton & Irvine; Willkie Farr & Gallagher; and Pollack Greenspoon & Singer, with hundreds of lawyers at their command. In the complex litigation that followed, my father almost won.

Another, similar case pitted him against the Glen Alden Corporation, a diversified company with vast holdings, presided over by the industrialist Albert A. List, whose ever-expanding assets included the Hudson Coal Company (the principal hard coal producer in the United States) as well as the RKO Theater chain. Once more, my father went up against two mighty law firms: O'Brien, Driscoll, & Raftery, and Battle, Fowler, Stokes & Kheel. The former boasted clients such as United Artists; the latter, several Presidents of the United States. Yet the stockholders, represented by my father, won a substantial settlement, and for about a year fortune's star glimmered above him in the sky. Then an Appeals Court reversed the judgment in a three-to-two vote. The deciding vote was cast by Judge George J. Beldock, who should have recused himself due to his interest in the case. Just before the appeal was heard, List had given $20,000 to an organization that Beldock had founded—and that List chaired! After he received a favorable verdict, List gave the foundation tens of thousands of dollars more. My father, learning of these dealings, which seemed corrupt on their face, claimed his clients had been deprived of due process, and equal protection under the law. In October 1967, the matter finally went to the Supreme Court. Though the Court dismissed the case, Justice Hugo Black voted for Certiorari, implying that the anomalies should have been explored.

These drawn-out cases were the backdrop to my life away at school, and I often came home to an environment charged with my father's frustration and rage. I vividly remember him returning red-faced from the office one day and pounding his fist on a table and shouting, "Court house justice stinks!" In a more philosophic mood, he had various homely expressions with which he voiced his discontent, such as "Man is a mistake-maker," or (a favorite) "The earth is the insane asylum of the universe."

One notable, if not particularly gainful, suit he won secured the right of artists in New York City to live in studio lofts. Throughout the 1950s, many artists had occupied lofts in buildings once devoted to manufacturing. Absurdly, they had been compelled to meet the same rigid fire and safety requirements as the industries had. In 1960, facing possible eviction, many had threatened to "strike" (that is, to boycott galleries and museums) and to take their protest to the streets. The city relented and allowed them to remain, but in December 1961 it reneged on its agreement. My father, representing the Artists-Tenants Association, took the case to Municipal Term court and won.

He rejoiced in the triumph. And it might have been a fine end to his career.

But his day was not yet done.

CHAPTER EIGHT

Meanwhile, after Tuxedo Park, I had gone on to Pomfret School, a boys' prep school founded in 1894 in northeastern Connecticut. It had a handsome, rural campus designed by Frederick Law Olmsted and a Romanesque stone chapel, radiant with medieval stained glass. Its Rose Window, above the entrance, as well as two of its arched, oblong side windows, had once belonged to the 13th century French cathedral of St. Julien of Tours. Various other campus buildings, designed by the architect Ernest Flagg, followed the Beaux Art style he had developed for the U.S. Naval Academy at Annapolis, which secured his fame.

Over the years, Pomfret had produced a number of illustrious alumni, including prominent bankers, diplomats, Congressmen, lawyers, financiers, scientists, and doctors, with names like Gulden, Morgan, Studebaker, and DuPont. In Edward Stettinus, it could claim one Secretary of State. Some artists, writers, and playwrights also emerged from its ranks, though they belonged to a relatively small subset of each class. The resident rector was Episcopalian; the school's "mascot" the mythical Griffin; and its motto, "Certa Viriliter" ("Strive Manfully"), which was oddly retained after the school later became co-ed. Just as oddly, the school's Coat of Arms was derived from that of the Lords of Pontefract Castle in the town of Pomfret, West Yorkshire, England where Richard II had perished in a crypt.

Pomfret's self-proclaimed purpose was to develop in its students "an alert and active mind able to grasp and solve the problems of the age." For such ambitions, it had a relatively small library, at least when I entered, but six playing fields, eight tennis courts, a hockey pond, and two ski slopes on its extensive grounds. Its faculty, however, was strong, newly diverse, and had a good deal to offer not only in athletics, but in the sciences, humanities, and arts. Under the enlightened direction of its new headmaster, Joseph K. ("Jay") Milnor (who had previously served as head of the American Academy in Istanbul), Pomfret began to embrace the wider world. There were exchange students from England and the Philippines and an African Seminar that went to Nigeria and Uganda. The color barrier was also broken with my class.

Pomfret should have been congenial to my soul. But by then I had already been in boarding schools too long. I had little enthusiasm, at first, for what I might encounter, and my stay was tinged with resentment at having to be there at all. Some of the faculty had curious or compelling pasts—there was a science teacher, for example, with a swarthy (or "sooty") complexion, who (it was darkly whispered) had worked on the atomic bomb; an athletic coach who had lost a testicle in a locker-room fight; an English teacher who had survived internment by the Japanese; a drama teacher who suffered badly from shell-shock from the war. The last was beset by a host of nervous tics, drank heavily, and, with a kind of touching futility, dusted his clothes each morning with talcum powder to try to mask the scent. One of my favorite teachers was Marcel Marcotte, who taught Philosophy and French. He was witty, wry, clever, good at explaining difficult ideas, and enlivened his cheerful commentary with bits of proverbial wisdom, such as: "If you don't know what you don't know, you're in trouble." He also directed an International Affairs Seminar that took students to Europe, and in the summer of 1964, he led the group to study the Common Market as an example of international accord. Another was Alice Dunbar, who taught sculpture and ceramics and did fine work herself in bronze, wood, marble, and clay. Under her guidance, much to my surprise, I created a well-wrought, glazed, clay image, in three-quarter profile, of a man smoking a pipe. She liked it so much she borrowed it for an exhibit in New York. This taught me that my artistic nature was diverse, for (as I was moved to recall) I had once learned to draw the truss work of bridges with skill. Later in life, I would make an interim living at a number of artistic trades—as jeweler, leather-craftsman, book-binder, and graphic designer—before I managed by my pen. Among the other faculty, I also had a good History teacher in Ben Williams and a good English teacher in Norval Rindfleisch, who later won the O'Henry Short Story Award.

My principal guide at Pomfret, however, was Hagop Merjian, who helped confirm my bearings toward a life of literature and learning and by his own, high example showed me what such a life could mean. Other teachers served as ancillary lights; but Hagop was my North Star. He taught English and Humanities and came to enjoy in my eyes an Olympian stature among his peers.

Though only a decade or so older than myself, he spoke six languages other than English—Armenian, German, Spanish, Arabic, Turkish, and Greek; had studied at Columbia under a number of notable poets and scholars (including Mark Van Doren, Louis Simpson, Jacob Taubes, and Walter J. Ong); had lived in Egypt and Greece; and brought to his teaching a scholar's passion for learning, a poet's passion for words, a prodigious linguistic curiosity and knowledge, and a humane devotion to his students and the impact of learning on their lives. Beyond his school obligations, he wrote himself when he could and occasionally published articles or poems in magazines. Meanwhile, at Pomfret Center, he built his own house and barn; established a farm; grew lettuce, spinach, onions, chard; raised and slaughtered his own livestock (turkeys, lambs, and pigs); and in general recreated a "little Armenia" for himself adjacent to the pristine campus of the school.

Beyond the usual syllabus of assigned reading (Hemingway,

Faulkner, Fitzgerald, O. Henry, and the like), Hagop introduced me to poets like Nazim Hikmet and Conrad Aiken, mythopoeic ideas of language, Greek literature (in particular Plato, in his Humanities class), and controversial social analysis by such figures as Eric Hoffer and C. Wright Mills. His exuberant energy and manifold range made him a force of nature; yet mingled with that gusto was a deep, mournful understanding of the tyranny of history over persecuted lives. Both of his parents had been orphaned, and after barely surviving the Armenian genocide of the Turks, had run a gauntlet of tribulations before making their way from eastern Turkey to New York. There Hagop had grown up in polyglot communities in Brooklyn and Queens, where his family mingled with Arabs, Greeks, Turks, Russians, and Jews. Every weekend, he once told me, his father (who cleaned oriental rugs for a living) would "rehearse and repeat 'good morning' and 'hello' and 'thank you' and 'goodbye' to me in a dozen languages, always repeating to me, in Armenian, 'a new language learned is a new world understood.'"

In addition to his teaching, Hagop counseled college admissions; advised the school's literary publications; and coached soccer and wrestling, among other sports. Some years after my time at Pomfret, he won the Gold Medal National Wrestling title in his weight class in the Master's Tournament at the age of 44.

Despite my ambivalence toward Pomfret, I was active in its life, and for the time I was there, on the staff of the school newspaper and literary magazine. In time, I became Editor-in-Chief of both. I was also a member of the International Affairs Committee and the Literary Society; Chairman of the Smoking Committee (a social post); a member of Pomfret's delegation to the Model United Nations, in which we represented Bulgaria; acted in a minor role in at least one play, *The Mad Woman of Chaillot*, by Michel de Chelderode; and earned a letter in athletics, for wrestling, in my 9th grade (or 3rd Form) year. In academics, my experience recapitulated that at Tuxedo Park. At first I struggled with the demands, then finding my level, rose.

Yet I was never sure I deserved the honors I received. It

seemed to me I had to work harder than most, and often gave the impression of knowing more than I did. At the same time, I took a sincere interest in large existential questions, and managed, in various ways, to accumulate an odd assortment of "advanced" knowledge unfamiliar to my peers. When not at school, my bohemian adolescence had allowed me to roam, from about the age of ten, unsupervised around New York; "hang out" in Greenwich Village; take in foreign films; and attend parties where avant-garde artists and political radicals mixed. I had been introduced to subjects like voodoo and the kabbalah, and at one gathering met Maya Deren, the famed avant-garde dancer, film-maker, and ethnologist. About this time, my father also remarried, and my stepmother—Elizabeth "Sherry" Most—brought new love and order to our home and enlarged my awareness of contemporary art and artists in whose circles she moved. When my father met her, she was living in a little apartment with a courtyard at Milligan Place, around the corner from E.E. Cummings. Willem de Kooning, Franz Kline, and other artists were among her acquaintances or friends.

Born Elizabeth Sharnoff on November 28, 1908 in Berdichev, Ukraine, she had come to the United States in 1909; won a two-year fellowship to the Jewish School of Social Work; married a journalist, Melos Most; traveled throughout Europe; and in 1939–1940 bicycled all over Greece. When World War II broke out, her husband became a wire correspondent for the Associated Press and she joined the American Red Cross. The German invasion of France overtook them, and together they were interned in Baden-Baden for thirteen months. After the war, she became a Welfare Officer for UNRRA (the United Nations Relief and Rehabilitation Administration) in a displaced persons camp at Wiesbaden, Germany. When Eleanor Roosevelt visited the camp, she gave her the tour. After she was divorced in 1949, she worked for the Margaret Sanger Bureau and Planned Parenthood, was connected by her friendships with the Abstract Expressionist movement, earned her doctorate in Social Work from Columbia University at the age of 52, and subsequently taught at the New

School for Social Research.

Meanwhile, in 1962 she had married my father (the year after I entered Pomfret) and we had all moved to the ILGWU Penn South Cooperative Housing Development in the Chelsea district of Manhattan. There we had three bedrooms (one of which my father used as an office), a living room, two bathrooms, a kitchen, and a balcony, with a clear view of the Empire State Building from the 13th Floor. The rent was cheap, but it was a spacious and luxurious apartment compared to what we had known.

My step-mother recounted her adventures to me in detail, which opened my eyes to many things; and years later when she was 93, I undertook to write her Memoir based in part on her words. It was privately reproduced and never published; but for the history in it at least, it ought to be preserved. Here is a page from a typical but memorable excursion she had with her first husband in the spring of 1940, as they pedaled through Greece:

> Macedonia was even wilder and more rugged than the more remote places we had seen in Spain. Often there were no inns to stay at, so we lodged with local peasants, who were very hospitable on the whole and glad to entertain strangers. Sometimes they were even reluctant to let us go when morning came. We enjoyed their company, and after a while learned to drink their resinated wine, which seemed to me at first to savor of kerosene. Eventually, I grew to like the taste.
>
> One afternoon we decided to cross the mountains to a village on the other side. The climb turned out to be difficult, and it was already dark by the time we reached the top. Suddenly, heavy flashlights were brandished in our faces and we were taken into custody by the mountain police. Their quarters were near the summit, and there they questioned us about out intentions. This was in May 1940, when no one expected to find tourists in such a place. So they kept us overnight, made radio contact about us with the authorities

in Athens, and explained they could not release us until we had been cleared. Meanwhile, they looked through our knap-sacks for clues of any seditious designs. By the next morning, however, a search of the criminal records in Athens had turned up nothing to incriminate us, so they let us go. A few hours later we came to the settlement on the opposite slope.

This was Larissa. From there we made a side trip by bus to a remarkable group of immense menhir-like columns of conglomerate rock that rose straight out of the ground. On the top of each cliff stood a monastery, and in former times the resident monks had to be hoisted up to their domi-ciles in baskets by pulley and rope. Later, crude steps were hewn out of the rock. We made our way up, visited some of the flower and vegetable gardens which the monks had culti-vated, and lunched with them on wine and marachina squares. We also had a chance to view more Byzantine frescoes, and in one place saw a pile of bone skeletons in a crypt. In fact, we were so absorbed in our adventure, that we missed the only bus back to town. At length, a man offered us his own car for hire, though he wasn't sure it could make the 12-mile trip. He had trouble getting it started, then it jerked along for two or three miles before giving out. There seemed to be no way to make it go further, and we were very sorry then not to have our trusty bikes.

So we began to walk. The road was rough, and the area wild. Mel found a stout stick to use against any dog that might attack us, since dogs in the area were kept mostly for guarding property, not as pets. But we made it through all right and finally reached our hotel in Larissa about midnight, where before going to bed I had to soak my blistered feet.

We proceeded along the coast to Athens, and by the time we arrived, the Easter holidays had begun. The streets were lit and festooned with decorations, and everyone looked their best. Our first night there we witnessed an imposing ceremony on the steps of the central cathedral. We had just taken up our own position in the crowd on the main square when it was surrounded by a mounted contingent of the king's royal guard. These 'Greek highlanders,' or Evzones, as they were called, sported colorfully embroidered blouses, blue and white kilts, tasseled garters, shoes and large pom poms, and other striking garb. Suddenly, the king himself appeared holding a long, slender candle, and just as he lit it, everyone else lit theirs. All at once, thousands of twinkling lights shimmered from the balconies of the surrounding houses and throughout the assembled throng.

The following day the royal guard invited us into their barracks, where they were busy roasting lamb over spits. They made a fuss over the fact that we were both Americans, and let us take pictures of them while they feasted at long tables set up in their courtyard and danced some of the slow intricate dances for which they are also famed. Then, to our astonishment, the king himself came in—the second time we had seen him in two days—and after he said a few words, distributed Easter Eggs to each table. We were invited to sit down and eat at one of them, and I was even given one of the Easter Eggs the king had brought.

These and other unique and vivid stories held me in thrall.

*

While at Pomfret, I finally began to know my grandfather as he was. He encouraged me in my studies, cheered on whatever I did in sports, and always closed his letters with a deeply affecting goodbye: "We send a shout of joy for it is always a joy even to think of you," or "Your grandmother and I hold you in our hearts and hopes day by day." Now and then there was a political aside: "Some of your Republican friends in that privileged school are probably being warned at home of the dangers of the welfare state. Meanwhile we are sharing in some of its privileges." He meant the government-funded "Talking Books" program for the blind, his sight having failed. Kennedy was president then, and he was glad that Kennedy hoped to extend social benefits. He "has a heart for others, including children," my grandfather wrote, which he felt the Republican Party lacked.

Of course, he took an interest in my reading (Hermann Hesse, Albert Camus, and other fashionable writers, some of whom he knew), but urged me to look as well at Alfred North Whitehead on education and William E. Hocking on theology and faith. His own reading (at age 84, by way of "Talking Books") included a book about Kennedy's circle of advisors, an account of "the Geophysical Year," and Jane Austen's *Pride and Prejudice* "which I should have read years ago and which drew upon my patience to read even now. Nevertheless it was a good experience." As I approached the age of independence, he warned me against the health-risks of smoking—"Please suffer the admonition and know that we count on you having a busy and useful life."

The summer of my 17th year, I worked as an usher at the RKO Palace movie theater in New York's Times Square. This was before its reconversion to a Broadway stage, and long after it had enjoyed fame as the best vaudeville theater in New York. Its ornate, gilded interior was still stunning, but the neighborhood was seedy; and I soon discovered that the first bags of kerneled corn brought up each day from the basement for popping were those gnawed through by rats. I also got hustled out of my first paycheck by a fellow usher at a pool hall nearby. The two movies I remember clearly are *Zulu*, released that June, about a fateful battle between Zulu warriors and British colonial troops in 1879; and Hitchcock's *Marnie*, released in July. As an usher, I saw them both, of course, a hundred times. I usually worked evenings, but on Sundays had the morning shift, when the theater was favored by prostitutes and pimps, early morning drunks, and, on occasion, unregenerate priests, who cheered on the slaughter of Zulu tribesmen from the incognito shadows of their balcony seats.

I had a pocket Latin dictionary with me that summer, and when not patrolling the aisles with a flashlight to embarrass smokers or loud talkers, tried not to waste my time.

Not surprisingly, my grandfather liked to imagine my summer in more positive terms. He hoped that I had turned it to account "as a study of photography and film making," for example; and that by my contacts with others in the workaday world, I had begun to acquire an "appreciation for 'unlikeness' which is one of the hardest things to achieve." He also tried to steer me onto a good path. In my senior year, he called my attention to an essay on T.S. Eliot in the *Saturday Review*. It examined the religious message of *The Waste Land* and explained that its central image was taken from Dante's seventh circle of Hell, the burning plain on which "the Violent and the Bestial" (murderers, war-makers, suicides, blasphemers, perverts, and usurers) were placed to condemn the spiritual wasteland of our times. In Eliot's view, the modern world was "cut off from all that joins men in love or touches the earth to its flowering."

A year later my grandfather commended another article (also in the *Saturday Review*) by Archibald MacLeish which contrasted the fashionable idea of human nature as debased with the more lofty idea of Man as expressed by the Chorus in *Antigone*—"Wonders are many on the earth and of these man is the greatest"—and the great soliloquy in Hamlet—"What a piece of work is a man! how noble in reason!/ how infinite in faculty! . . . /in action how like an angel!/ in apprehension how like a god!"

*

As an editor at Pomfret, I must have had a critical eye, but my own writing was incredibly turgid and heavy-laden with involved expressions and abstract words. What might have been said simply was often mouthed over and obscure. There was a tortured quality to it, like a voice in chains. I can barely understand what I was saying; or why I said it as badly as I did.

The general quality of the *The Pomfret Review* (the school's literary magazine) was high. In 1962, for example, there were essays on Joyce and Aristotle, Copernicus, Debussy, Thomas Mann, Augustine and Boethius, Conrad's *The Heart of Darkness*, and

William Golding's *Lord of the Flies*; in the following year, on George Bernard Shaw, Robert Browning's "Rabbi Ben Ezra," Adam Smith, Bishop George Berkeley; and so on. Other issues had papers on "The Folk Tale as Psychic Revelation," "The Aftermath of the Expulsion of the Bonus Army, July 28, 1932," concepts of Time, and "Echolocation in Bats."

That spoke well for the school.

However, the best thing about the *Review* in my day were the blurbs with which Hagop introduced each piece. Here, for example, is how he prefaced a paper on "A Study in Time: Mythic and Religious": "The Western consciousness, our consciousness, contains within it three basic time motifs: 1.) cyclical time: the idea of time as a natural, regenerative thing, manifested and witnessed in the seasons of the year, believed in the festivals of man, and worshipped in the perpetuation of life year after year. 2.) vertical time: the Graecic contribution to our consciousness that drives man out of time, for it awakens our souls to the idea of perfection, of absolute forms and divinely perfect ideas. The dialectical quest for absolute truth must end in a goal outside of history, suprahistorical, and so it does—the immortality of Socrates. 3.) horizontal time: out of the Hebraic experience of the Old and New Testaments comes the idea that time has a divine origin, is divinely ordained and is progressing toward a divine conclusion. Time becomes invested with sacrality: is holy. History becomes, therefore, sacred; the arena where man's relation to God is revealed."

There is a whole education in that paragraph.

In general, Pomfret's students were engaged. When the school opened its own on-campus paperback bookstore in the fall of 1963, for example, the bestsellers in its first two weeks were: *Brave New World*, by Aldous Huxley; *Rabbit Run*, by John Updike; *Go Tell It on the Mountain*, by James Baldwin; *1984*, by George Orwell; *Hiroshima, Mon Amour*, by John Hersey; *Doctor No*, by Ian Fleming; *Four Great Elizabethan Plays: Doctor Faustus, The Duchess of Malfi, the Shoemaker's Holiday*, and *Volpone*, with an Introduction by John Gassner; *The Bridges at Toko Ri*, by James

Michener; *The Future of Architecture*, by Frank Lloyd Wright; and *Seven Short Novels*, by Anton Chekhov.

Although schools like Pomfret tend to turn out members of the "ruling elite," perhaps because my class was fired in the kiln of the 60s, it proved more diverse. It produced a dedicated Civil Rights lawyer; two or three gifted artists; a famed ornithologist; a celebrated song-writer; an outstanding musical director; a master craftsman; two accomplished architects; a high-minded banker; two prominent physicians; a leading expert on community and regional planning; one writer (maybe two); and a pioneering entrepreneur in the farming of cannabis, before the law allowed! No doubt there are others who might be singled out.

Memories of friendships, some fleeting, abide. One was with Miguel Delgado de Torres, whose older sister, Ines, would marry the poet Galway Kinnell. Ines, then an editor at Scribners and a woman of statuesque beauty, introduced me to the work of Malcolm Lowry, whose *Under the Volcano* (like Hermann Hesse's *Siddartha*), was then almost obligatory reading for those in their late teens. Lowry's doomed life story naturally appealed to me, as perhaps she thought it would; later Ines and I would form a more mature friendship when our paths re-crossed.

Miguel's parents were among the loveliest, warmest people I had ever met. They embraced me like a long-lost son and welcomed me with joy in visits to their home. I was also fascinated by their past. During the Spanish Civil War, Miguel's father had served in the Republican government of Juan Negrin, and kept key government resources—funds, documents, gold, and so on—from falling into Fascist hands. Through his own deft arrangements, these assets were secretly dispersed to depositories in Russia, Mexico, and France.

Another friend and classmate was Bill Rukeyser, the son of the poet Muriel Rukeyser, who came to Pomfret one day in March of 1964 to read. She was then about 50, large and heavy, but with a commanding presence, and had just published her translation of the poems of Octavio Paz. After the audience fell silent—a silence her patience seemed to impose—she read her fine short lyric "Song" in a slow and measured fashion, with such a sonorous, noble, and dignified voice, that it indelibly imprinted itself on my mind as the way a poem should be read. In her following talk, she remarked, among other things, that "poetry is noticing," and closed with a poem about a bridge. I saw her on a couple of other occasions when she came to visit her son, and in addition to an inscribed copy of her *Selected Poems*, she gave me her own copy of *The Autobiography of William Butler Yeats*.

In her public stance, she was a poet-prophet of Biblical fire, wrote poems that were "primordial and torrential," at times mystical, or full-throated jeremiads against injustice in the world. Her work was occasionally disparaged for its lack of restraint, but what I remember most about her now was her majestic presence and self-respect. Many years later, when I was deeply immersed in Elizabethan studies, I was delighted to discover her excellent book on Thomas Hariot, a pioneering figure and magus of the English Renaissance.

*

Since my father had been an activist, I was probably more aware than most of my classmates of the great struggles on the world stage. By our senior year, the Vietnam War had begun to take possession of the national psyche and I joined an anti-war march on Washington on April 17, 1965. A month later, I graduated with a scholarship to Columbia University. When the headmaster, Jay Milnor, gave me my diploma, he shook my hand and said: "You're a credit to the school." That was more than gracious. The year before I had almost been expelled. As editor of the school paper, *The Pontefract*, I had approved a series of articles and cartoons that criticized the school administration and some of the programs (in particular, a compulsory chapel program) recently put in place. Moreover, instead of clearing the issue with the faculty advisor, as required, I had managed to get it printed surreptitiously for distribution on Commencement Day. That way it got into the hands of the parents unchecked.

It caused a stir, and soon after the summer recess began, I (and my co-editor, Robert J. "Buzz" Yudell) were summoned back to school with our parents to answer for our deed. I remember the court-martial-like proceedings, and the stern faces of the chosen faculty in their chairs. We apologized profusely and showed ourselves contrite; in return, we were granted a reprieve. My contrition was inwardly reluctant then, but grew to be sincere. Yudell later became a trustee of the school.

The summer before my freshman year at Columbia began, Hagop sent me a letter of advice. Wondering how I would manage, he advised me to "get a haircut," find practical employment (if possible at a big corporation); urged me to check out the Thalia Movie Theater (famed for its foreign and avant-garde films); explore the bookstores below Herald Square; remain an activist; but "stay out of trouble with the law." He also offered to read (and critique) anything I wrote: "I always have time for this," he said.

Two years later, he and his wife, Aggie, came to the East Village, where my Pomfret classmate, Peter Murkett (then also at Columbia) and I both lived. He wrote afterwards: "Very fine to see you last week. Very painful to leave so early; there is no doubt about it, we should not get together again unless we have a full day or even a few days to spare .... [Aggie] finds both of you beautiful and quick; the only alternative in the Nicene Creed—remember?? I will keep in touch with you somehow .... For any old thing, keep me posted." He included a calendar of poems: "Each day of the year's avarice will perhaps be satiated by flowers rather than cadavers if it is met with one of these poems. Enjoy this calendar. I do so much. It is and has been the greatest and most meaningful anthology of poetry for me—and perhaps for our carcinogenic nation."

Thirty-two years would pass before I saw him again.

CHAPTER NINE

At Columbia, I went somewhat wild with my new freedom, found my own apartment at the outset, lived in Spanish Harlem, then the East Village; got high on hashish (but stayed clear of psychedelic drugs); was often "in love" (driven by desire); and refreshed my thirst at the West End Bar, then a fabled university hang out on upper Broadway. My brother, Pete, two years my senior, was also at Columbia, where he majored in Chinese. I chose English, with a sub-major in Classics, in emulation of my eldest brother, Jim. My literary taste (not unlike his) also inclined to Medieval and Renaissance Studies. But I was interested, too, in disparate figures like Karl Popper and Ludwig Wittgenstein, and the scholastic philosophies of St. Thomas Aquinas and St. Augustine. My particular texts of reference in the history of ideas were by Paul Oskar Kristeller, John Herman Randall, Erich Auerbach, and E.R. Curtius; the art history books of E.H. Gombrich, Erwin Panofsky, and Edgar Wind; various Oxford Companions to English Literature (especially those by C.S. Lewis and Douglas Bush); E.M.W. Tillyard, Rosemond Tuve and Rosalie Colie in Renaissance studies; and Moses Hadas, Gilbert Highet, and Henry Steele Commager, Jr., for the literature of Greece and Rome. Some of these scholars (Highet, Kristeller, Randall, and Commager) were on the Columbia faculty then, and I was privileged to hear them; Moses Hadas had died the year I enrolled. In philosophy my guides were Etienne Gilson, for scholastic thought, and a ten-volume history of philosophy by Frederick Copleston, S.J. I was driven by a tremendous mania "to know." I had more or less tortured myself over Existentialism in my teens; and in my freshman year at Columbia remember imposing upon a friend—who was trying to prepare for a date—for a clear explanation of the difference between Aristotle's Universal Specific Concept and the Platonic Idea. The matter seemed so urgent to me I couldn't put it off.

Now and then my dormant faith stirred. I remember one night at the West End Bar, when all the raucous sounds around me seemed to fade, and I was seized with a longing for some divine presence on which I could rely. I then found myself repeating those iconic, once familiar lines that every student of the Middle Ages used to know: "Everyman, I will go with thee and be thy guide, in thy most need to go by thy side."

My roommate for Freshmen Orientation Week was Faris Bouhafa, an "Irish-Tunisian" who (when I knew him) seemed mostly to love fast cars. He used to take me at night for hair-raising rides of tremendous speed on back roads in New Jersey while we waited for the week to pass. I thought of him as a kind of playboy then; as I discovered much later, he was more. When I came upon his obituary in 2006, I learned that he had been a force in contemporary music, promoting Bob Dylan's career; had managed the famed rock club, Max's Kansas City, where he featured Bob Marley and Bruce Springsteen, then both fairly unknown; and, later, when the American Muslim community was under attack, served as a rational spokesman for the Arab-American League during the first Gulf War.

For all my hectic living and distractions, I was also a dedicated student, studied hard, mindful of the scholarship I held, and of my need to repeat it year to year. In my anti-war activity, however, I took real risks. Before college I had helped organize a community teach-in (possibly the first) against the war at P.S. 11 in Chelsea, on July 30, 1965. As a freshman, I took part in a number of demonstrations, churned out leaflets, and attempted one brief speech from the campus Sundial (a time-honored soapbox) on College Walk. In the following year, on February 8, 1967, as a member of SDS (Students for a Democratic Society), I also joined with seventeen others in a sit-in against C.I.A. recruiters in Dodge Hall. It was the first sit-in on campus, and an early act of civil disobedience against the war. In its aftermath, there was a "trial" in Low Library, which nearly led to my expulsion. At the time, a still-moderate-seeming Mark Rudd, the future "Weatherman" extremist (who sat behind me in my Humanities class), sharply criticized me for my "radical" action on the grounds that it might "alienate undecideds" at the school.

The folly of the war, and its horrific carnage, was the obsession of just about everyone who was politically aware; and though students and others split into many groups and factions, in the generally mobilized marches and demonstrations, all tended to merge—the War Resisters League, Youth Against War and Fascism, SNCC (the Student Non-Violent Coordinating Committee), SDS, the WSA (Worker Student Alliance); and so on, along with more doctrinaire groups like the Socialist Labor Party, the Progressive Labor Party (which was Maoist), and the Trotskyite Spartacist League. The latter had their own long-term agenda and tried to exploit the naive goodwill of student unrest. On the other side, government informers and agents provocateurs tried to lure the well-meaning into violent schemes. Both plied the same sinister, seditious trade. It was a treacherous time for any young activist enraged by social injustice and a calamitous war.

In one way or another, almost everyone became involved. One day at Book Forum, a store across from the campus on upper Broadway, I encountered a Pomfret alumnus who was a prominent Trotskyite. He had been three grades ahead of me at school, where I had known him slightly, and was astonished to find he held the dogmatic views he did. More than a convert, he was a founding member of the Spartacist League and its "leading theoretician on trade union work."

Later that year, I moved to the East Village. Though my apartment was far from campus, its distance accorded with my divided world. When not absorbed in my studies, I went to a strobe-lit nightclub on St. Mark's Place called "The Balloon Farm" (afterwards, "The Electric Circus"); to the Fillmore East Theater to hear Linda Ronstandt, the Fugs, and other current bands; Janis Joplin at Tompkins Square Park; art movie houses like the 8th Street Playhouse; or roamed (as I had for years) about Washington Square Park. One day, walking there with a girlfriend, we caught sight of W.H. Auden sitting on a bench. In a sense, I owed him my life. A few months before, as I was walking home with his *Collected Poems* and a notebook under my arm, a demented derelict, or addict, had tried to stab me. With the help of his book, I just managed to deflect the blow.

Those living on my street—I had now moved from 10th Street between Avenues A and B to 5th Street between 1st and A—were also occasionally harassed by someone who threw eggs at them from a roof. One afternoon the great jazz musician Charlie Mingus came up the street with a bow and arrow shouting, "Ok, egg-man, come on out!" And—to everyone's surprise—the harassment ceased.

For a time, I dated a girl at Brooklyn College, and on one of my long subway rides home from her family apartment in Brooklyn, I wrote a dejected poem—conceived as a sonnet, less one line (to represent my own incompleteness); and of course it was bound up with my faltering speech:

> I wonder at my place among these lives –
> The Brooklyn to Manhattan train
> Stammering the darkness, speech
> Lost to the coherent, simple sleep
> Of other men. I wonder at these eyes
> Like dusk before me in this subway dawn,
> What secrets of disaster each pair hides,
> What words, unspoken, each had wished to say –

On this, the last-mile shuttle of their longest day.
How many times, perhaps, such eyes were stunned
By gun-shocks of some sudden love –
Now tired, staring at the ads above,
These people are all haunted by their names.

Not long afterwards I met someone whose aunt had been a friend of my mother's, and whose great uncle had been my grandfather's colleague at the University of Illinois. She was a gifted artist, jeweler, leather-craftsman, and painter, played the guitar nicely, and sang well. Our friendship became romantic, in part inspired by our remarkable family ties. But we were more like brother and sister, and the romance was brief. During our time together, however, she taught me how to make jewelry—pendants, rings, earrings, bracelets, and the like—out of gold and silver wire. In my studio apartment, I had a great sheet of plywood for a desk, now strewn with books and papers, now cleared for craftwork, where I assembled my tools and soldered together my pieces with an acetylene torch on an asbestos block. From that process of step-by-step creation I first came to understand what went into the construction of a well-made artifact.

In a risky move that left me open to the draft, I took a year's leave of absence from school in the following year. It seemed to me then that I had reached a breaking point. The uninterrupted strain of years of pressurized study, combined with the daily exhaustion of coping with my speech, had taken an untenable toll, and made an intermission imperative for my mental health. My faculty adviser, A. Kent Hieatt, the noted Medieval and Renaissance scholar, wisely advised me not to take incompletes, but return to a clean slate. "You don't want all that unfinished work hanging over you when you come back," he said. "Take failing grades and put it out of your mind."

During that "year of living dangerously," I found part-time work with Alex Munsell, a former publisher of progressive books (under the imprint of "Marzani and Munsell") who owned a brownstone in Chelsea and whose father had invented the color wheel. Though Alex claimed to be working on an autobiography, he seemed more intent on having an eclectic assortment of left-wing people around him (mostly for company, I suspect) helping him sort through a basement full of boxes of things he had acquired. At 73 (a bit older than I am now), he was fussy, eccentric, wary of being exploited (as the wealthy often are); yet wore a jacket spangled with so many protest buttons you could hardly make out the cloth. Included in our group of mostly students was Solon De Leon, the son of Daniel De Leon, a founder of the Socialist Labor Party. Solon, then 84, was a witty, genial, sardonic little man who had been expelled from the S.L.P. in 1918 by his own father for refusing to tow the Party line. He had once edited a guide to American Labor, done some teaching, and translated works from the French by Gustave Herve and Eugene Sue. I liked him for his playful nature, and because he was blessedly free of the morbid intensity of some of the other activists. Of equal interest to me, he was adept at macaronic verses that combined English and Latin words to comic effect. Here is one delightful piece he gave me, first published in 1902 in *Mercury,* the magazine of the City College of New York:

CARMEN AMORIS

> Once a puer amabat maiden,
> Sed dolore was he laden,
> Et his forma fast was fadin'—
>   Cur? She non amabat.

> Omnem diem he, a-weary,
> Wandered, nihil, visum cheery,
> Praeter window where his deary
>   Videbat vesperi.

Hic, at night, in shade arboris,
Flebat to his "Lux Amoris"
Till the aer cum sighs was porous
    Still her cor was glacies.

But, quum he, multum repining,
Mortuus, on his lute reclining,
Virgo tunc, her vis declining,
    Heu! perivit also.

Maids, O virgins pudentes,
Be not thus till death morantes,
Sed unto your lorn amantes
    Date vos dum vivant.

*

During my leave of absence from Columbia, the turmoil on campus had grown. In October, SDS had stepped up its protests; Mark Rudd had gone off to Cuba and returned a zealot, espousing confrontation; and on March 13, 1968 he was elected chairman of the university chapter of SDS. His first act was to disrupt the Martin Luther King, Jr. Memorial Service at the university's St. Paul's Chapel as a "hypocritical obscenity." A little over a month later, on April 23rd, a thousand students took over several buildings. When the police were called in, the campus was transformed into a battleground. The buildings were stormed, 700 people were arrested, and 150 others injured to varying degrees. In the midst of it all, SDS issued a series of demands, accompanied by Rudd's notorious "Up Against the Wall, Motherfucker" manifesto, in keeping with his style.

My brother, Pete, and I had taken part in the C.I.A. sit-in together, but then went our separate ways. I don't remember what his stance was with respect to these protests; I do remember he had become doctrinaire. In high school, he had been a model of balance—an excellent, well-rounded student; superb athlete;

member of the Student Council, the Honor Society, the Glee Club, and so on. At Columbia, he excelled in Chinese, his chosen field. Yet something went awry. From considered social analysis, he veered to dogmatic extremes—first left, then right, and so ever since, with increasing family estrangement, through the years.

I am sorry for that.

*

My grandfather supported my anti-war activity completely, though he cautioned against "blind protest," "irrational words and deeds," and urged me not to imperil my future by getting into trouble with the law. By then I had come to understand what a remarkable man he was. I had once thought of him as a stately Victorian figure of quaint beliefs who belonged almost to a bygone age. But his massive propriety (and he was certainly proper) was joined to a political spirit that was not conservative at all. He was a gentleman—and a very gentle, manly man—who served God and Man with coherent fervor. He was righteous, and his liberal soul was righteous. He was all of a piece. As for my own political thinking, he urged me to read beyond the "radical writers" I favored, suggesting, for balance, three books by Catherine Drinker Bowen—*Yankee from Olympus* (a biography of Oliver Wendell Holmes), *The Lion and the Throne* (about Sir Edward Coke), and *Miracle at Philadelphia* ("one of the great books of our time") about the Constitutional Convention. He also commended Samuel Eliot Morrison's one-volume *History of the United States*. He hoped by reading these—despite all that seemed wrong with America just then—I might better appreciate some of the "positive purpose and idealism that went into our nation's life."

Bowen's book on Coke described the evolution of the Common Law—its gradual, incremental growth by right reason, crystallizing into precedent; her book on Holmes showed that the life of the law was not only based on logic but experience. In her view, the wisest judges "possessed historical as well as judicial awareness" and "construed the Constitution" not as inscribed in stone but "according to the needs" or (in the words of Holmes himself) the "felt necessities" of the times.

The book on Coke, however, was also about a long, affectionate marriage, and growing older, and the loneliness of advanced age. He had recommended it to me when he was near the age Holmes was when he died; and so he hoped, I think, that I would better understand by example why he longed for my letters and my voice. "I get so lonesome for news of my family sometimes," he wrote, "that I just have to cry out." My heart aches to read these letters now, not remembering how promptly or often I might have replied. I was therfore immensely grateful when I finally read: "Dear Barry: I wish I could make you really realize what a marvelous thing it is for me to have your letter, so warm in affectionate remembrances. It means so much to me and so remarkable in its revealing of your interest and evidence of the heights and depths of what goes on in your life . . . . I have read and re-read it, that is to say, I have had it read to me several times." After my grandmother died, my great aunt Susan wrote to tell me that my grandfather carried my letters in his pocket wherever he went.

Yet as a self-involved young man, I was too caught up in my own drama to fully appreciate his yearning. And I had a defective sense of time—of my own mortal coil and of his running out. Thankfully—providentially!—I saved most of his letters, which has allowed me to carry on a posthumous dialogue with him in the eternal present of the soul.

Among the letters I cherish most was also one of his last, written on October 24, 1968, less than a year before he died:

"Dear Barry:

"It is a beautiful autumn day, here in California—the kind of weather you would love. I suspect you would wander out of doors or up the mountains or somewhere.

"I frequently wonder about you and the other boys, and what I would call your inner life. I hope there is a developing richness in that direction. I confess I feel a little happier about the studies you are choosing which have to do with the rich-ness of the spirit of man. If you were moving in the direction of science I can still hope that the inner side of your life is also developing; and when you write of Spenser and John Donne, I am strangely comforted, if I may so put it.

"All this may seem to you a strange way in which to begin a letter but the longer I live, the more I hope that the greater traditions, may I say, of your family may be cleansed and deepened and made beautiful ....

"I wish you could see me as I near my ninetieth birthday in this little home which so expresses the life and spirit of your grandmother and mother. I am sitting in the living room, with its furniture and piano and pictures and draperies which your grandmother placed. And on the lovely Korean chest which I think you have seen are the pictures of your mother and grandmother. It is now almost 830 days since your grand-mother went away from me, after we had lived together 65 years. On every one of those days there has been a red rose for her picture and the picture of your mother ....

"Really, I don't know why I started in this way—maybe it is because I do so long to know about your surroundings and of your general life, and so was moved to give you a little picture of the life I live.

"When I really started this it was to say that I was so grateful for your letter ....

Your mother used to call you 'Fellow.' And so I say, God bless and keep you, Fellow, and may your days be ever richer and richer. Grandpa."

At the end of his life, he lived alone in a small cottage on the edge of Claremont Manor, a United Methodist retirement complex in Claremont, California. In the distance, the lofty Sierra Madre Mountains rose into the sky. A half dozen or so friends helped keep him up-to-date with a regular schedule of readings (from newspapers, journals, books), and, as before, he made use of government book recordings for the blind. His liberal politics never wavered and included an abiding concern "for student life and work." When asked on his 80th birthday what he prized most, he had replied promptly, "The affection and confidence of the young." In January 1969 (to the chagrin of some of his peers), he defended anti-war protesters and the general youth revolt in an interview with *The Los Angeles Times*.

His Claremont home, though small, was beautifully furnished with wall hangings, gongs, inlaid chests, rugs, vases, figurines, fans, trays, urns and other Oriental objects. One item that eventually fell to me was a lovely Korean rug with a bamboo pattern that had been especially made for my grandmother around 1929. For many years, it adorned my study—my magic carpet, as I felt—until it was worn out.

My grandfather had a magnificent memory and after his sight was gone, he would sometimes cheer himself up by reciting remembered passages from the books he loved. Now and then he would feel along the shelves for some favorite volume, pause and recite something from it, often in verse. "A fine poem," he once said, "sings its way into your mind and heart."

If my grandfather was ever kindly, my grandmother had seemed forbidding—though she was really just more formal in her ways. When she died of a stroke on July 14, 1966, at the age of 90, she received many fine tributes, which spoke of her "aristocracy of character and grace," "queenly bearing," "personal dignity" and "deep humanity, hating cruelty in any form." Such virtues allow me to imagine her as I would have liked to have known her; and as the perfect companion my grandfather found.

Scattered, often endearing details, fill out my picture of his life. At his first pastorate in Ashland, Massachusetts, for example, he had a white cat named "Teddy," named for Teddy Roosevelt, who kept him company each morning and waited patiently as he got the fireplace going, "never asking for his breakfast until I was done." Afterwards, Teddy followed him to the train depot for his daily commute. From his travels I have pictures of my grandfather on the deck of a trans-oceanic steamer; mounting the steps of the Army Transport plane that took him to Japan; at conferences in New York, Geneva, Tokyo, Pyongyang, Seoul; bedecked with garlands in Hawaii; riding an elephant in Indonesia; or standing by an Ipoh tree in Borneo or Malaysia. The tree, known for its poison sap, is pockmarked with hundreds of holes from arrows or spears.

I suppose he had many adventures. When I was a child of four, he told me that one day he had been riding a bike along a jungle path in Burma when he stopped to rest on a log. "I sat down," he said—"*and the log moved!* It was a huge snake! So I jumped on my bike and pedaled off as fast as I could."

The last time I spoke to him—in one of our rare (somewhat awkward) trans-continental phone conversations, on Christmas Eve 1968—he said, as he prepared to say goodbye: "You won't forget me now, will you?" "No, Grandpa, I won't," I said. "Promise me, now," he said. "I promise," I said. And that exchange, a half-century or so ago, remains with me still, and gave rise to this Memoir, which was begun as an attempt to fulfill my vow.

My grandfather had six siblings, three of whom died before he was 18. He also lost his own two children—my mother's infant sister, Elizabeth, in 1916; and my mother, in 1955. On September 26, 1969, he died of a stroke. Psalm 121 was read at his service, and one of his favorite hymns, "O Thou Who Camest from Above" (No. 344 in The Methodist Hymnal) was sung. Most of his papers, library, and artifacts went to the Claremont School of Theology in California, the College of the Pacific, and the University of Illinois. My brothers and I also received a handful of things; and I subsequently located and acquired a fairly large body of material that I placed with the Boston University School of Theology in 2018. One item that came my way was his heavily annotated copy of Edgar J. Goodspeed's 1924 "American Translation" of The New Testament. Three documents were tucked inside: An article by Jimmy Cannon, from May 12, 1947, entitled "Lynch Mobs Don't Always Wear Hoods," about attempts to run Jackie Robinson out of baseball; the closing paragraph of Albert Schweitzer's *Quest of the Historical Jesus*; and "Simon the Cyrenian Speaks," a poem by Countee Cullen, a leading poet of the Harlem Renaissance. Cullen's poem was paired with another—"Golgotha," written in 1905 by Frederick Lawrence Knowles—which my grandfather had copied out and seamlessly joined to the first in a threnody of power.

He is buried beside my mother and grandmother in Mountain View Cemetery, Altadena, California.

CHAPTER TEN

At Columbia, my studies advanced. In 1969, I came under the spell of Edward W. Tayler, who taught celebrated courses on Shakespeare and Milton, and whose Senior Seminar on Renaissance Literature was the most compelling class I took in my college years.

A short, spry, graceful man, about 5'4", with blond hair, blue eyes, and a disciplined bearing, he had tremendous presence, an affable demeanor, and a heavily defended reserve. When irked he sometimes glowered, but more often his eyes had a plangent look of supplication, as if he wanted you to understand your complex plight in a fallen world. His teaching style was crisp and provocative with a nimbly orchestrated plan, and he managed the class dialogue so ably that it moved inexorably through a series of epiphanies to a pre-determined end. In his own Socratic fashion, he declined to divulge "answers" to questions raised, yet was triumphantly happy to confirm them once they were grasped. He was witty, sometimes funny, commonly intense; engaged each student directly; and chain-smoked as he taught. The control he exerted was complete, marked at times by startling asides. On one occasion, for example, after quoting Wallace Stevens on metaphor and analogy ("Identity is the vanishing point of resemblance"), he remarked: "I mean, it's ok to think of the confession booth as a psychiatrist's couch—

so long as you don't try to go in and lie down!"

On the first day of his Milton course, he handed out a "Self-Help Sheet" with guidance on standard English usage (grammar, punctuation, and the like) interspersed with telling advice. It is the kind of advice few students today are apt to receive:

> Proofread your manuscript carefully. (It is difficult to feel respect for a work whose author appears to despise it.)
>
> Even when responding to an assigned topic, take care to make the subject your own, writing as if you had set yourself a given task; that is, present An Essay, not An Exercise; avoid becoming a mechanical contrivance.
>
> Do not suppose that it is necessary to begin a new paragraph after every inset quotation; since the end of a paragraph has rhetorical importance, it should be reserved for your own use.
>
> Do not be afraid to say things simply and clearly; otherwise you will produce 'English-Teacher Talk' or some related form of pretentious discourse. This talk may occur on Madison Avenue or in the Pentagon—anywhere, in fact, that words are used to insulate rather than to communicate—but most often it appears in the teaching of literature when the instructor feels he has to sound important. Having been taught by English teachers, he then becomes one of them by perpetuating unintelligibility.
>
> Colombia is a country, Columbia a university. Tayler is an instructor; tailor refers to a vanishing professional; Taylor might be almost anybody.
>
> Almost invariably locutions like 'the fact that' and 'in terms of' betray your unwillingness to revise a badly-begun sentence.
>
> The designation 'respectively' has become a verbal tic in modern prose.
>
> Be alert when using forms of the verb 'to be,' the abuse of which led to the rise of philosophy; find more accurate, active verbs where possible.

A thing does not center around. It centers on or in. Point of view is more elegant that viewpoint. If you say 'overview,' you will go to Teachers College when you die. Never use 'life-style,' as in: I have decided to adopt the life-style of a nun. Do not 'opt' for things, as they do in the Pentagon: be a man—and choose.

If you feel obliged to say 'in the above quotation,' 'as I mentioned above,' or 'as I hope to elucidate in succeeding pages,' you will know that you need to re-organize what you've written.

Do not end sentences slackly—unless a comic or feeble effect is intended—with, for example, participial phrases. End with a bang unless the rhythm of the paragraph demands a terminal whimper or change of pace.

Use subordinate, adversative, and other constructions in preference to co-ordinate: 'and' merely hooks ideas together in a rudimentary way, without making the (usually) necessary distinctions. To subordinate indicates your awareness of the relative importance of ideas, while the overuse of simple declarative sentences (or constructions such as 'It is significant that ....' reveals how habits of language have stunted your intellectual growth.

Remember that A Pedant is merely some person whose standards of accuracy happen to be higher than your own.

With proper allowances for human weakness, you may reasonably hope for a meticulously attentive and sympathetic reading of your manuscript, a kind of reading you may not reasonably hope forever again and many good authors never receive.

Tayler's teaching methods were inspired by two great teachers of his own: Theodore Baird at Amherst and Yvor Winters at Stanford. Baird "always wanted to ask two questions," Tayler recalled: "Where are you when you talk that way? and "Who are you when you use those words?" The same questions were implied by many of the questions Tayler asked. He insisted that our taste in reading showed us who we were (or the state we were in) and to our astonishment he seemed at times to read us like a book. In his Senior Seminar on Renaissance Literature, for example, he used to ask each of us to choose the ten "best" poems from a given poet's work, arranged in descending order of their worth. With what seemed like clairvoyance, he often knew in advance the poems we would choose.

There was a good deal of Yvor Winters in him, too. From Winters, Tayler had learned—or perhaps found in him confirmed—the idea that the merits of a work of art, including its moral value, could be objectively assessed. As a teacher, and critic, Winters had been categorical, combative, dismissive, provocative, and arch. But he had real knowledge; a well-grounded point of view; and a profound understanding of the poetic tradition in English literature that few could match. He probably knew more than anyone about the development of the short English lyric, and the "plain style" tradition fundamental to English verse. In addition, he was an accomplished poet himself, and a few of his poems ("Sir Gawain and the Green Knight," for example) belong in any anthology of the best 20th century verse. He was therefore a formidable figure, dogmatic, relentless, and demanding, and though sometimes wrong, also often right. He schooled Tayler at Stanford; and Tayler, with a good deal of Winters in him, schooled me.

To Winters, a viable poem was "a rational statement about a human experience" in which the emotion appropriate to it was also expressed. The poem was therefore "a complete judgment of the experience." Most poets, he thought, had implicitly embraced this notion in the past; but in modern verse (due in part to the doctrinal innovations of the Imagists and Ezra Pound) thought and feeling had been divorced. Since ideas were said to arise from sensory impressions, mere impressions (so Imagists claimed) could express ideas. Yet poetry had seldom been governed by "concrete images" in that sense. Some images, in fact, were "metaphysical" (linked by idea); ruled by logic (as in Andrew Marvell's "To His Coy Mistress," which unfolds as a syllogism); and turned on paradox. The interplay of meter and rhythm (often confused by critics) had been the life of poetry, too. "Meter," noted Winters, "is the arithmetical norm," rhythm the "controlled departure" from it, by which emotion is expressed.

Under Tayler, I became acquainted with the various canons of style, the art of the metaphysical conceit, the four different kinds of meter (quantitative, accentual, syllabic, and accentual-syllabic), the creative tension between metrical and rhetorical stress, and the deep moral wisdom of many poetic texts. For an understanding of meter, he recommended Nabokov's essay on the subject, appended to his translation of *Eugene Onegin*, and Robert Frost's pointed remark that a poet "must learn to get cadences by skillfully breaking the sounds of sense with all their irregularity of accent across the regular beat." In this way, Frost explained, "the speaking tone of voice" becomes "entangled in the words." The poet John Frederick Nims once nicely summed it all up this way: "The meaning of poetry is a concord, or sometimes a discord, of many elements: of rhythm, of the sound of words and all it conjures, of the way our lips and throat relax or struggle to pronounce them, of the way words rebel against or nestle with each other, of their past record in the language and the company they have kept, of all their haloes, induced currents, and blue leaping arcs."

Tayler's knowledge of poetry seemed complete; but his field was the Renaissance. As a scholar, he was deeply versed in Biblical studies, exegetical methods, the fourfold reading of a sacred text (literal, figurative, moral, and mystical), typology, and all things having to do with patristic thought. He also had a taste for metaphysical wit that was much attuned to Donne's. I believe he was the first to show that the linear, five-stanza structure of Donne's "The Canonization" corresponded to the five-step process of canonization as prescribed by the Catholic Church; that Donne's two long "Anniversary" poems were organized into tripartite divisions corresponding to the three faculties of the soul—Memory, Judgment, and Will, as derived from the Holy Trinity—"a trinity from the Trinity," as set forth by St. Bernard; mastered the prelapsarian astronomy of Milton's "Paradise

Lost"; and was the first to note that Satan's course through the universe in that poem is through the Serpent in the constellation Ophiucus ("the Serpent-Bearer"), proceeding through his mouth and departing from his anus or tail. Beyond that, he illuminated many difficult poems, and uncrossed many a crux. His academic writing was sometimes dense, if not opaque; but his superb Introduction to *Literary Criticism of 17th Century England* (his own compendium) is a tour-de-force of clarity and wit.

In general, Tayler's teaching was organized around several touchstone texts which stressed that we live in a world of interdependent opposites, and that the knowledge of good and evil, in all their infinite permutations and guises, are as two halves of the same apple "cleaving together"—in Milton's punning phrase—like twins brought forth into the world. To help explain what he meant, he called our attention to Freud's essay on "primal words," as inspired by the work of the philologist Karl Abel, where words were said to have originally meant two opposite things. Tayler pointed to surviving examples: the Latin word "altus," which meant both "high" and "deep," and "sacer," which meant both "sacred" and "profane." The Old English word "cleave" ("to sever" and "to cling,") was a third. These reflected the fabric of reality itself, as well as our understanding of it, in which "contraries, though they destroy one another, are yet the life of one another," in the words of Sir Thomas Browne. We can only know things by their opposites—light by dark, cold by hot, wild by tame. Therefore, "every experience must have two sides," wrote Abel, and "either every name must have a double meaning, or else for every meaning there must be two names."

In such a world, moral choice can be murky, as we are pulled in opposite directions, or feel two ways about the same thing. Yet the God who put us in this fix—a "God of long division," as Tayler put it—also gave us Reason, that is, "freedom to choose." We have to make our way. Not surprisingly, Tayler disliked it when students used passive phrases, such as "My homework got misplaced" or "It slipped my mind," and would sometimes say sharply: "Don't you have a choice?!"

In his own reading, he favored poetry and theology; considered most modern critics "Biblical illiterates"; disliked newfangled literary theories like Deconstruction; agreed with Moses Hadas that all great works were inherently "iconoplastic"—not shattering the old but bending old forms to accommodate the new; and thought most novels "a waste of time." Yet I know he loved novelists as diverse as Melville, Anthony Burgess, Kurt Vonnegut, John Barth, and Thomas Mann. Needless to say, he rejected the notion that a work of art means whatever we want it to, and insisted that art can best show us where we stand in relation to the standard it sets. Otherwise, we risk bringing it down to our own current level, without making the effort to rise. He liked to recall a final exam once given in a Great Books course by Raymond Weaver, the famed Melville scholar, that had one question on it: "Which of the books (*The Odyssey, Isaiah, The Aeneid, Dante's Inferno, King Lear, Moby Dick,* and so on) that we read this year didn't you like, and to what defect in your character do you attribute this?"

In Life as in Art, we find love and truth (perhaps true love) only by understanding another on their own terms. A new self is thereby created, or the old one transformed. As Tayler explained to one freshman class: "You're here to build a self. You create a self; you don't inherit it. One way you create it is out of the past."

Perhaps Tayler's greatest gift to me was the idea that a poem can change you. That opened me up to literature as a source of moral power. Some poems have meant the world to me, in fact, and (I hope) wrought their will: among them, John Donne's "Good Friday, 1613. Riding Westward," and Milton's two great sonnets on Time and obligation, "How soon hath Time, the subtle thief of youth," and "When I consider how my light is spent."

*

My recollections of some of my other teachers are a scattered mix: Paul Oskar Kristeller in the library stacks, where he did all his own scrupulously self-verified research; Sacvan Bercovitch, later prominent in American studies, who was my freshman instructor in the Advanced Placement Seminar in English: he had each of us write a poem at the outset, which he promised to save. I can't quite recall mine, except for the last line, which I think worked well in context: "Birthdays remind us that we're still alive." A couple of years later, I became his research assistant, when he was working on "Horologicals to Chronometricals: The Rhetoric of the Jeremiad," and a vast bibliography on *Typology and Early American Literature*. In my copy of the first, he wrote: "For Barry Bobrick, A short guide to the approaching apocalypse."

One day I was talking to A. Kent Hieatt when the poet Kenneth Koch came in. Koch asked for the skeleton key to a closet. "Oh, Kenneth," said Hieatt, "all my keys are skeleton." Though Hieatt had been my faculty advisor, I didn't know him well. I was better acquainted with one of my Latin teachers, Steele Commager, Jr., the son of the Harvard historian. Among academics, he was almost unique in having gained tenure without an advanced degree. He was more a literary scholar than a linguist, witty (often at his own expense), agitated, neurotic, smoked heavily, drank, and died of a heart attack at 51. He refused to give up smoking and once explained, "Why should I become a slave to my will power?" He held up a Marlboro: "It's better to breathe the foul air of New York through a filter anyway." He was hilarious in ridiculing one of Ezra Pound's Latin translations, which seemed to have been done by free association; and urged me, as a student, to notice how words connect. As an example, he told me that he had been proficient in Latin for a long time before it occurred to him that the English word "peninsula" simply combined "paene" (almost) with "insula" (island). I read his books on Horace and Propertius, but I remember him mostly as a high-strung, nervous young man striding across campus with his book bag slung over his shoulder and some clever thought playing in his head.

CHAPTER ELEVEN

❦

Of words, and the murder of words, he dreamed,
Whose very syllables are the sounds of fears . . .

These are the only lines I can remember now, as I wrote in *Knotted Tongues,* "from a poem I wrote when I was about nineteen about Caedmon, the tongue-tied Anglo-Saxon poet, whose speech was freed by an angel who appeared to him in a dream. Notwithstanding my passion at the time for early English verse, the poem's dark wellspring was my own experience with stuttering; and though I suppose I was past believing in a divine or miraculous cure, I do remember that my poem ended with a prayer."

So far as I know, I first began to stutter at about the age of eight—at least I first became conscious of my stutter at that time. As everyone develops their own theory as to where it comes from, "mine," as I explained, "was that it was somehow connected to my mother's death. Since she had stuttered (at least occasionally), I thought I might have acquired her impediment as a way of holding on to some part of her once she was gone. It was only as an adult that it occurred to me that since my eldest brother stutters too, it was highly unlikely we would have both adopted the same curious psychic stratagem."

To an extent others might find surprising, my stutter dominated the first half of my life. My handicap was pronounced, and included a tendency to "block" or stop dead on certain sounds. Roughly one hundred muscles are smoothly coordinated in the normal (and normally automatic), simple act of speech, and any glitch in that process can lead to involuntary repetitions or prolongations of sounds, spasmodic interruptions, blinking and other facial tics, tremors of the lips and jaw, gasping, stamping of the feet, jerking of the head, contortions of the whole body, and even foaming at the mouth as in an epileptic fit. Stuttering has been ascribed to any number of physical or psychological causes, and treated in a hundred different ways. Sound clinical evidence today suggests that it is an inheritable, physically-based problem involving a neurological defect in the auditory feedback loop, pertaining to anomalies of sound transmission through the skull.

In school (again, as I wrote in *Knotted Tongues*), "I tried to say as little as I could and used all the avoidance behaviors I have ever heard of to conceal the secret of my speech. I became adept at word substitution, clever at paraphrase, and an ambulatory thesaurus of synonyms as a means to help me evade 'difficult' sounds. I also cultivated a reserved, even abrupt manner of speaking (interspersed with many 'thoughtful' hesitations), and in this way succeeded at times with my masquerade." Yet that afforded me no inner assurance or relief. "Each day, I would set forth determined, as if my life depended on it, to slay this dragon, only to find that my speech had a life of its own. Moreover, though expert at avoidance and a covert stutterer to a high degree, I was nevertheless among those comparatively rare individuals who stuttered even when reading aloud to themselves."

By the time I entered college I felt better able to manage in informal settings, and wondered briefly if, by some strange luck, I might actually 'outgrow' my malady. Yet in retrospect it seems to me that I wasn't so much better as more of an adept. Besides, I had reached an age when I could drink, and I found, frankly, that that helped me to relax. And of course I continued to avoid stuttering situations when I could. Classroom participation was seldom obligatory; but seminars were a trial.

Even so, my academic record seldom suffered, and despite the failing grades I had taken in the spring of my sophomore year, I graduated Magna Cum Laude from the College in the winter of 1971 with a two-year Kellett Fellowship to Oxford.

Columbia offered me a Graduate Fellowship, and I stayed.

From the East Village, I moved to Amsterdam Avenue and 87th Street (around the corner from the famed Barney Greengrass Deli); then to 106th Street between West End Avenue and Riverside Drive. My fellowship was not enough to live on, so I worked at various jobs—as an after-school counselor for children at Greenwich House, a settlement house in Greenwich Village off Sheridan Square; at Butler Library in the stacks; and as a weekend nightwatchman in a building at 110th Street and Riverside Drive. As a nightwatchman, I had two indelible experiences. On one occasion, I saw the figure of an elderly woman—a tenant—pass through the lobby late one night, only to learn the following week that she had died about the time I had seen her wraith-like form. I also had a religious experience that gave voice to an inchoate desire. Early on, at about the age of fifteen, I had been struck by Goethe's epigraph to *Faust*—"Wer immer strebend sich bemüht, den können wir erlösen": "Whosoever unceasingly strives upward, him can we save" (in the stilted translation of the Modern Library text). I knew at once that this was something I must not forget. But I did forget it, of course—and then at times recalled it with a start. One night, after being transported by the "Alto Rhapsody" of Brahms, which I had just heard for the first time, I suddenly said to myself out loud, "Thank God I was born with the impulse to strive!" I didn't say this, to be sure, from any sense of self-assurance; only hope.

Nightwatchmen are often viewed with some ambivalence, and my duties gave rise to an ironic poem on that score:

THE NIGHTWATCHMAN

He was like their conscience—How they spent
Their time at night, with whom they came and went,
Or if along, their dark-entrusted states
Were shown him with misgiving where he'd wait.

Though he was hired for them, and they his charge,
As things are reckoned at the going rate,
They felt they paid enough for him in rent,
Which reckoned up, the tips were seldom large.

Meanwhile, in 1972, I had earned my Master's Degree with a thesis on Sir Thomas Browne and, mindful of my speech, began, as I wrote, "to look down the road toward my doctoral orals a couple of years away. Time came; time went: the day drew near. When it finally arrived, I hid my terror as best I could behind some extremely eccentric verbal behavior and clouds of cigarette smoke. Actually, by the time I walked into the room I was almost as worried about having a heart attack as I was about my speech. For weeks I had more or less lived on brandy and cigarettes, and for three nights running been virtually unable to sleep. Thanks to the magnanimity of my examiners, I passed," but I left school shortly thereafter, convinced I was unfit for a teaching career. I also felt, in an intensely personal way, that I had disappointed the great poets I admired, and in the following weeks, in a penitential act of homage, wrote a series of poems "in the manner of" Donne, Milton, Greville, Herbert, and others to expiate my sin.

From the heights, I fell into the depths. Over the next year or so, I took a number of odd jobs—as leather craftsman, file clerk, book binder, book production assistant, and so on—as I tried to find my way. In the rat-infested basement annex of one leather shop on Bleecker Street, I cut out patterns for the top and bottom soles of sandals. The patterns were closely drawn on wide leather sheets, and as I turned them on a band saw, I had to follow the wavy lines exactly to make the cuts clean. I could hardly fail to notice that the other two "cutters" had fingers missing from their hands. Later, I worked for a year at a leather shop on the upper East Side, where I made sandals, briefcases, belts and other items, hand-finished and adorned, stained with aniline dyes, and designed, where possible, to take advantage of interesting patterns of the grain. After that, for a month or two, I worked for Spink and Gabor, a bookbinding company founded in 1927 with a second story industrial loft on 6th Avenue and 26th Street. Their long, wide louver windows had, I think, never been washed, and their accumulated grime dimmed the outside light as much as drawn shades. Some of the fine or decorative binding in the shop was done by the owner, Edward Spink, but everyone else worked on reinforced library bindings, which meant rounding the spines—smeared first with protein glue, a colloidal collagen extract made from the boiled connective tissue of rabbits—on an anvil. The books were then encased in acrylic-coated buckram stiffened with paste over boards. It was old-fashioned, jarring, assembly-line work, done in enforced silence, since the owner supposed that even simple conversation would distract us from our tasks.

After my stint as a bookbinder, I spent a few months as an assistant to Nahum Tschacbasov, a once-prominent artist who had a large, working apartment in the Chelsea Hotel. When I met him in the fall of 1976, he was in his late 70s, married to the artist Irene Zevon, much younger than himself, and ran a profitable business supplying college art departments with slide collections from his suite. The slides were organized into packets by artist, period, and style (Gothic, Baroque, Neo-Classical, Roccoco, and so on), and genre (architecture, sculpture, painting and the minor arts) from Paleolithic to modern times.

Tschacbasov was a burly, irascible little man, energetic, feisty, and robust, who looked, in the striped shirts he favored, like a Russian stevedore. He had a flamboyant temper and often began the day in a rant; but between his theatrical fits, he could be amusing and astute. He thought New Yorkers had acquiesced to de facto chemical warfare—"Stand on a highway overpass," he said to me one day, "and look down at the fumes!"; was scathing in his assessment of Freud—"He was a sick man. I never had his dreams!"; and held forth on local crime. In his determination not to be a victim of it, he wore a holstered derringer strapped to the calf of one of his legs. But he reserved his greatest wrath, bulging with expletives, for Saul Bellow, to whom his daughter, Sondra, had been married for three years.

In the course of his long career, Tschacbasov's work had ranged from socialist realism, inspired in part by his friend Max Weber, to Expressionism, as a student in Paris of Fernand Leger. His late style combined Cubism and Surrealism after the fashion of Picasso and Chagall. His Expressionist paintings had influenced the work of Anais Nin, and he had items in the collections of prominent museums around the world. From time to time, he also wrote poems, but his fame had vanished, and he resented the obscurity into which his work had been cast.

One day he said to me quietly: "I can see that you're a man of quality. What are you doing here?" which, though direct, was not unkind. I could only answer, truly: "I don't know." Shortly thereafter, on January 21, 1977, I told him I was leaving. He gave me an inscribed book of his paintings and said, "Good." His wife, Irene, gave me a hug.

I never saw them again.

At about this time, I had been invited to become poetry editor of *Ais-Eiri*, the magazine of the Irish Arts Center in New York. No one else then wanted the job, on the grounds that they couldn't tell a good poem from a bad one.

I thought I could.

CHAPTER TWELVE

✿

Ais-Eiri filled a brief and happy interlude. Meanwhile, in the fall of 1976, I had married a singer, Danielle Woerner, and in the following year we founded a New York City recital management, Woerner/Bobrick Associates. Danielle and I had met the previous winter at the leather shop where I worked, dated intensely, married that fall, and honeymooned at Mohonk, where I had gone to school as a boy. With luck, we booked the "Tower Room" favored by Stravinsky and his wife, Vera, which still had a *Ballet Russe* poster on the wall.

In our venture, Danielle took charge of the public relations work; I did the graphic design. I had no musical training to speak of, but my oblique family connection to the Kneisel Quartet perhaps served as a cosmic prompting; Danielle, for her part, had once worked in the office of a theatrical agent, Sheldon Soffer; as an assistant to Lennie Tristano, the great jazz pianist; and sang in the Collegiate Chorale. Our principal goal was to survive in the arts. While Danielle developed her singing career, I hoped to find my writing voice. The day we were legally established, I jotted down this rhyme:

MY WIFE & I GO DOWN THE ROAD

Blest pair of Sirens, Voice & Verse,
Keep the hollow from our purse,
Now that we have put you first;

Give us both enough to eat,
Shoes below to clothe our feet,
Rafters up above from sleet;

Tea & honey for the throat,
Pen & paper for the notes,
And the lines for which I hope.

By "lines" I meant poetry, of course. Writing history was then far from my mind.

We started on a shoestring (my first "light-table" for design was a window the sun shone through); but working out of our Greenwich Village apartment—a spacious floor-through with a skylight and stuccoed arch—we soon earned a good reputation for the high standards of our work. Over the next decade or so (for as long as our marriage would last), we were, it is fair to say, a dynamic if fleeting force on the New York music scene. There was scarcely a recital we managed that didn't draw several critics, including from *The New York Times*; and though our income was modest, we found ways to economize. Every flyer I designed doubled as a mailer, and tripled as a poster when enlarged. To save on the expense of color printing, I hand-painted the enlargements displayed in the great glass cases before Lincoln Center and Carnegie Hall. We also served as our own ad agency, to claim the commissions paid for placements; did strategic mailings; and made diligent use of public service postings and announcements to help fill halls. My flyer designs were also competent enough to bring in outside work.

Our clients included the Thouvenal String Quartet; the Western

Wind Ensemble; The New York Choral Society; the Da Capo Chamber Players; the American Composers Orchestra; the Manticore Chamber Orchestra; the Naumburg Orchestra; the Group for Contemporary Music; the Jupiter Symphony; The Kings Singers (a famed English a capella group); The Collegiate Chorale; and The Concord String Quartet. We also worked with a number of prominent composers, often with works in premiere—including Elliott Carter, Ned Rorem, Virgil Thompson, Otto Luening, George Rochberg, Laurie Anderson, Gunther Schuller, Ellen Taaffe Zwilich, and William Bolcom; as well as such performers as Malcolm Bilson, Keith Jarrett, Phyllis Bryn-Julson, Sharon Zuckerman, Ursula Oppens, Oscar Shumsky, and Robert Black.

I name them out of pride.

Our principal venues were Alice Tully Hall at Lincoln Center, Carnegie Hall, the Merkin Concert Hall, and the Carnegie Recital Hall. We had church concerts to manage, too, along with events at various centers and schools.

Many of our programs featured traditional repertoire, from medieval motets to Richard Strauss; others, modern "classical" music, which meant lending our ears to atonal sound. I never got used to it, though I tried to make a place for it in my aesthetic world. At its tolerable best, it had the abstract, intellectual appeal of an algorithm; at its worst, its dissonant, disconnected sounds assailed the nerves. Some of its composers were agreeable, personally—and one, Otto Luening (whose later career developed around electronic music)—became a friend. But it was fostered mostly by academic theorists, and some of the music parties I attended were as pedantic as the grids on which their twelve-tone rows were mapped. Otto Luening, on the other hand, was brilliant, sympathetic, and engaging, with a charity of feeling that had sprung from personal despair. He was also an excellent flautist, active till the end, and with his impish visage and upturned mustache, resembled, at age 80, a King of the Elves. In his youth, he had known James Joyce in Zurich where he belonged to Joyce's English Players, a theatrical troupe; studied with Feruccio Busoni;

and performed in the Tanhalle Orchestra under Arthur Nikitsch and Richard Strauss. He had a superb memory for the typical traits and eccentricities of all these men, whom he evoked in his autobiography, *The Odyssey of An American Composer*, published in 1981.

*

In September of 1978, as our concert management business gained traction, Danielle and I decided to go on a holiday to France. We stopped over in London (since it was cheaper to go by way of England), roamed about for a day, saw a play, then took a Hovercraft from Dover across the Channel to Calais. At Calais, we boarded a train for Paris and arrived at night at the Gare du Nord. We were tired and sought accommodations in a shabby hotel across the street. We were told there was no room, but in response to our pleading, were given a kind of half-room, for an exorbitant sum. As we settled in, roaches appeared. "C'est la guerre," Danielle said. "Non," I replied, "c'est la gare."

Though I could read French fairly well, my pronunciation was poor, which might have hampered our excursions. Fortunately, Danielle had a perfect Provencal accent (acquired from a semester of study abroad); and despite the proverbial impatience of Parisians with those who don't know the language well, we got about without much trial. We visited the Ile de la Cite, the Musee de Cluny, the Cathedral of Notre Dame, La Place Pigalle, the Moulin Rouge, the Louvre, and took an unforgettable day trip to Chartres, where the inexpressible perfection of the cathedral incarnates, in all its human proportions, the mystery of Man. After exploring the labyrinth that adorns its nave (disparaged by the local priesthood as a pagan relic), and the secret astronomical device set into its floor, we returned to Paris, having, as we felt, glimpsed the divine. The following day (almost as confirmation of the fact), we came upon the lovely little church of St. Germaine des Pres, just at dusk, at Vespers, as the congregation was singing a beautiful hymn by heart.

In the meantime, we had found a quaint little room, much like an artist's garret, six flights up in the Latin Quarter in the Rue de Cujas. Although the shared shower for tenants was on the ground floor, our room had a bidet and a small trellised balcony that looked out over the rooftops where at night, in a kind of trance, I listened to the church bells ring.

On our last day in Paris, we exchanged most of our francs for pounds sterling, went out for an elaborate dinner, but lingered too long. We had a train to catch, and rushing with our luggage out into the stormy night, finally found a cab, but got to the platform of the Gare du Nord just as our train receded from view. It was the last train of the night to anywhere; and the next London train (which was also the last that could connect us to our flight home) left at 5:30 a.m.

We were not allowed to spend the night in the station, and with the Bureaux de Change all closed, didn't have money enough for a room. As it happened, Danielle had an Israeli friend, Aviva, who had an apartment outside Paris. It was now about midnight, an unseemly hour to intrude; but in desperation, Danielle called. Her recollection of the following events is somewhat more vivid than mine. Aviva answered at once and, thankfully, was in the midst of hosting a big family party, and said, since her couches and beds were all taken, we could crash on cushions on the kitchen floor. Great, we said, how do we find you? "Take the Boulogne Metro to the very last stop, and when you get out, look for the road that goes into the Bois de Boulogne. Follow that road and keep the woods on your right. You'll soon see a little side street on your left. Walk to the next. That's ours. We're at 16, rue Maurice Barres. I'll wait up."

We had just enough francs for our round-trip fare. After waiting some time for the train, it then proceeded to make every local stop. At length, we emerged (about 1 a.m.), passed the first street, and continued on into the park. We walked a good way, our luggage gaining weight. It was a cold September night, and we were lightly dressed. At length, we realized we must have gone too far. Though we had followed the road, few streetlights flanked it, and few cars had passed. Suddenly, from behind a tree, some thirty yards distant, emerged a huge, garish figure—a man the size of a linebacker, smeared with rouge, bizarrely dressed in a silver miniskirt and tight sweater, wearing a fuschia wig. We knew at once he had to be desperate—perhaps a psychopath. Then we saw—could it be? In his hand, he held a butcher knife. He began to run toward us; in turn, we ran. Soon he was gaining. A terrible death seemed sure. Just at that moment—as in a grade B Hollywood film (a genre I now exalt)—two headlights appeared in the distance. Waving our arms wildly, we stepped out into the road. As the car slowed, our pursuer retreated. The driver (who had to stop or kill us) turned out to be a personable Swede. He spoke English as well as French; accepted our pleas for help; and from the city map he happened to have with him, we discovered that we had passed our turn two miles back. We climbed into his Saab and he kindly brought us to Aviva's door. We collapsed on her kitchen floor for a couple of hours and tiptoed out before dawn.

Had we imagined all this, or made it up, in part, by repeated telling? Some friends may have thought so. Forty years later, however, my brother, Jim, happened to be reading Edmund White's memoir *The Unpunished Vice*, when he came upon White's description, from his own Paris days at this time, of "Brazilian transvestite prostitutes as made-up as mass-produced cream cakes, with soccer-player calves, tall as clowns on their stilts or stilettos, breaking through the bush of the Bois de Boulogne!"

No, we had not dreamed it. But we had encountered one gone mad.

On another holiday, less fraught with danger, we spent a week or two in England. To avoid being a conventional sightseer with the usual map and guide, I took *The Pub Crawler's Guide to London*, so I could happen upon sites by surprise. Aside from enjoying an occasional pint at an historic pub, I "happened upon" the Houses of Parliament, the Tower of London, Dr. Johnson's house, London Bridge, and so on, without ever knowing in advance what I would see. This turned my roamings into a series of stunning finds—like some imagined wanderer in the desert wastes of Egypt who might suddenly encounter the Pyramids at Giza, the Temple of Karnak, the Great Sphinx, or the Valley of the Kings.

During that relatively brief vacation, we also went to Brighton (where I found a period poster of Graham Greene's *Brighton Rock*), Salisbury to see the cathedral, and rented bikes and pedaled to Stonehenge, where after exploring small church cemeteries along the way, we arrived just as the sun was setting, bathing the ancient ring of stones in crimson light. A few days later, we visited the ancient Roman springs and Abbey Church in Bath.

These brief excursions (which were my first abroad) altered my sense of Time. Nothing that I had experienced in America outside of geological wonders like the Grand Canyon seemed to compare in antiquity with what I had glimpsed in England and France. Perhaps every traveler has this sensation; but it gave me the feeling of belonging to a measure of things incomparably beyond my own mortal span.

CHAPTER THIRTEEN

❦

In the winter of 1979, Danielle and I joined forces with the composer George Rochberg, whose three new "Concord Quartets" were being readied for their New York Premiere. The works had been commissioned by the Concord String Quartet and the group's manager, Sheldon Soffer, considered the logistical demands of a mere recital a waste of his time. So he asked us to take it on.

We grasped opportunity by the forelock and made the most of our chance.

Rochberg was an unusually compelling figure—"part of that remarkable generation of Eastern European Jewish emigrants and their children," as one scholar put it, "including Aaron Copland, George and Ira Gershwin, Leonard Bernstein, and Irving Berlin—who propelled American music into the forefront." A prodigy of sorts, he had been featured on the radio in his teens; worked his way through college playing piano in clubs and bands; and studied composition under Gian Carlo Menotti and George Szell. In between, in his mid-20s, he had fought as an infantry lieutenant, 90th Division, in Europe, where he was wounded in Flanders, before taking part in Patton's relief of the U.S. First Army in the Battle of the Bulge.

He returned from the war resolved to live a life of creative affirmation in the face of the destruction he had seen.

In the early 1950s, upon a trip to Italy, he came under the influence of the serialist composer Luigi Dallapiccola, a leading figure in the avant-garde. Dallapiccola convinced him that twelve-tone composition was the music of the future, and, as he later explained to me, "I signed on." Upon his return from Italy, he taught at the University of Pennsylvania and the Curtis School of Music; directed publications at Theodore Presser, the music publishing house; wrote on music theory; and as a composer made his mark. Almost from the start, his work was performed by major orchestras and chamber music groups, and by the early 1960s, he was considered "America's first and greatest master" of atonal composition, in the manner that Arnold Schoenberg and Anton Webern had pioneered.

Atonal theory reflected the times. The nightmare of two world wars, new concepts of time and space, and the dislocations in modern life, were all mirrored in the arts: by the rejection of traditional perspective, distortion in depicting figures, dissonance in music, and the lack of traditional poetic harmonies (including rhyme and meter) in free verse. In music, the twelve pitches of the octave were now organized—by the serialists—into melodic sets in rows. This rigidly detached and mathematical system created a neutralized and neutered sound that (to unconvinced ears like mine) was divorced from the well-springs of life. Many of its proponents were academics who composed for their peers. Their music, in fact, "didn't have to be defended by the way it sounded," as Rochberg would later write. "It could be justified by . . . its description." Meanwhile, its adoption had been dogmatically urged in 1952 by the young, influential French composer Pierre Boulez, who declared: "Any musician who has not felt . . . the necessity of the twelve-tone language is of no use!"

Rochberg's view was more mature. He thought the new sound filled a need. Its severe chromatic palette, full of "the cutting, dark dissonances of emotional uncertainties and aural confusions— essentially neurotic, constricted gestures....of certain kinds of experience—the worst ones (alienation, trauma, nihilistic-destructive withdrawal, etc."—stood to capture such features of modern life. And so (intentionally or not) it often did. One day, my eldest brother, Jim, joined me at one of "The Group For Contemporary Music" concerts at Symphony Space. Mid-way through, he whispered in my ear: "This sounds like something written for a horror film!"

Despite Rochberg's esteem for Dallapiccola as a man, whom he loved and admired, he came in time to feel that "there could be no justification for music, ultimately, if it does not convey eloquently and elegantly the passions of the human heart." In "Tradition and Twelve-Tone Music," an essay first published in 1955, he wrote, "Twelve-tone composition, if it is to win final acceptance…must be a way of producing significant works which will be listened to and performed not as curiosities or strange novelties, but as music." By 1959, he had become convinced that "a completely rationalized system of composition" was "incapable of mirroring subjective experience." At the very least, it tended to suppress the voice of the individual by mechanical rules. *In Four Lines, Five Spaces: The World of My Music*, written at the end of his life, he nicely described the difference between tonal and atonal thought. Tonal thinking, he wrote, is "open, always en route to completing itself, to closure"; twelve-tone thinking is "self-consciously circular . . . [without] melodic extension." It has "no inherent points of rest. A composer wanting to simulate a cadence in twelve-tone music" has to "invent a pause." Finally, "the process of breathing, inhaling and exhaling, without which music cannot exist," was simply "more 'natural'" to tonal thought.

One might go further and say that tonal music is an expression of Man's organic self, with his cardiovascular system and neuro-logical pitch. It is tuned to us—or by us—from within. The tonal key of a piece is its emotional center, that is, its felt center of gravity of understanding, in an organic sense. Or as Rochberg put it, tonal music goes "directly into the channels of the Central Nervous System to reform itself there as an intensely convincing experience."

This was not, for him, an academic idea. Personal calamity had transformed his world. In 1964, confronted with the death of his 20-year-old son, atonal music had failed him completely as a means for expressing his grief. In the works that followed, he began to reincorporate traditional music into his sound—first in collage fashion with quotations from other composers (*Contra Mortem et Tempus* and *Music for the Magic Theater*, for example, composed in 1965), followed by *Ricordanza*, a tonal, elegiac work for cello and piano; and his *String Quartet No. 3*, in 1972, which included a set of Beethoven-like variations and an adagio that some thought Mahleresque. With it, he said, he had rediscovered the "energy of pulse." After its world premiere, Donal Henahan wrote in *The New York Times*: "Mr. Rochberg's quartet is—how did we used to put it?—beautiful. It is one of the rare new works that go past collage and quotation into another, fairer land."

In three subsequent quartets—his 4th, 5th, and 6th, written in 1977 and 1978 (known as the "Concord Quartets") Rochberg boldly confirmed his new stance. A private, preview performance took place on November 26, 1978, at the stately home of a patron in a Philadelphia suburb. It was there that I first met George and formed a friendship with him that would last until his death. The preview performance was stunning, and I remember a tremendous sense of being "present at the creation." Time has borne that out. His quartets are considered among the finest of modern times.

At the party afterwards, George and I discovered a shared enthusiasm for Herman Melville, and talked at length about *The Confidence Man*, which he was just then developing into an opera in collaboration with his wife, Gene. At the time, he was 60, I was 31; but perhaps because I had also begun to ponder some of the same artistic questions, we seemed to breathe the same air. I soon came to regard him as a kind of elder statesman, mentor and guide. With characteristic generosity, he treated me as an equal, which raised me up.

Toward the end of the evening, I suddenly noticed out of the corner of my eye that his wife, Gene (who had once been a dancer) had done a flip and was standing on her head. George turned to me and said: "When Gene starts standing on her head, I know it's time to go home!"

In his person, George was a rather tall man, with a long, somewhat rabbinical face, a lofty brow, and kind and sympathetic eyes. He had a tremendous intellectual range—as amply displayed in his fine collection of essays, *The Aesthetics of Survival*—and an open curiosity and understanding for anything of interest one might say. He considered himself (at times) a "lapsed Jew" without faith in a resurrection, but had a mystical sense of his own connection to invisible realms. He also had a liking for striking images that expressed intense ideas, and our conversations often took the form of a fiercely empathetic exchange.

His work had passion. "There is a fire in the mind," he wrote, "which comes from the universal fire that makes solar systems and galaxies, asteroid belts and comets, huge orbiting spirals, circles, loops that bend back on themselves in giant symmetries and stream out across millions of miles." The purpose of the artist, he declared, quoting Robert Browning, was to make beautiful things that "have lain burningly on the Divine Hand."

The premiere of George's new quartets took place at Lincoln Center's Alice Tully Hall on January 22, 1979. My wife and I did everything we could to promote it, and through our considerable exertions helped draw an unexpectedly large crowd. Every seat, as I recall, was filled. As the evening unfolded, it became abundantly clear that George had adopted time-honored forms—fugues, serenades, sonata movements, rondos—for his quartets, that resounded, as one critic put it, "with passages of warm lyricism, rich harmonies, frolicsome rhythms, and sheer joy in music-making, with an occasional touch of modernist astringency for zest." The audience saluted his achievement with a tumultuous ovation, and Leonard Bernstein, in the forefront, embraced him and declared the works a "masterpiece." Most critics concurred. Raymond Erickson of the *Times*, for example, found their phrases "gorgeously harmonized," "incredibly sure, lucid, and brilliant," and described a fugue in the 4th quartet as "one of the gentlest and loveliest imaginable." Another, writing for the *Detroit News*, said that it was "hard to think of a more brilliant and beautiful array of chamber music produced by any composer in recent years."

As broad as this praise was, so were the attacks upon him by the serialist avant-garde. He was denounced as a heretic and "shameless apostate" for having "betrayed the progress of music"; in reply, he urged the serialists to "stop tormenting themselves, each other, the musicians, and the audience" for the sake of their strained ideas. In their work, he went on, they mistook "demonstrations of theoretical-analytical thought processes" for true musical ideas. Even the best work of Elliott Carter, Milton Babbitt, Leon Kirschner, and others he considered mere "stylistic efforts" of no lasting account. He also had no use for the random or "aleatoric" music pioneered by John Cage. It "rested," in his view, "on thinly developed notions of chance, uncertainty, and indeterminism" that required no talent, knowledge, or training. It therefore allowed composers to disclaim responsibility for what they wrote. As for the new electronic music (then allied with atonal practice), it was "incapable of expressing passion on any level. There is no love in it . . . Music must be a form of love conveyed through sound—shaped by the human need to say, to utter, to project its painful knowledge of life . . . ."

George's expansive, discursive essays were learned and provocative, and in "The Avant-Garde and Modernism" (1969)—his most famous, perhaps—he conclusively demonstrated (or definitively proved) that atonal music was doomed by being opposed to how the Central Nervous System makes sense of sound. Music, he pointed out, must conform to the nature of the physiological system that receives it—as a structured, intelligible succession of synchronized sounds. Otherwise, the Nervous System will experience it as an affliction. Its memory function is also unable to absorb music without the self-perpetuating features of repetition, variation, and recall—the very things that make a piece distinct. By analogy (in my view) we might say that meter, rhyme, alliteration, assonance, and other traditional mnemonic, "self-perpetuating" poetic techniques are the very features of a poem that enable us to take it in.

In his contest with the serialists, George prevailed. His work broke the grip that atonal dogma had on the world of his peers;

and by the force of his example, given his stature, he "opened the way to greater freedom and latitude in the way composers could write." By the end of the twentieth century—freed from the absurdly stringent dictums of Pierre Boulez—there was once more a vast range of stylistic choices from which they could choose. Some of the best of the younger composers, including David del Tredici, John Corigliano, and William Bolcom, followed his lead.

George's own work continued to evolve. He was in touch with all traditions; "had a soft spot," as he put it, for American popular songs, especially from the 1920s and 1930s; and was ever seeking to enlarge his palette of sounds. Some of his pieces might be called Neo-Romantic—his 5th Symphony, for example, premiered by Georg Solti and the Chicago Symphony Orchestra in 1985; *Slow Fires of Autumn*, for harp and flute, based on a lullaby; *American Bouquet*; and the Violin Concerto he wrote for Isaac Stern. Toward the end of his life, he also made use of chromatic dissonance at times; but his final conviction (as he expressed it to me) was that atonality had been an "experimental interlude" that expanded the range of sounds for expressing the pathological in life. But it could hardly supplant the music of the past.

George composed over 100 works, including six symphonies; seven string quartets; concertos for violin, clarinet, and oboe; works for harp and guitar; song cycles; several pieces inspired by Old Testament texts; and the Melville opera. His fine collection of essays, *The Aesthetics of Survival: A Composer's View of 20th-Century Music*, will be read for a long time. He was also a vivid teacher, and it was said that when he taught Brahms or Mahler it was as if they were in the room. In 1979, he became Annenberg Professor of the Humanities at the University of Pennsylvania, a title he held until his retirement in 1983.

At the beginning of 1988, George had surgery and, to beguile his convalescence, read the work of Robinson Jeffers, whom he had encountered before. He shared Jeffers' doubt about a caring God; embraced his pantheistic love of creation and his disdain for certain modernistic artistic trends—in particular, the process, which he dated from Mallarme, of "divorcing poetry from reason and ideas for the sake of melodic effects." That could only lead in time to "further renunciations"—as, indeed, it did: "Ideas had gone," wrote Jeffers, "now meter had gone, imagery would have to go; then recognizable emotions would have to go; perhaps at last even words might have to go or give up their meaning, nothing would be left but musical syllables. Every advance required the elimination of some aspect of reality, ... It was too much like putting out your eyes to cultivate the sense of hearing, or cutting off the right hand to develop the left. These austerities were not for me; originality by amputation was too painful." To George, it seemed as if the abstract austerities of twelve-tone composition had done the same thing. "Modernism ended up by allowing us only a postage-stamp-sized space to stand on," he wrote. "We cut the rest away."

His favorite writers were Yeats, Rilke, Borges, and Blake (a quartet I could embrace); admired the novelist Kazuo Ishiguro; enjoyed the off-beat character of the Coen Brothers films; and (among my other incidental recollections) scorned Deconstructionists like Derrida as "leaving the mind, the spirit & the universe even thinner than the old positivist notions" by "stripping every possible layer of 'natural' meaning from experience." Much contemporary music criticism seemed to him absurd. I vividly remember him doubled over in laughter as he read me the beginning of an essay by one trendy critic who alleged that the pounding opening bars of Beethoven's *Fifth Symphony* signified the pelvic thrusts of a man about to climax in intercourse.

*

My concert work introduced me to a number of remarkable people, but none as compelling as George. One other was Otto Nathan, a Socialist economist who had been Einstein's colleague at Princeton and the co-executor of his estate. In mid-March of 1979, Otto asked me to help organize a concert in Einstein's honor, to which he would lend support. For various reasons, it failed to coalesce, but thereafter, over lunch and at his apartment at 24 Fifth Avenue, I had a chance to talk to him a handful of times. He told me something of his struggle with Princeton over Einstein's papers; of his great reliance on Helen Dukas, Einstein's secretary and co-executor, who was "so thoroughly familiar with our Archives that I feel confident that, if anything was available, she would be able to lay her hands on it"; and of his own insignificance in anything having to do with world affairs. What I remember about him most was his modest, self-effacing manner; his simple, steadfast Socialist convictions; and his frank confession (to my amazement) that his diminutive stature had been the dominant fact of his life. "I never got over it," he said, adding that the critical thing is often not even guessed at in people's lives.

Einstein had indirectly crossed our family's path before. When I was growing up, I had three honorary "aunts": Marion, Louise, and Claire Severn. Their father, Louis Svecenski (a Croat of German-Jewish stock) was a celebrated violist, and a founder of the Kneisel Quartet, the first string quartet in the United States. Almost every composer and musician of note came through his door. Albert Einstein, too, was a familiar guest, and always brought along his violin. In Marion's vast upper East Side apartment (which she shared with her sister Louise and seven or eight cats), there were three or four pianos, a priceless Gasparo da Salo viola (later acquired by Lillian Fuchs of the Juilliard School), and signed photographs and other memorabilia and artifacts pertaining to Puccini, Dvorak, Verdi, Brahms, and other musical giants of the past. Svecenski had helped introduce the work of the Viennese masters, including Hadyn and Beethoven, to the American public; promoted the work of Dvorak, who wrote several pieces for the Quartet; and had performed at the White House for both Theodore Roosevelt and William Howard Taft. From 1888 till 1917, when it disbanded, the Kneisel Quartet had been fundamental to the world of classical music in the States.

None of his three daughters ever married. Their mother, Bertha—once a promising young pianist herself—was often "ill," impossible to please, rejected all her daughters' suitors, and made them emotionally dependent upon her by her demands. Louise had once run off with a circus acrobat only to be brought back;

Claire taught piano in Mexico City for most of her life; Marion became a patent attorney in New York.

One of Marion's dear friends was the writer Rachel Field, who gave her the nickname "Swish." Marion had been close to a number of people in the theater, where Rachel Field first made her name, and as a child I remember once sitting happily on the lap of Eva Le Gallienne, the actress, director, and translator of Hans Christian Andersen's fairy tales. After Marion died, Louise gave me a box of Rachel Field's papers, which are now part of the Arne Nixon Center for the Study of Children's Literature at California State University in Fresno. The box included manuscripts, letters, original illustrations, family photographs, clippings, and other documents, author's galleys for two books; Rachel's original, corrected typescript of three plays for young adults (later published by Scribner in 1924); her hand-written notes for a work she was planning on Lola Montez; and the original typescript (perhaps received as a gift) of a number of charming animal poems for children by Laura Benet. Aside from her celebrated books for children and young adults, Rachel wrote some wonderful poems and a few best-selling adult novels that were made into films.

As maiden aunts, Marion and Louise were typically eccentric and devoted to their cats, with many of their household decorations, such as cigarette boxes and coasters, cat-related in design. They would rise together at dawn and grind out fresh liver for them all in a hand-grinder and set it out in separate bowls. Each cat seemed to know its own, and raced to its respective place, as if choreographed.

Marion was unquestionably my father's oldest and dearest friend. They had been active together during the 1920s and 1930s in the Socialist Party and in 1938 appeared on the radio together to discuss the Spanish Civil War.

Every year on his birthday at Christmas, Marion gave my father a box of Cuban cigars. I assumed this was because the cigars were exceptionally good. Later, when I saw old pictures of them together on a beach in Havana, I realized that it also commemorated that by-gone time.

CHAPTER FOURTEEN

❦

Despite the success of my concert work, I could not see it as my fate. There was an egomania about the music world I disliked, as typified by flyers that featured the name of the performer in large letters, with Beethoven, Brahms, or Mozart in smaller type. I often preferred opera stagings and recitals, for example, at the Juilliard School of Music, where the talent was superb, the voices fine, the music in the forefront, and no one yet a "star." I became partial, too, to the selfless beauty of choral music and medieval chants.

Meanwhile, I was intent on a writing life. From time to time in the mid-1970s, I had unsuccessfully applied for grants from the Guggenheim Foundation and the National Endowment for the Arts; worked, in fits and starts, on a blank verse drama based on Herman Melville's *Pierre*; compiled notes for an historical novel about the Inquisition; thought up a story about self-discovery set in Corfu; and compiled a list of topics for a collection of essays, among other projects—all groping in the dark. As I struggled to find my bearings, I took some comfort from a passage in Kafka's *Diaries*, in which he lamented the many failed or incomplete efforts of his life:

It was as if I, like everyone else, had been given a point
from which to prolong the radius of a circle, and had then,
like everyone else, to describe my perfect circle round this
point. Instead, I was forever starting my radius only constantly
to be forced at once to break it off. (Examples: piano, violin,
languages, Germanics, anti-Zionism, Zionism, Hebrew, garden-
ing, carpentering, writing, marriage attempts, an apartment
of my own.) The center of my imaginary circle bristles with
the beginnings of radii, there is no room left for a new attempt;
no room means old age and weak nerves, and never to make
another attempt means the end. If I sometimes prolonged the
radius a little farther than usual, in the case of my law studies,
say, or engagements, everything was made worse rather than
better just because of this little extra distance. (January 23, 1922)

And yet I thought to myself (without any pretense to comparison),
"he did all right in the end." So I copied it out and pinned it
above my desk.

In 1977, I came up with the idea for my first book. It had
begun to take shape in my mind the year before when I was working
as a paste-up artist for a small, mid-town, graphic design firm affili-
ated with Schocken Books and Stein & Day. On my lunch hour,
I used to walk over to the New York Public Library, sift through
pertinent material, and became convinced that its uncovered riches
were substantial enough to justify my idea. The book that would
emerge was *Labyrinths of Iron: Subways in History, Myth, Art, Technology & War*. I put together a proposal; set out to find an agent;
and just at that juncture learned from Danielle (who had a contact
at *Newsweek*) that Newsweek Books needed urgent help on a paste-
up job someone had botched. I offered my services, got it right,
and as the publisher, Alvin Garfin, was inordinately grateful, seized
the day and proposed the book to him. He liked it at once, and
I soon had a contract in hand. The advance was modest but at least
I now had a chance to show what I could do. I wasn't, in fact, sure
what I could do, frankly; but I had conceived my topic broadly, to

engage me completely; and I was full of determination not to fail.

Over the next two years, I wrote the book largely at night. Nights were really all I could spare from my concert labors; and there was always enough anxiety about money to keep me at overlapping tasks. From my study in the back, I looked down on a courtyard, which adjoined the town house of the playwright Israel Horovitz, who was then working on *Author! Author!*, a movie script. I used to hear him pounding away at his typewriter at all hours of the day and night; and though we never met, his disciplined productivity was a positive reminder to me of what was required. I owe him that. Occasionally, for a change of scene, which often helped, I wrote in the back room of the "Café del Artistes," one flight up, on Greenwich Avenue, a few doors down from where I lived.

Before *Labyrinths of Iron*, I had never tried to construct a compelling narrative, let alone a large one, with complex matter in the mix. One can only learn to do this by doing, in a process governed by your own sensibility and tact. One afternoon, I happened to hear an interview with the director, Peter Brook, who remarked that he had recently been looking at some rushes for a film he was making that seemed to go on too long. Yet when he timed the sequence, it was really no longer than those that went at a good clip. He puzzled over this awhile until it occurred to him that it had to do with how the film was lit. The sluggish sequence was dark. Darkness had become duration. When he brightened the film, its pace picked up. It occurred to me, in turn, that this might apply to writing. I noticed that some of my pages dragged because the writing was dense, or cluttered, or obscure—by analogy, dark. I could think of various ways to address this; but the most important discovery for me was the manner in which anecdotal material, even as it enriched the story, let in light and air.

However, no one had more of an influence on my writing and early development than my eldest brother, Jim. From a young age, he was well-read and articulate, in an original and striking way, with a startling gift for expressing himself in memorable, often dramatic, turns of phrase. It would be hard to overstate the impression this made on my sensibility, except to say that it established standards of expression of the most exacting kind. I wish I had saved his earliest letters, which were much beyond their years; but in his later writing, too, he was always interesting to read. When he introduced me to John Berryman's *Love & Fame*, for example, he commended it for its "unzipped wit & pathos," which was aptly witty itself. Upon meeting a woman he'd begun to date, he conjured her up sharply as "an elegant gamin from Chicago with a voluminous chevalure, hard chic, and vespid glitter," which made her as alluring and elusive as a hologram.

That was his style.

Jim was also an accomplished poet, with a meticulous knowledge of his craft. Each piece was exquisitely well-wrought with seldom a wasted word. Here, for example, is a fine little poem that turns on the vernal equinox:

> Once more in Aries day and night
> The sun and clearest constellations shed
> The eastern Garden's priscal light.
>
> On punished flesh the sweetness gathers back,
> As you, Spring's sigil in its stead,
> Climb to the flashpoint of the zodiac.

Another evokes precisely the ritualized, superstitious obsessions of someone in love:

ANSWERING MACHINE

> Scared sick you'd call it off, I came to be
> as strung-out on the messages you'd leave
> as you on those blue pills that got you free.
> Reaching my winter rental on the bay
> alone at night, I'd conjure a reprieve
> by climbing the dark staircase the same way,
> and (as though terms were spells) "triangulate":
> I'd gaze—call indicator out of sight,
> consciously breathing—seaward through the plate

glass till the blood that juddered in my head
calmed to far pulses from the Cleveland Light,
then sideways…fixed on what I hoped flashed red.

His gift for memorably apt, ironic turns of phrase was epit-
omized for me early on by the closing lines of his translation of
Baudelaire's "Daybreak," which describes the noble city of Paris
in all her ignoble, tawdry rites of waking up:

Shivering in her hues of pink and green,
The dawn proceeds down the prostrate Seine;
As diehard Paris rubs blear eyes and turns
To traffic in her urinals and urns.

Jim was about twenty-two when he wrote this, when he was
also working on a verse translation of part of Book XXII of Homer's
Iliad, his Senior Honors Thesis in college. He introduced it this
way: "Although most of the lines in the following adaptation stand
in at least an oblique relation to the original, I have not aimed at a
photostatic reproduction of Homer's idiom; such attempts, however
ingenious, usually result in translationese, not English. I have tried
to present the essential action as vividly as I could and have pruned
and grafted to that end. My guides have been mostly negative: my
own sense of what is possible in contemporary writing and a
desire to avoid both dullness and overstatement which are, as
Yvor Winters remarks, the Scylla and Charybdis of narrative
verse. I hope my adaptation may be read with enjoyment for its own
sake, and I urge my readers to do so before they consider its relation to the text itself."

That was modest. In his young but accomplished hands, the
force and beauty of the poem at once came alive. Here Apollo,
who has adopted the guise of a Trojan prince to lure Achilles into
a chase away that draws him away from the walls of Troy, turns to
confront his pursuer:

"You overstep yourself. Give up, you fool,
before I lose my temper. No mere man,
not even you, can spear and strip a God.
The broken Trojans scramble back to Troy
while truant to your own intent, you run
regardlessly off to play tag with me."
Achilles answered:
                    "Many others, lord,
would have taken between their screaming teeth
the final wafer of communal dust,
had it not pleased you to deceive my eyes,
decoying me out here, defrauding me
of glory. If I could, I'd make you pay,
but no man can get even with the Gods."

Turning, he jogged towards Troy, his boots trampling
a decade's dead, the human humus which
enriched and stratified the rotting plain.

Dog days: and heat fracturing the scorched earth,
with Sirius rising, disastrous star,
livid and brilliant, a red warning hung
far through stupendous arcades of starlight;
when fevers rage and men begin to die.

So, on the plain, Achillles' breastplate shone.

With equal originality and power, the translation continues
for several hundred lines, recounting the prelude to the great battle
between Hector and Achilles, as well as the battle itself, with
perfect artistic control over the exact metaphor or image, all within
a brilliantly modulated iambic pentameter line. Had Jim chosen
to translate the whole of the poem in this way, I believe he would
have achieved, by the age of 25, a kind of masterpiece.

After graduating from Boston University, with a major in Classics, he continued his studies at the University of Texas, returning to Boston to earn his doctorate in 1973. Subsequently, he taught at the Swain School of Design before becoming a Professor of English at the University of Massachusetts, South Dartmouth.

Jim's prose was equally vivid and succinct. The simple opening to his doctoral dissertation on *Giles Fletcher and the Hexaemeral Tradition* is a good example of his style: "Although widely regarded as the best of the biblical brief epics in English after *Paradise Regained*, Giles Fletcher's *Christ's Victorie and Triumph* has seldom been examined on its own terms. Some critics discuss Fletcher mainly in light of Spenser and Milton; others emphasize stylistic elements or attitudes of mind that Fletcher shares with Southall and Crashaw, the metaphysicals closest to the Continental baroque; but no one has offered a satisfactory account of the poem as a coherent whole." That sets up his discussion of the poem's numerological structure as well as anything could.

Jim was of tremendous help to me in giving *Labyrinths* its shape. By his editorial suggestions and, at times, close editing, he showed me how to form paragraphs of optimal length, quote sources deftly, and improve the pace. In certain respects, my style developed through his.

Our fraternal natures have always been mystically linked. Our horoscopes are similar but opposite (our Ascendants being reversed); we have almost the same voice; have lived, to some extent, analogous (if not parallel) lives; suffered analogous (if not identical) ills; shared many of the same studies; and even, independently, and at about the same time, allowed ourselves to be inducted into an underground Gurdjieff group—Jim in Boston, myself in New York. We mainly differed in the end in our convictions—Jim adhering to an Epicurean, secular view of life, as I became more devout.

*

My editor at Newsweek Books was a woman by the name of Marion Wheeler, who had formerly worked at MacMillan and might have been expected to have some literary sense. Unfortunately, she had no capacity for second levels of meaning, and her general knowledge was poor. When I referred to the Cumaean Sybil of Roman mythology, for example, her query in the margin was: "Sybil who?" Moreover, all her marginal notations were literally expressed in beauty parlor terms: this passage needed "a face lift," that "a tummy tuck," and so on. She also exhorted me to emphasize the carnage of subway accidents, to give the text "verve." This was my first experience with editorial ineptitude and I was in something like a state of shock.

The thought of reshaping and degrading the book in her image was unthinkable, but Wheeler, with Garfin's backing, assumed I would acquiesce. After all, this was my first book, and both thought I would agree to anything to get my name in print. When I refused, Garfin threatened to sue me to recover the advance. Fortunately, my contract, which granted me few other rights, included a clause that allowed me to reject my editor, if I chose. I stood on that; and at length the book was assigned to a copy editor, who did a respectable job in straightening out mundane grammatical errors or oversights.

Labyrinths of Iron was well-received, widely-reviewed, and helped on by a generous tribute from Lewis Mumford, the great social historian. Needless to say, I sent a copy of my book to Edward Tayler, whose teaching had done so much to shape my thought. My admiration for him had been next to unbounded, but my diffidence, as a student, had made it hard for me to form a connection with him at the time. He had found merit in my papers; delight in my "Empsonian" habit, as he called it, of unearthing layers of meaning in a text; but I had seldom taken advantage of his office hours or spoken up in class. Moreover, though he presided over the "Major Author" part of my doctoral orals (and politely grilled me on Sir Thomas Browne), I had neglected to seek his counsel in my hectic preparation for that day. It was only later that we began to establish a real friendship, exchanged letters, and visited each other in New York, New Hampshire, and Vermont. We had been out of touch for about a decade when I wrote him in January of 1982. He replied, nicely: "I knew there must be some reason why I had been teaching [Allen] Tate's [poem] 'Subway' all those years."

As I considered what to write next, I received a call from the venerable engineering firm of Parsons, Brinckerhoff, Quade & Douglas. They were about to celebrate their centennial history and thought their story should be told. The founder of the firm, William Barclay Parsons, had been the chief engineer on the first electrified subway in New York, and one of the firm's directors had seen the review of *Labyrinths of Iron* in *The New York Times*. I was wary of a commissioned work; but Parsons himself had led a fascinating life, and the firm had been involved in a number of remarkable projects, from the Cape Cod Canal and the 1939 World's Fair to military airfields and hardened defense facilities like NORAD (the North American Air Defense Command). I signed a contract to do it, but wisely insisted on a clause that allowed me to write as I pleased. The firm obliged; and when attempts were later made to alter the text, I stood fast and prevailed. That ultimately redounded to the company's benefit, since Van Nostrand-Rheinhold decided to publish it as a work of independent worth.

While I was working on this book, my father died.

CHAPTER FIFTEEN

Over the years, my father's legal practice had gone through numeous gyrations, but fairly late in life, in a triumph of timing, he made his mark on the national stage. In 1966, when I was a sophomore in college, he became the attorney of record in the first case to question the legality of the Vietnam War. The case was David Henry Mitchell 3rd against the United States of America and it eventually went to the United States Supreme Court (October, 1966, No. 1012). Mitchell had refused to report for induction and was indicted, convicted, and sentenced to prison for five years. His defense had been that the war was one "of aggression" conducted in violation of certain treaties the United States had signed—in particular, the Treaty of London of August 8, 1945, which declared that waging such a war was a "crime against peace." Article 8 of the Treaty, moreover, held individuals responsible for their involvement, even under command. Having taken the case, the Supreme Court declined to rule on its merits; but Justice William O. Douglas wrote a notable dissent, stating that the major issues should be explored. He quoted Justice Robert H. Jackson, the United States prosecutor at Nuremberg, who said: "If certain acts in violation of treaties are crimes, they are crimes whether the United States does them or whether Germany does them, and we are not prepared to lay down a rule of criminal conduct against others which we would not be willing to have invoked against us." Douglas further noted that Article VI, clause 2 of the Constitution states that treaties are part of "the supreme law of the land; and the Judges in every state shall be bound thereby."

Five years later, with Richard Nixon in office, my father founded the National Committee for the Impeachment of the President and ran a two-page spread on May 31, 1972 in *The New York Times*. As noted at the outset, it was the first public call, prior to the Watergate Scandal, for the President's impeachment, charged Nixon with conducting an illegal war, and created a sensation nation-wide. The ad, which reproduced the text of House Resolution 976, of the 92nd Congress, 2nd Session, cost $17,850 and was substantially funded by Alexander Calder an his wife. The Committee named Ernest Gruening, the former U.S. Senator from Alaska, as its Honorary Chairman; Richard A. Falk, Milbank Professor of International Law at Princeton, as Vice-Chairman; my father as General Counsel; and my stepmother, as Secretary-Treasurer of the enterprise.

Seventeen days later, the Watergate Break-In occurred. Both the House Resolution and the ad were fiercely attacked by Attorney General John N. Mitchell, later imprisoned for conspiracy, perjury, and obstruction of justice; but strongly supported by General Telford Taylor, the chief United States prosecutor of Nazi war crimes at Nuremberg.

Nixon of course was apoplectic. John Dean was told to add my father and step-mother to Nixon's "Enemies List" (in the haste to do so, misspelling my father's first name); and on June 20, 1972— the same day Nixon and H.R. Haldeman had their infamous 18 ½ minute, self-incriminating chat, later erased—Nixon met with his counsel Charles Colson to discuss the ad. It dominated their conversation, as they wondered if the *Times* might be charged with libel, or the Committee with a violation of the campaign finance laws. On August 18, the Justice Department brought suit against the Committee in the U.S. Court of Appeals, Second Circuit, where the case was decided on October 30, 1972.

My father, joined by other attorneys, won. The Court ruled that the mere running of an ad did not constitute "a political" action group, subject to campaign finance laws, for if that were held to be true "every position on any issue, major or minor, taken by anyone" and "any comment upon it . . . be subject to proscription . . . Such a result would, we think, be abhorrent. . . .The dampening effect on first amendment rights and the potential for arbitrary administrative action that would result from such a situation would be intolerable." In conclusion, the court quoted Judge Learned Hand, who had "so eloquently described . . . 'the spirit of liberty' . . . as the spirit of Him who, near two thousand years ago, taught mankind that lesson it has never learned, but has never quite forgotten; that there may be a kingdom where the least shall be heard and considered side by side with the greatest." In short, the government's authoritarian presumptions had been condemned by Christ Himself!

Meanwhile, in late August 1972, Randolph Phillips, as Chairman of the National Committee; my father as General Counsel; and Vern Countryman, Professor of Law at Harvard, distributed a booklet to the delegates of the Republican National Convention that claimed that in order to obtain his nomination in 1968, Nixon had "sold" a Supreme Court seat to South Carolina Senator Strom Thurmond in return for delegates he controlled. The charge could not be proved, but Nixon's subsequent nominations of Clement F. Haynsworth, Jr. and G. Harrold Carswell suggested they were right.

Two years later my father and stepmother moved to New Orleans, where my stepmother was teaching at the Southern University, an all-black school. While there, my father, age 70, made his "theatrical debut" as the corrupt judge in Charles Gordone's Pulitzer Prize winning play "No Place To Be Somebody." How much he must have relished that role! He also debated the Judge Advocate of the VFW on the subject of Amnesty at the First Unitarian Church.

After he returned to New York, he suffered a series of strokes, was progressively disabled, subjected to an unnecessary operation, and underwent pointless physical therapy, almost to the end. He suffered badly. I was with him when he had his last stroke. We were sitting in the waiting room of a dentist's office. He had taken out his wallet and was anxiously counting out the money he had. He did this over and over, with the same set of bills. A few moments later, his hand motions slowed and his speech began to slur. He was 78 at the time and on Medicare; but the pinching cost of health care was still on his mind.

In the hospital one day a few months later I found him sitting up in bed, trying to handle a doctor's questions. His speech was almost gone and the words wouldn't come. After the doctor left, I asked him how he was. He looked at me with astonishment, raised himself a little in his bed, and, with an eloquent sweep of one hand that took in the entire room, said, distinctly, "Are there any pleasures here?" "No," I replied; and at that, with an expression of satisfaction, he leaned gently back against his pillow and closed his eyes.

He never spoke again.

He is buried near his sister, Frieda, in New Montefiore Cemetery, Pinelawn, Long Island.

After my father's death, I put together an album of family photographs. There were dozens of pictures I had never seen, including some of my father as a young man—climbing a mountain in Russia, drinking at the Morocco Club in Hollywood, romping on a Cuban beach, in New York canvassing for votes. There were other pictures of my mother, too, from the 1930s in China and Korea; putting on lipstick; on the gangway of a great ship; drinking a beer at home as she read an issue of *Life Magazine* with a picture of F.D.R. on the front. There was also my great uncle Charles in a First World War uniform holding my mother (then eight) on his knee.

Nine years after my father died, on April 20, 1990, I joined in a séance of a kind, at a Ouija Board. My friend Peter Guttmacher was "at the controls" and was hoping for advice about his acting career. Unexpectedly, my father appeared. He said he wanted to speak to me, if he could. He had a question: "Are you angry with me?" "I have been," I said, "because I didn't know why you did certain things." He replied obscurely, then repeated "Anna," or "Nana," which I took to refer to his mother, for that was her name. My friends (who didn't yet know his name) asked him what they should call him. He replied, "Bob," which was how he was known. Again, he said he wanted to talk to me, and used the name "Benson." I said, "Are you sure? Why do you call me Benson now" [instead of "Barry," my familiar name]. He replied, "Bona fide" (using a term he was fond of, which seemed to mean that he wanted to use my proper name). I asked, "What do you want to tell me?" He replied, now all in caps: "HAVE A GOOD LIFE." I asked, "Are you holding on to things?" (i.e., worries). He replied, "Yes." I asked, "Is my being angry one of the things that is keeping you from being happy?" He replied, "YOU CARE N YOU ARE A MAN EACH OF US LIVES LIFE AS WE BEST KNOW HOW LOVE YOU TALKING DAY AM." I said, "Can I ask you one more question?" He said, "Yes." I said, "How is Mother doing?" He replied, "LOVES ALL NANA." Peter asked, "Is Nana an all-embracing term?" My father replied, "No." Peter: "A specific term?" My father replied, "OPENING." Peter, "What kind of opening?" My father replied: "NAME."

Though I tend to think of Ouija boards as engines of malevolence, yet . . . good angels having been invoked . . . .

I recount this for what it is worth, exactly as transcribed.

*

When my first book was published, my faltering speech impaired its prospects, as I failed to take advantage of interview requests that arose. Over the years, as I recounted in *Knotted Tongues*, "I had seen a speech pathologist, a hypnotist, and a psychotherapist. None of them had done me any good. Then one day I happened to watch a movie on one of the new cable channels I had just hooked up called *Talk to Me*, which dramatized a relatively new therapy devised by Ronald L.Webster at the Hollins Communications Research Institute in Roanoke, Virginia." An experimental psychologist, Webster had been working on the problem of stuttering since 1966. By 1974, through computer analysis, speech spectography, and other techniques, he had been able to identify "a series of tiny but absolutely critical speech movement characteristics" that appeared to be precursors to fluent speech. These were precisely and empirically defined and incorporated into several muscle movement patterns, or "targets," which became the basis for the now-famous Hollins "Precision Fluency Shaping Program."

In a fundamental paper entitled "The Establishment of Fluent Speech" presented in September 1979, Webster, summarized the new evidence and the conclusions to be drawn: that stuttering is a physically based problem; tends to run in families, whether or not the affected members are known to each other at first hand; and that a tendency to the disorder, if not the disorder itself, is inherited, as evidenced by the fact, that (1) it occurs throughout the world in all language groups, with an incidence of about 1 percent; (2) the developmental course of the disorder is universally consistent, with about 95 percent of all cases occurring by the age of seven; and (3) the sex ratio of the disorder, which affects four times as many males as females, is also consistent worldwide. Adopting a cybernetic paradigm (according to which there is an abrupt increase in the level of a system's output when a feedback signal is disturbed), Webster noted that the repetitions, prolongations, and blockings characteristic of stuttered speech all represented forms of "overshooting" in which muscle movements were made with undue force. In further evidence that auditory feedback was involved, he noted that ways of enhancing fluency—by whispering, singing, choral reading, and so on—had their "loci of effects at either the larynx or the ear." He concluded that stuttering was essentially "a motor control disorder," and that the probable mechanism responsible was a defect in the auditory feedback loop.

"For a stutterer to speak fluently," he wrote, "the movements of speech must be held within certain limits of rate and force." His detailed therapy taught patients how to do that, and through tactile and proprioceptive feedback, to acquire the feel of correct speech.

"There are many other therapies to be had, of course, some resembling Webster's, some not. But," as I wrote in *Knotted Tongues*, "this was the one that worked for me. In mid-April 1986, I enrolled in a version of the Hollins program taught by a clinic in New York.

I saw the head clinician there, Catherine Otto, who interviewed me at length, and variously assessed my speech. She had an opening in a summer program, and I took it; I have seldom stuttered since."

A daguerreotype of my great grandfather, Benjamin W. "Webb" Baker, when he was a Civil War soldier, ca. 1862.

"Webb" Baker and Martha Frances Henry at the time of their marriage, ca. 1870.

My paternal grand-
parents, Paul Bobrick
and Anna Lindner,
on their wedding day
in Warsaw, Poland,
ca. 1900. Paul's
parents (names
unknown) are seated.

My maternal grandparents,
James C. Baker and
Lena Benson, at the time of
their marriage in 1901.

*My great uncle,
Charles G. Howard,
with his son, Peter,
ca. 1930.*

*My mother's passport photo,
1928.*

My mother, ca. 1933.

My father's parents, on the steps of their home in Brooklyn, in 1951, the year before they died.

My father, with my eldest brother, Jim, 1942.

My mother, already ill, in 1952, with my older brothers and myself.

My stepmother, Elizabeth "Sherry" Most as a Welfare Officer for UNRRA (the United Nations Relief and Rehabilitation Administration) at a displaced person's camp at Wiesbaden, Germany, after World War II. Here she is shown escorting Eleanor Roosevelt on a tour.

My father, ca. 1962. *My grandfather, the Bishop, in his late 70s.*

Hagop Merjian,
at Pomfret School.

My brother, Jim, in his early twenties,
ca. 1965.

Edward W. Tayler
(photo taken at the wedding
of a mutual friend), in 1986.

159

P.L. Travers as a young
Shakespearean actress.

Danielle, about the time of her
New York Recital debut, 1986.

George Rochberg at home,
autographing a copy of his book,
Four Lines, Five Spaces:
The World of My Music, in 2005.
(Photo: Michael Garber)

George and Gene Rochberg
at our home in Brattleboro,
Vermont, July 1997.

Hilary, when I met her, with three of her seven pets (the other four were cats).

Below: Around the time of our wedding.

Above: Jasper, our Shiba Inu, at the vet. We adopted him on the same day we adopted our Chow Chow, Zuzu (whom Hilary named for "Zuzu's Petals") when they were both eight weeks old. Remarkably enough, both had also been born on the same day.

Zuzu. She was completely devoted to Jasper, and died not long after him in 2018, at the age of 15.

Correcting the page proofs, July 2019.

Part Two

꙰

"Many thousand things that I now
partly comprehend I should have thought
utterly incomprehensible, many things that
seem to me lucid and enlightened now they are
seen from inside I should honestly have
called dark and barbarous seen
from the outside . . . ."

—G.K. Chesterton,
St. Francis of Assisi

CHAPTER SIXTEEN

At about the time I had come to know George Rochberg, another great figure crossed my path. This was P.L. Travers, of Mary Poppins' fame, who completely transformed my understanding of what it meant to be alive. As with my encounter with George, literature forged a bond. I was ushered into her New York apartment on York Avenue, where she was seated in an erect and stately fashion, neatly attired in a white linen dress, her wrists and fingers bedecked with silver jewelry fashioned by Indians of the American Southwest. Her hair was not abundant, but seemed more so by being curled; and when she turned to greet me, I was struck by the bright blue clarity of her eyes. At the same time, their concentrated core had a kind of metallic luster, like polished orbs of hematite. Her knowing gaze was full of expectation, perhaps assessment: I felt at once I must not disappoint.

Travers was 76 at the time, focused but relaxed, and in a reserved yet congenial way we talked about my studies and certain writers, including Sir Thomas Browne, whom she knew well. T.S. Eliot came up. "He was wonderful with children," she said. "They used to follow him about." That surprised me, since I thought of him as dour. Later I learned that Travers had served with him on the board of A.R. Orage's *New English Weekly* for several years. We came to William

Blake. She had recently had an amiable argument with the poet-critic, Kathleen Raine, over whether Blake held "categorical" beliefs. Travers was doubtful. I agreed. I said I didn't think he would have been *categorical* about anything. Her eyes flashed delight.

*

Though Travers was mainly known to the public for her celebrated nanny, her writings were diverse, and she was a much-loved and respected figure in the world of humane letters when she died in 1996. Well into her 90s she remained a woman of regal presence, and to those who knew her, as I did, as luminous as the Northern Lights. Her pronouncements were always to be heeded and had an oracular kind of wisdom to them drawn deep from the well of folktale and myth. That wisdom seemed almost incarnate in her, like the Wise Old Woman of many a fairy tale.

She was one of the great students of folklore of our time.

Toward the end of her long life she wrote, in a kind of summing up: "The cauldron of plenty in each of us seethes with its ferment, sweet and bitter—the world to be carried and no plaint made; love to suffer long and be kind, not vaunting, not puffed up; the seed that we carry to be threshed, freed from its crusty husk; the aching question of who we are and for what made, answered only by its echo; the need to stand before the Unknown and never ask to know; to take our leave of the world, head high, no matter how hard the parting . . . ." That was her "way," as one friend put it: open, honest, brave.

Born Helen Lyndon Goff in Queensland, Australia, on August 9, 1899, she lost her father (a tea planter and bank clerk) at the age of seven, after which she moved with her mother and two sisters to New South Wales to live with a great aunt. By her own account, her childhood was loving, and she grew up on folk tales and the star lore of the hugely expansive southern skies. By her early 20s, she had begun to publish poems and articles in newspapers and periodicals, took up theater and dance (adopting "Pamela Travers" as a stage name), and toured with an acting troupe.

But the romance of Ireland was in her blood, and in 1924 she sailed for England with Ireland in her sights. She sent the brilliant poet A.E. (George Russell), who edited *The Irish Statesman*, a poem, and to her surprise he took it, paid her two guineas, and asked for more. She embarked for Ireland to meet him, and he became her tutelary deity for many years. Through him she met W.B. Yeats, James Stephens, Sean O'Faolain, Oliver St. John Gogarty, Padraic Colum and other leading lights of the Irish Renaissance. They all "cheerfully licked me into shape," she wrote, "like a set of mother cats." Although a Dublin uncle objected to her "gallivanting around with men who see fairies," it was in the visionary company of Yeats and his compatriots that she came to understand the mythic world.

One of her early poems, accepted by A.E., lamented the passing of that long ago time when poets had been inspired by heroic themes. No subject could have pleased him more. Called "The Dark Fortnight," it began:

> Oh, I could weep with despair
> in this blind, barren time,
> for the themes that have loosened their hair
> and dangled the glittering strands
> for other eyes than mine
> and hands that are not my hands.

Another, "Coming Toward Meadows," was a prayerful lyric on the end of a romance:

> In the dark heart of the forest
> Is a terrible splendor—
> We have hidden there
> All our love's thunder.
>
> Now I can look in your eyes
> Without fear, without stirring

The quiet tides of my breath
Or a bird in my breast murmuring.

Beauty grows merciful
And apples of amazement are
Red-ripe upon the branches,
Unplucked, familiar.

Give me your hand and kiss
Me in this quietude
O bitter honey, O grief
For the dark lost heart of the wood.

Love, have we come to the end
Of our wild sojourning?
Into the passionate wilderness
Is there no returning?

O whitethorn blowing with red lip
Fire after fire along the wealds
Light us a way from the cold brakes
To the friendly fields!

A.E. showed her work to Yeats, who thought it had "merit"—which, A.E. told her, "means a good deal from him," for he was notoriously sparing in his praise. Time, however, passed before Yeats and Travers met. Then one day, as she told it, she was on her way to Dublin by train when she realized she would be passing through County Sligo near the lake Isle of Innisfree. Thinking to honor his great poem with a trophy, she hired a boatman to take her across, found a roan tree, stripped it of its branches, re-crossed the lake in a storm and, soaked through, hauled them onto the train. When she got to Dublin, she went straight to Yeats' home where "his housekeeper," she recalled, "met me at the door. I'm afraid I was a sorry sight, dripping wet, clutching this huge gathering of branches. The housekeeper took them from me and ushered me into another room to dry off. By the time my clothes were dry, I had grown mortified by my behavior and was about to slink out when the housekeeper said, 'The master will see you now.' Yeats was bubbling over with enthusiasm. His canary had just produced an egg and he was eager for me to see it. As we talked, I noticed out of the corner of my eye that there was a vase on his desk with a tiny slip of roan from the huge bundle of branches I had brought. That's when I learned you can say more with less."

When not exploring the Irish hinterland, Travers read deeply in the folklore of all cultures and wrote bold poems that expressed their deepest themes. Here is her startling "Christmas Song for a Child":

> Child in the manger laid,
>   Take now your myrrh and gold
> And incense as we kneel
>   With the Three Kings of old.
>
> Child, on this winter night,
>   Do you know that we mean
> To crucify you
>   When the leaves are green?

She knew, of course, what the three gifts meant: gold for Christ's Kingship, incense for His Priesthood, and myrrh for His embalming sheet. The Magi, after all, were astrologers, and had read his meaning in the stars.

For a time, Travers worked as a film and theater critic, drafting stories on the side. Then in 1934 she published the first of her *Mary Poppins* books, about a magical nanny, which began her fabled enchantment of readers worldwide. In 1964, Walt Disney made her stories into a film. Her struggles with Disney over its making were epic, and his distortions brought her, literally, to tears. But in time she came to accept the movie as "a colorful entertainment" if "not true to the meaning" of her tales. "What wand was waved," she asked, "to turn Mr. Banks from a bank clerk into a minor president, from an anxious, ever-loving father into a man who could cheerfully tear into pieces a poem that his children had written? How could dear, demented Mrs. Banks, fussy, feminine, and loving, become a suffragette? Why was Mary Poppins, already beloved for what she was—plain, vain and incorruptible—transmogrified into a soubrette?" The errant wand, of course, was Disney's opportunistic imagination; but his greater failing was to make the world of children childish, where pity replaced compassion, and justice was sentimentalized as the desire for fair-play. The result was a domesticated garden of good and evil, where cuteness was a virtue and painted sorrows all we know of tragedy and grief.

Over the years, Travers wrote a number of other books, including *Moscow Excursion*; *I Go By Sea, I Go By Land*; *Friend Monkey*; *The Fox at the Manger*; *About the Sleeping Beauty*; and *What the Bee Knows*.

At the outbreak of World War II, she came to the United States, worked in the Office of War Information, and lived for two summers with the Navajo Indians in the American southwest. She later traveled the world over—to Africa, the Near and Middle East, India, China, and Japan (where she studied with a Zen Master)—and became a reliable authority on Islamic, Buddhist, and Hindu thought. Meanwhile, she had come under the influence of the esoteric teachings of P.D. Ouspensky and George Ivanovich Gurdjieff. Although she remained their unwavering adherent to the end, her understanding belonged as much to the allusive world of story and symbol as to the tenets of any school. In this, Shakespeare was her guide: "By indirections find directions out."

Travers had been introduced to Gurdjieff around 1938 by A.R. Orage; attended Gurdjieff's Prieure Institute in France; worked in England with his student Maurice Nicoll; and when I first met her some 36 years later was a principal group leader at the Gurdjieff Foundation in New York.

Gurdjieff held that the ordinary waking state of Man is a kind of sleep; that such sleep is marked, psychologically, by mechanical reactions and associative thoughts; that our thoughts, sensations, and emotions belong to as many shifting selves; and that among them there is no coherent, reliable "I". In his view, the path to redemption from this disordered—essentially soulless—state was a disciplined process of "self-remembering," which, through constant effort, could create a conscious, conscientious Self.

Travers embraced this doctrine as divining profound truths, which she found reflected in other great teachings as well as timeless tales. For her, the "Sleeping Beauty" was the paradigmatic fable of the slumbering, unclaimed Self, enclosed within "the automatically growing forest of our habitual nature." In her own extraordinarily alert, forthright presence she seemed (to me at least) to exemplify what self-study might achieve.

There appeared to be nothing of importance she didn't know. Children also gathered around her wherever she went, and I remember one memorable Christmas assembly in the Cathedral of St. John the Divine, when they were spell-bound by her story-telling gifts. Though she was said to be a "children's book" author, she herself doubted there was such a thing as "children's literature," for in the world of our imaginations, where does childhood end and adulthood begin? "If it is literature indeed," she said, "it can't help being all one river and you put into it, according to age, a small foot or a large one. When mine was a small foot, I seem to remember that I was grateful for books that did not speak to my childishness, books that treated me with respect, that spread out the story just as it was, *Grimm's Fairy Tales*, for instance, and left me to deal with it as I could."

Myth and fable were alive to her at all times, and she saw many of the narratives in life around her as reenactments of ancient tales. "If one was willing one could not open a newspaper," she wrote to me on one occasion, "without noticing that the myths simply cavort in it." She was even a bit intrigued to learn that I was the youngest of three brothers, since many tales cast that unlikely figure as the hero of a quest. And why not? "There are times in every man's life," the Scottish poet, Edwin Muir once observed, "when he seems to become for a little while a part of the fable, and to be recapitulating some legendary drama . . . . The Fall is one of those events, and the purifications that happen in one's life belong to them, too." For "the life of every man is an endlessly repeated performance of the life of Man." More broadly, Thomas Mann, in his essay on Freud, suggested that all lives, *in their essentials*, potentially conform to archetypes.

Travers strongly believed in a dialogue with the dead—in the need, as she advised in a letter, "to *work* with & repair the past—[both] for ourselves *and* the past." In her story, "The Unsleeping Eye," she wrote, in that vein, of building a ladder back to the sun: we must "climb up through the length of ourselves, on each rung repairing what had been—the wrong roads taken, the forgettings, the long stretches of nothingness—and preparing what was to come." Or as Muir put it: "I must live over again the years which I lived wrongly . . . . everyone should live his life twice, for the first attempt is always blind."

A part of the work of life (if one lives long enough to do it) is a process of reintegration and repair. Can the past be repaired? In eternal recurrence, everything is done both once and forever—that is, forever and a day. The past is therefore re-lived, and potentially corrected, *right now*. This can only be done by changing the mind and heart, where all things—for all time—live, move, and have their being: in our soul, which belongs to the Mind of God. In *that* Mind are joined together all other souls, which know and feel the change so wrought in us.

So I believe.

Finally, Travers was convinced, as she taught in another fable of her own, that the judgmental side of our nature must learn to forgive the indulgent part, caught up in the stream of life, just as the latter must forgive that which in us is stern. The two together, joined in compassionate understanding, make one healing whole. After all, "Good" in isolation, "in life as in story, is pallid and color-less," she wrote. "It needs to be touched by Bad to blush and know itself." It is the villains in a story that provoke the heroes to virtuous acts—not only in the world without, but *within* ourselves.

For Travers, life was a mission, which all the great stories confirmed. When we are born, she wrote, we enter into an obligation—"there are no rights of any kind, but only a purpose to be served." The hero (of whom every person is a type) is the one who "puts his foot upon a path not knowing what he may expect from life but in some way feeling in his bones that life expects something from him." The end of the quest—on one level, surely—is the recovery of the Self; but "all one can say for sure is that Myth makes it clear that we are meant to be something more than our personal history." In one interview, she gave a clue: "Accept everything that comes and make jewels of it ... you can only be the hero of your own story if you accept it completely." At the heart of it all (knowing Travers as I did) lay St. Paul, for true happiness, in her view, involved not just pleasure and joy but was "a moral virtue, come to by grace and discipline and not without suffering. It requires a poignant letting go of what has been most cherished and learning a new vocabulary—the grammar, as it were, of the heart. The 'I' that knocks upon the door must become, in answer to 'Who is there?' inevitably 'Thou.' Love, as noun, must become verb and lose itself in Loving; and Passion assume the syllable that makes of it Compassion. Only thus, when what was lost has been found, is it possible to enter the city with bliss-bestowing hands."

All her gestures had meaning. On the same Christmas occasion I saw her read at the Cathedral of St. John the Divine, she gave an ostrich egg to its Dean, James Parks Morton, who hung it in a chapel arch as an Eastern Orthodox symbol of resurrection and re-birth. How so? "Because," said Travers, in her typically paradoxical fashion, "the ostrich is a forgetful mother!" For it was thought—and in Biblical times believed (Lamentations 4:3; Job 39:13-16)—that the ostrich left its eggs in the earth to be hatched by the sun. So their birth (a type of our re-birth) was achieved by celestial warmth and light.

Travers was also given to memorable observations and asides. In a talk I attended at the Jung Foundation on folk tale and myth, she said of Robert Graves, "He was right even when he was wrong." And in speaking of Hans Christian Andersen's more "mawkish" plots observed, "Sentimentality is the obverse side of cruelty," in summing up the tenor of his tales. At the end of the talk, a woman in the audience raised her hand and said, in a kind of rebuke to Fate: "I didn't ask to be born." Travers replied sharply: "I'm sure I did! I'm sure I insisted on it!" (For so we must.) Someone else objected to the violence in some stories as unsuitable for children, pointing to "The Three Little Men in the Wood" in *Grimms'* in which the villain is rolled down a hill in a barrel stuck through with nails. Travers disagreed. "Children love justice," she said (quoting G.K. Chesterton). "It is we who need mercy."

*

When Danielle and I married, Travers presided as a kind of fairy godmother over our union, and did her best to guide us. But we were not yet ready for the deep wisdom she dispensed. "Dear Danielle and Barry," she wrote in one lovely letter, "I shall be thinking of you on your wedding day & sending you my thoughts—wishing for you both a long life together full of mutual loving-kindness. Love, like the rainbow, comes & goes unless it is LOVE, which is something we mortals can't always rise to. But loving-kindness, which is what St. Paul in the Corinthians meant by charity (caritas), is a jewel of great price—to be sought for & won. And the English language is the only one that has this word. Other tongues try to approximate it but cannot—It is our own. Cherish each other! And God bless you."

Travers had just moved into her new row house at 29 Shawfield Street, Chelsea, London, and before giving up her New York apartment, had offered us some of her furnishings, including a dressing table (which we took) and her bed, which we did not. Then or slightly later, she also invited us to join her in London. But we were bound to our lives in New York.

In subsequent letters, she often mingled advice with insights into life and art. "Let ideas just go into you," she wrote on one occasion to Danielle. "By 'standing under' I mean to let it come down upon you as you would if you were willingly and restfully standing under the rain. Or sunshine, if you like. Be defenseless. Do not 'try' so hard . . . . The trying can become merely muscular; the mind has muscular gestures as well as the body. Let the ladder, as it were, draw you up rather than forcefully putting your foot on each rung. A friend who lives up a great many stairs told me that he climbs them with ease by doing it very lightly, almost on tiptoe. I tried that and the stairs seemed to be lifting me."

In the same letter, she recommended *Zen in English Classic and Oriental Literature* by R.H. Blyth and, with it, Robert Louis Stevenson's story, "The Poor Thing," in which an unborn child arranges the circumstances that bring about its birth. "Try to get into you the idea—Kafka discovered it—that 'it all doesn't depend on me.' Yes, I must submit myself to the Great Work which is Life with a capital, I must indeed make efforts, but I must also allow that the Great Work in fact works! If I allow for the existence of Grace I am in the necessary state of humility."

While I was working on *Labyrinths of Iron*, she exhorted me "to remember the Labyrinth, a fundamental idea. And the catacombs, the journeys to the underworld of the heroes of myth." I did so, and framed the book in that light. In my subsequent writing, I tried to remain attuned to the storied subtexts of the facts.

She rejoiced in my early work (the only part of it she would know); likened *Labyrinths* to "descending into the Underworld with Persephone"; and commended my poetic determination to give the subject a "largeness and meaning, mythological meaning without which we cannot live." When I later chose to write about Ivan the Terrible, Russia's first tsar, she saw it as a challenge to my "gentle" disposition, and hoped Ivan would not prove "so terrible after all." Beyond that, she pressed me to persevere. Not surprisingly, she worried about the obstacles I faced in making a living in the arts; urged me to keep in touch with the business world ("It can make the bread while you make the butter"); yet (addressing Danielle, too) "where shall we get if we do not take risks—anything to do with the arts is risky. You note I do not say 'creative arts.' I have long held, with C.S. Lewis, who said 'There is only one Creator. We merely mix the elements He gives us.' And I add, 'gratefully.'" A year later, she took the time to recommend me for a Guggenheim Fellowship despite her struggles with ill health.

In the summer of 1981, I wrote a poem for her inspired by an image she had used in a talk:

> Whatever the weather, let it be extreme,
> Let the Sun bake out of me the dross,
> The rain come down in sheets, and wash
> Me through, the wind blow through my seams.
>
> Let nothing of me remain but what
> Innately is, archaic, seer—
> A glass in which, as in a crystal sphere,
> The whirlwind-water-fire are caught.

She thought it "good"— akin in spirit to Donne's Holy Sonnet "Batter My Heart Three-Personed God"—and tried to place it in *Parabola*, a magazine she had helped to found. She was annoyed at its rejection, and taking my part, explained: "I do not think [the chief editor] understands poetry—either in words or other ways . . . I am sorry an inch wasn't found for it."

She was now far on in years, spoke often of "wanting to rest"— though not, she said, "from writing which is not a work but a difficult joy"—and in the summer of 1981, still hoped to go to Switzerland, if only for a brief stay. Even so, she maintained her Gurdjieff group in London, and produced a steady stream of allusive and poetic essays and stories, later collected in *What The Bee Knows*. Some of her stories are as wise and riddling as the timeless tales she pondered and retold. Meanwhile, she wrote two more *Mary Poppins* books when well past eighty years old.

Like the bee itself, she took pollenated sustenance from any flower in which she found it. Offhand, I can think of a host of authors who gave her a tell-tale line: e.e. Cummings, Thomas

Traherne, Dylan Thomas, ("The force that through the green fuse drives the flower"), Isak Dinesen (one of her favorites), Theodore Roethke ("I learn by going where I have to go"), D. H. Lawrence (who "deserved to be canonized for pointing out that there is the truth of fact and the truth of truth"); James Joyce ("My childhood bends beside me"); G.K. Chesterton; Robert Louis Stevenson; William Blake (who said of myths and legends, "Their Authors are in eternity"); St. Augustine (for his belief in truth "uncreate"); Meister Eckart; Robert Graves; Shakespeare; Plato; E.M. Forster (for his injunction, "Only connect"); Homer; the great Eastern sagas (the Rig Veda, the Upanishads, the Ramayana, and the Mahabharata); and the Greek poet Aratus, who declared: "Full of Zeus are the cities, full of Zeus are the harbors, full of Zeus are all the ways of men!" That combined in my mind nicely with a Hermetic description of God I loved: "God is a circle whose center is everywhere and whose circumference is nowhere."

I once had a conversation with Travers about what it is to be a "good man." She declined to venture a definition, but said: "It's more important to be a good *man* than a *good* man." By that I understood her to mean that virtue, to be true and strong, must proceed from the fulfillment of one's nature. And perhaps that is what Robert Greville (the friend and colleague of Milton) meant, at least in part, when he said: "The good you know, you are."

In 1982, her Gurdjieff group gave a Christmas performance which, despite a minor blizzard, drew a sizeable crowd. A few months later, she went to hear a concert of Tibetan music performed by members of the New York Harmonic Choir. "It was a very moving evening," she wrote. "I know about and to some extent have experienced, the sort of humming done in Zen, which is not dissimilar . . . . Gurdjieff said that the proper way to say the Lord's Prayer is by this humming. And think of the word 'Amen.' It is not very far from Om."

She was seldom well enough to travel now and in the summer of 1984, when was 85, wrote that apart from a sojourn to Kent, she had to remain close to home. "It has been a difficult six months for me, . . . But I go on writing: Give us this day our super-essential bread—let me make a super effort no matter what." She ended her letter sweetly: "Love and blessings and news when it is ripe to be news, of whatever kind. Ever your friend, PLT."

As important as she was to me, I do humbly know that I was but one of a host of people for whom she cared. Our contact was intermittent; spanned only a decade and a half; and (I suspect) occupied one of the outer rings of her ennobled world. Those who belonged to her study groups were perhaps her heart's first care. When I last saw her—in her grand old age, now a "Dame of the British Empire," at her small townhouse in Chelsea, London— she allowed me and Danielle to take tea with her, a privilege (she announced in Mary Poppins fashion) not granted to anyone she had not known for at least eight years. Her house had a famously distinct pink door, and there was an antique rocking horse in the hall. Her terraced sun-lit studio, furnished with a camellia, a bay tree, and a marble Buddha, was at the top. Her conversation had "vertical take-off" (to borrow a phrase from Sheamus Heaney, who applied it to Joseph Brodsky) and we had a good talk.

"Everything we know, " she declared, "our immemorial memories, all the great stories, are carried in the hemoglobin of our blood. They are nearer than the vein in our neck." We touched on names. ("A nickname in childhood," she said, "is often a key to a person's essence, or real nature"); on prayer: ("Prayer is different than thought. To pray, you must make yourself transparent in some way"), which struck me at once as true. She confessed happily to being superstitious—noting that the root, *super stitia*, means "that which stands over," i.e., "that which remains" as a fragment of something that once had truth and meaning, and referred me to lore about mistletoe and clues in nursery rhymes. When I voiced some apprehension about the future, she said, "Never do anything out of fear." At one point, she also remarked on the different physical gestures by which gender is expressed.

Tea was followed by brandy and then a brief tour of her garden, which included a rose bush, herbs for cooking, lettuce and beetroot plants. As we left, she gave us a sprig of rosemary "for remembrance."

Travers was one of the immortals. For those who believe in significance—in an ordained imperative at the mysterious heart of life—she belongs on the choicest shelf beside Homer and Shakespeare, Donne and Milton, Stevenson, Browne, and, of course, the Brothers Grimm.

*

My encounter with Gurdjieff's core teaching was a watershed in my life. Under its aspect, I saw many things clearly that I had only glimpsed before. At about this time, a number of discrete threads in my understanding began to weave themselves into one cloth. Just as Webster's therapy had shown me that by conscious monitoring one could become responsible for the mechanics of one's speech—which meant that stuttering no longer "happened" as if it were the result of an independent force—so self-remembering (a form of self-monitoring) provided the key to one's deliverance from the mechanical reactions that typify our sleep-walking state. The thought of a sleep-walking life had long filled me with dread. I vividly remembered a T.V. drama I had seen in my teens about a young woman whose entire life was spent in a coma—or state of amnesia, I don't remember which—after an accident, and who at last awakes, only to discover that her whole life is past. Yet I had almost come to believe what the mother in O'Neill's *Long Day's Journey Into Night* believes, or says she believes, that "None of us can help the things that life has done to us. They're done before you realize it, and once they're done they make you do other things until at last everything comes between you and what you'd like to be, and you've lost your true self forever."

Here, to lead one out of that labyrinth, was a Thesean thread.

Just as the alchemical distillation of time-honored words and phrases often preserve certain truths as in a vial, so it seemed to me that the principle of self-remembering was embedded in ordinary descriptions of our errant state: "absent-minded"; "lost in thought"; "preoccupied"; "self-absorbed"; "beside oneself"; "scattered"; "carried away," and so on, which all tell us the same thing: that we are not there. For when we identify with any thought or feeling, as our habit is, we are absorbed into it and become the thing itself, which is not us. And for that moment—let us say, "being beside ourselves with anger," and so the Incarnation of Anger—that is all we are. Machines have no souls. Insofar as you act like a machine—and live a life of simple reaction to stimulation, with your thoughts in a constant associative stream—you have no soul either, but are like an automaton.

From then on, my life began to acquire a new dimension—not of altered space or time, but of an infinite point in the middle of Time which the Self began to fill.

*

It used to be axiomatic in Gurdjieff circles (and perhaps still is) that Ouspensky intellectualized the system, whereas Gurdjieff was the Teaching itself—the more complete man. I wonder if that's true. Gurdjieff introduced some of the ideas Ouspensky caught hold of; but Ouspensky developed them and thought them through. Gurdjieff may have had the stronger, more charismatic personality, but he was also an opportunist, by his own admission, as well as a showman. Without Ouspensky's "translation" and transmission of his teaching, he would scarcely be known at all.

Not long after I had been introduced to Travers, I was encouraged to join the Gurdjieff Foundation in New York; invited to a private screening of Peter Brook's new movie, *Meetings With Remarkable Men*, based on Gurdjieff's recollections; and interviewed by a group leader, who suggested I read Ouspensky's *In Search of the Miraculous*. But I was profoundly averse to belonging to any "school." After all, I had come out of Tayler's course on Milton where I had learned that Truth, like the dismembered body of the Egyptian god Osiris, was dispersed throughout the world and had to be gathered up "limb by limb." So I had a dogmatic aversion to anything that smacked of "dogma"—and to some extent, still do.

*

As a singer, Danielle's greatest strength was probably the art song. When she made her own New York recital debut in the fall of 1986, she featured that genre in the program she chose. Tim Page wrote it up nicely (October 6, 1986) for *The New York Times*: "As a founder and co-director of Woerner/Bobrick Associates, a New York public-relations and concert management agency, Danielle Woerner has long been well known in the musical field, and she has seen many young artists through the anxiety and excitement of a debut recital. Last Tuesday night, it was Ms. Woerner's turn to experience these emotions firsthand when she made her formal recital debut as a soprano at Merkin Concert Hall. Ms. Woerner has a fresh, agile voice of moderate size and ingratiating sweetness. Although her high notes were a little tight throughout the evening, she negotiated the tessitura artfully, and her singing was intelligent and idiomatic in several repertories." I cheered her on, but our marriage by then was dissolving and we divorced two years later with a rough equality of blame. In time, we reemerged as friends; and are to this day. In a fine gesture that was also an homage to our bond through Travers, she sent me an ostrich egg with a perfectly round break in it where the hatchling had come forth.

CHAPTER SEVENTEEN

My book on Parsons Brinckerhoff had taught me much about the history and business of American engineering; but I was looking for another kind of story that might engage me completely, as *Labyrinths* had. One day, as I was browsing in the Strand Bookstore on Lower Broadway in New York, I came upon Paxton Hood's *The World of Anecdote*—a compendium of odd lore published in 1897. It had some pages on Ivan the Terrible, the first Russian tsar, whose complicated story spanned most of the sixteenth century and therefore coincided with the late Renaissance in the West. My academic field had been Renaissance studies, yet it occurred to me at once that I knew little about the impact, if any, of Renaissance culture on Russian life and art. I doubted others did, either. A biography of this inscrutable man—whose capacities in some respects had a Renaissance largeness—would, I thought, allow me to explore that era of Russian history to the full. I also soon discovered that there were many tantalizing interconnections between Ivan's Russia and the English Renaissance.

My agent at the time was John Hawkins, who had recently acquired the Paul R. Reynolds Agency from his father-in-law. Founded in 1893, it was the oldest such agency in the United States and its imposing roster of clients had once included William and Henry James, George Bernard Shaw, Joseph Conrad, Leo Tolstoy, and Stephen Crane. In the hallway outside Hawkins' office framed letters of gratitude from some of these authors lined the wall. As if this weren't intimidating enough, several doors down from his suite, then located in a building on 23rd Street which he owned, was an office occupied by "The Knights Templar," according to a placard on the door. Hawkins himself had done well as an agent, and his own chief clients at the time were Alex Haley, James Clavell, William Shirer, Gail Godwin, and Joyce Carol Oates. To celebrate his success, he had decided to change the name of the agency to John Hawkins and Associates and under that rubric, for a while, continued to thrive. I was naively thrilled to be his client, since I was then ignorant enough about publishing to think it mattered who his other clients were. In docile obedience, I therefore languished in his stable for the next three years. During that time, a junior associate had hammered out the details of the Parsons Brinckerhoff contract; but, not surprisingly, Hawkins greeted my idea for a book on Ivan with weary condescension, on the grounds that Ivan's story—and that of his Muscovite realm—was remote and obscure.

Practically speaking, he was right. It was unlikely to make much money, and not the "big book idea" he'd hoped I'd find. Nevertheless, the topic had come to engage me and I eventually secured a relatively small advance from G.P. Putnam's Sons which, though not a living wage, kept my career alive. Despite my straitened means, I also felt sure in my resolve.

Ivan's reign, though chronologically remote, had relevance, in my view, for anyone caring to understand the Russian people and their world. As I would later explain in my Foreword, some part of the Russian soul will always remain "Muscovite," and to a degree most might find surprising, the Soviet state elaborated under Stalin was less a repudiation of the world of the tsars than a recrudescence of the realm Ivan ruled. Traces of old Muscovy continue to this day, and are broadly reflected in everything from popular customs to government organization and foreign affairs. It is in Ivan's time, for example, that Russia's great confrontation with the West begins, and ideas formed then seem almost to have been cast and set in a mold. "Evil Empire" speeches belong to a long tradition, and one urgent admonition delivered in 1569 by the king of Poland (who described Russia as "an enemy to all liberty under the heavens") stands as the progenitor of all such diatribes.

Ivan was cruel—and "terrible"—and great. His considerable reign saw the conquest of the Tartar strongholds of Kazan and Astrakhan, and (despite a disastrous drive to the Baltic) the consolidation of Russia as a nation from the Caspian to the White Sea. His ongoing duel with the princely aristocracy, or boyars, laid the foundation for an autocracy supported by a nonhereditary serving class, while his permanent initiatives in opening up diplomatic ties to Europe bound Russia ever after to the West. No ruler of the age had more staying power. Eight popes would succeed each other to the Holy See; four monarchs each to the thrones of France, Poland, Portugal, Germany, and England; three to the throne of Sweden, and three Turkish sultans to the Sublime Porte before Ivan met his own demise. Within Muscovy itself, his judicial and other reforms for a time made him an exceptionally popular ruler, and though his security apparatus eventually developed into a terror machine, features of its organization brought lowborn gentry into the councils of government and arguably, at first, had the welfare of the people at heart.

Yet however great his achievements, they were matched by his despotism and atrocities; and despite his colossal stature, historians disagree about him on almost every level and on many important details. He has remained the most controversial of tsars, and part of his fascination for a student of history lies in the changing fortunes of his fame. One contemporary miniature remains for me inimitably succinct: "He was a goodlie man of person and presence, waell favored, high forehead, shrill voice; a right Sithian; full of readie wisdom; cruel, bloudye, merciles."

One day when I was in The New York Public Library Rare Book Room parsing my way through a little volume on Ivan in

Renaissance Latin (*Ioannis Basilidis Magni Muscoviae Ducis vita*, by Paul Oderborn, published in Wittenberg in 1585), a man came in, saw what I was reading, and (against all odds) began to talk about it, since he had read the book himself. He was evidently an accomplished Latinist, but sixteenth century Russian history also lay within his ken,

This was Hugh F. Graham, then Professor Emeritus of History at the University of California at Bakersfield. He held degrees in Classics from the University of Toronto, a degree in Byzantine Studies from Princeton, a doctorate in classics from the University of Southern California, and degrees in Russian, Church Slavonic, and Russian history from Berkeley. He was also fluent in German, Polish, and French. He had been the first American historian to teach Russian History *in Russian* at Leningrad State University (in 1981–82), and (such was his range) was also a virtuoso jazz pianist with an Oscar Peterson-like drive. To support himself as a young student, he had played piano at jazz clubs in Toronto at night. We began a friendship, and over the next several months, his knowledgeable guidance on source material helped my research along.

As with *Labyrinths*, I worked on the book night and day, and two years later, my biography, *Fearful Majesty: The Life and Reign of Ivan the Terrible* was published, in 1987. Though my labor had not been gainful (by any normal financial standard), in the course of it I had acquired a working knowledge of Russian and a substantial understanding of Byzantine culture, the Russian Orthodox Church, the politics of the Baltic states, Polish history, Elizabethan diplomacy and commerce, and some of the lasting issues that set Russia against the West. My fascination with these subjects must have made itself felt, for my book was well received, and the publisher (scarcely a given) was even moved to advertise. Hugh Graham also commended the book to scholars in a generous review in the *Journal of Canadian-American Slavic Studies*.

Ivan's reign had come to an end just as Russia's conquest of northern Asia began. A book about Siberia—with its broad array of curious, besotted, and heroic characters; fantastic expeditions;

"Wild East" sagas; tales of exile; and the awesome power of the land itself—seemed a natural sequel. I conceived the story in epic terms; changed agents; held out for a proper contract; and threw myself into research. In changing agents, I followed the advice of an editor at Doubleday who was also a friend. She recommended Russell Galen, then with the Scott Meredith Agency. He undertook to see that my ideas were properly funded, and from then on I was gainfully employed.

My thirty-two page proposal for the new book was capacious and I secured a sizeable advance from Poseidon Press, a division of Simon & Schuster. The editor who acquired the book had once been the poetry editor at W.W. Norton. She had literary intelligence, and so I felt my own ambitions might now be understood. It was therefore with a high heart that in the summer of 1989, I embarked for Gorbachev's Soviet Union to see for myself what Siberia had become. I had a sentimental reason for going, too, for it allowed me to follow in my mother's footsteps across that vast terrain.

Once more, Hugh Graham lent a hand. He knew everybody in the field of Slavic studies, pointed me to sources of value and interest, and at the American Association for the Advancement of Slavic Studies Conference in Honolulu in November 1988, squired me about from one talk to another in the appropriate khaki shorts and floral shirt. I can picture him now—a debonair man, elegant, well-spoken, down to earth, practical—sipping daiquiris on the verandah of the hotel where we stayed. The theme of the Conference—"The Soviet Union and the Pacific Rim"— was also perfectly suited to my task.

Before striking east to Siberia, I spent time in Moscow and St. Petersburg, then still called Leningrad. My flight in had taken me through Helsinki, Finland (which seemed like an island in a forest from the air), and as my plane circled Moscow's Domodedevo Airport, I was surprised at how much forest surrounded Moscow, too. Once I touched down, I was aware of being in a third world country—impoverished in all but its military might. At Helsinki, each restroom stall had been furnished with its own small sink—exquisitely civilized and quaint; at the Moscow airport, every stall was awash with backed-up sewage and stank. On the drive to my hotel, I passed miles of dreary, Soviet-era standardized housing with their balconies converted into flimsy outside rooms.

In the middle of one thoroughfare, an abandoned, vandalized car was ablaze.

In my room at Moscow's Cosmos Hotel, even elementary accessories, like shower curtains and toilet paper, were lacking and the bed was not quite made. An unfinished glass of juice stood on a desk. There was an old T.V. that worked on three or four channels, and a radio that went dead after an hour. The sterilizing unit for my contact lens case exploded when I plugged in the adaptor I had brought from the States.

Russia at the time was plagued by sudden, unexplained shortages of basic goods like detergent, and some of the supplies in Russian grocery stores were so meager as to be almost symbolic—two cuts of meat, four jars of jam, one fish. The day I arrived, even coffee was being rationed and I had to pay forty kopecks a cup above the indicated price. Though *glastnost* (openness) and *perestroika* (restructuring) were taking hold, Gorbachev, to my surprise, was not yet admired. He was thought to be corrupt, and it was rumored that he had recently passed laws to curb alcohol abuse in order to profit, personally, from organized crime. That might seem absurd to us now, but not to those familiar then with the machinations of Kremlin power. Sugar, in fact, was scarce because bootleggers had reportedly begun to hoard it for their stills.

I would soon discover that the newspaper tear-sheets of Gorbachev's speeches were also being used as toilet paper on the Trans-Siberian line.

In Moscow, I took in some of the sites—the Kremlin, St. Basil's Cathedral, Red Square and the changing of the guard at Lenin's red granite Tomb; a few museums, including the famous Tretyakov Gallery on Lavrushinsky Lane; attended a big "Music Peace Festival" (guarded, notably, by skinheads); browsed in a used bookstore on Gorky Street; and explored Izmailovo Park. Whenever possible, I took delight in Russian cuisine: fresh sturgeon, pike, or perch; cucumbers in sour cream; bliny (akin to a French crepe); pelmeni (Russian ravioli); and pirozhki (baked or fried rolls filled with cabbage or meat). For dessert, I often had éclair-like pastries or ice-cream congealed from cream and buttermilk.

From Moscow, I went to Leningrad. All commercial flights at the time were in heavily guarded planes, and to prevent hijackings were surrounded by submachine gun-bearing troops. The pilots also wore side-arms and armed security personnel patrolled the aisle.

At the front desk of the Hotel Leningrad, where I stayed, I picked up a promotional magazine on "The U.S.S.R. Today." On the cover was a montage of colorful photos showing Gorbachev and Reagan sitting comfortably together in the Kremlin on a white divan; a Russian woman in her wedding dress; a church; a skier; children; a band. It touted the laudable goals of glasnost and perestroika, Soviet efforts at international cooperation and disarmament, and offered a "candid assessment" of the need for reforms. Some things were comically expressed. "Even unemotional economists become enthusiastic when speaking about the Soviet Union's potential," one item read. Another confessed: "Our electoral system remained unchanged for too long. Candidates were handpicked and then presented to the electorate at the rate of one candidate per vacancy. This resulted in a lack of public interest."

Yet some things could be admired. Homelessness was rare; rents low; public entertainments, like the ballet and theater, cheap; and almost everyone seemed able to get by. Many did so, too, with part-time work, and some of the professionals I met (electricians, plumbers, and the like) had time for artistic and other pursuits. In the underground economy, people found a way. Most were content to share moveable goods, like records and books; and their daily lives were not driven by a mania for gain. Bus fare (in Leningrad, at least) was also on the honor system, which could only impress. It was also not uncommon for someone relatively poor to have a dacha or little country house.

According to the official exchange rate, the ruble was equal to the dollar, but on the black market it was about ten rubles to one. Russians were eager to obtain "hard" or foreign currency for goods like electronics (available only at "Beriozka" or hard currency stores), and I stretched my money considerably by exchanging it at the black market rate. In Leningrad, my chief contact was the son of an army major, stationed "somewhere in the north." I used to meet him occasionally on a street corner off Krasny Prospekt, and in gratitude for our arrangement he gave me a handsome watch that ticked off the time in half-seconds, uniquely, which I prized.

Wherever I went, I encountered a strange mixture of expectation and decay. Hope abounded in reform, but the collapse of the old order had set the nation adrift. Even the security services seemed in disarray as their members moved sideways into parallel or analogous professions, like drug-dealing and prostitution, to thrive in new developing underworlds. Among all walks of life, there was a tilt toward crime. Many Russians had been introduced to the idea of free enterprise in its most mercenary form, while others could only find employment on its seedy fringe. One intelligent young couple I met in Moscow had university degrees in both French and physics, worked part-time for Intourist, the Soviet tourist agency, but failed to find regular work consistent with their skills. They were desperate for a decent life and had a new-born child. To survive, they enrolled for three months at "Interclub Moscow," run by Casino Royale, where they were trained as croupiers. Eventually, they ended up on a casino boat (the "Carnivale," as I recall, "to see the world"), destroyed their marriage, and abandoned their infant daughter to foster care in Tver.

Such stories, of course, might be told of many couples in the States; yet it somehow typified how things in Russia were.

While in Leningrad, I struck up a friendship with Svetlana Gorokhova, then a professor in the Department of Foreign Languages at Leningrad Technical University. She was fluent in English, devoted to her students, a linguistics expert on slips of the tongue (which she subjected to algorithmic rules), and wrote arcane articles on such things as "Probabilistic and Algorithmic Strategies of Grammatical Structuring in Speech Production" and "The Semantic Decomposability of Idioms Predictive of Speech Errors." Even so, she was lively, clever, sardonic, and (at least with me) not at all academic in her ways. Though a de facto member of the intelligentsia, with independent views, her father was a distinguished geochronologist, specializing in isotopes, and a decorated member of the U.S.S.R. Academy of Sciences. Her grandparents on both sides had achieved standing in economics and the arts. One had been a Commissar for the Red Army; another Vice-Rector of the Leningrad Conservatoire.

Svetlana had an intimate knowledge of the city and its history, its secret haunts and exotic spots, and to earn extra money occasionally led guided tours. She had a big, loveable St. Bernard ("one of the two high-jumping St. Bernards in St. Petersburg," she told me) named Larry, which she strove, amid shortages, to keep properly fed. She also had a relatively pleasant one-bedroom apartment of her own. It was located in a so-called "Khrushchev apartment house"—a five-story walk-up building, famous for its tiny kitchens, low ceilings, and other compressed features to economize space. Nevertheless, she had made the most of it, dividing its small expanse—330 square feet—into a study and a bedroom/ sitting room combined. To her mother's dismay, she also covered the floor with rope mats to give her dog better traction. She would have liked a larger place, but in those days all apartments had a waiting list, for which you could only qualify if you lived in outright squalor or had nowhere else to live.

Like other Russian Jews I met, she thought of herself as more Russian than Jewish, though it concerned her that anti-Semitism was on the rise. Recently, for example, she had encountered someone in a local park shouting murderous nonsense about "Zionist spies." Meanwhile, she had established her own niche in Soviet life. She had been a "Young Pioneer" (the Soviet equivalent of a Girl Scout), and as an accomplished academic with exceptional language skills, had been obliged to undergo some military training, with military rank. Her innate intelligence was valued, and after she left off teaching for a while, she was paid to just "come up with ideas."

We used to meet under the statue of Lenin at the Finland Station—where Lenin had disembarked to lead the Revolution of 1917—and during my time in Leningrad she was my devoted friend. Together, we went to a new museum devoted to Anna Akhmatova (at 53 Liteiny Prospekt, housed in the southern wing of a palace once owned by a Russian count); the "Literature Café" on Nevsky Prospekt, where Pushkin and other famous writers used to dine; to a performance of "Gizelle"; a concert of Tchaikovsky's music, with chorus, at Smolny Cathedral; a philharmonic concert by the Academic Symphony Orchestra, featuring Bizet's Symphony in D Major and Samuel Barber's "Adagio For Strings"; to the Kirov Ballet; and to an environmental film where instead of being offered popcorn and candy, we were served little cheese and meat sandwiches with wine.

One day, we took a hydrofoil across the Gulf of Finland to the great Peterhof Palace and gardens. On another, as evening fell, we roamed along the unguarded parapets of the famed fortress prison of Peter and Paul where we came upon lovers in a recess of the walls. To celebrate one of the fabled White Nights, we deliberately stranded ourselves on the far side of the Neva (after its lovely, arched draw-bridges went up) with a bottle of white wine, and sat on one of the embankments and talked till dawn.

*

In my Russian travels, I ventured beyond the major cities when I could, crossed Siberia twice, and traveled down into Central Asia to Tashkent and Samarkand. In Uzbekistan, the people smiled broadly through their creased, weather-beaten faces, but seemed a captive folk, patient, enduring, detached, self-contained. Though Soviet-style banners everywhere exhorted the virtues of work and Party with monuments to Lenin, Kalinin, and other such icons of the State, they seemed like relics of the past. Indeed, the first thing

I saw in Tashkent as I was about to enter my hotel was an old-fashioned shoot-out, as one car sped past, chased by another, shooting at the car ahead. As I settled into my room, Arabic music came over the terrace, followed by silence; then a muezzin called the faithful to prayer.

In Samarkand, I explored the "Registan" or old city center, with its historic mosques and mausoleums, which included the great turquoise-domed tomb of Tamerlane. Majestic portals, roofed galleries, and the friezes of minarets were embellished with ornamental designs and inscriptions, azure mosaics, gold leaf, majolica, and glazed tile. Of particular interest to me was the great Ulughbek Observatory, built in the early 15th century, where, with the help of a giant marble sextant set in a trench, accurate tables had been compiled for over a thousand stars.

At a bazaar in Samarkand, one merchant asked me if I was Jewish. "Perhaps," I replied, truthfully, thinking of myself as "half." He smiled without malice and we bargained reasonably over a pendant of amber beads. Another sold me two jeweled daggers with blood grooves on the blades.

I will never forget the speed with which he produced them from under his robe.

*

One day on the platform of the main Moscow Station (from which the Trans-Siberian embarked), I noticed a gypsy with a knapsack on her back. She set it down, untied it, and with a kind of somersault, a child tumbled out. It went about the platform begging; then, when the train was about to board, tumbled back in. None of this was legal and I stared. She saw that I remarked it all closely, and came up to me and cursed me for three minutes straight. I have no idea what she said, nor would I care to. But I was mortified.

The Trans-Siberian carried me 5,300 miles in six days across seven time zones from Moscow to Khabarovsk—from the fields of European Russia over the Ural Mountains into Asia; through the vast Western Siberian lowlands; across the Volga, Irtysh, Ob, and Yenesei rivers; past hundreds of miles of evergreen forest; to the mountains around Baikal, the world's largest freshwater lake. At length, my journey came to rest on the Amur River on the Chinese frontier. My recollections are a bit faded now, but I remember a blue and gold astrological clock at the Kazan Station, just beyond the Urals; banners praising work, glastnost, and perestroika— "Perestroika is the business of the Party and the Nation," read one—in passing towns; heroic statues; old women on wooden benches outside their log houses, their weathered faces glowing in the sun; farmers facing the train with shovel, rake, or pitchfork in an image of "Siberian Gothic"; nude sunbathers on a roof; tilled garden patches; and men working the fields with scythes. On the platform of every station, vendors sold vegetables, soft drinks, pastries, and fruit.

The Trans-Siberian was then (and may be still) like a great traveling slumber party, with people lounging about all day in their jump suits or pajamas, talking, drinking, and playing cards. My own coupee, which I gaily decorated with Russian posters, was a magnet for entertainment, and I had many visitors interested in what I could tell them about life in the States. My own curiosity about their lives was just as keen. Much of the talk was about popular American culture and icons like Marilyn Monroe, but now and then something more somber came up. From one Ukrainian family, I learned that the average life expectancy of a Ukrainian miner was 39. The man who told me this was a miner, with two young children by his side. I had given one of them my camera case to play with; the wife took it all in with a sad smile.

The train proceeded at a great rate, and to feel the force of it, I slept at night on the bottom bunk close to the wheels as they churned across the land. For most of the way, I had a compartment to myself, but one night I was awakened by a man who came clattering in with bags of vodka bottles he had smuggled on to the train. He was hugely apologetic, spoke in bursts, and soon explained that he had just been stabbed in the leg. As he clutched his calf, blood oozed between the fingers of his hand. I soon learned that he was an Iranian, not Russian, by birth (though he considered himself a Russian national); dealt in bootleg liquor; thought America must be a great place; and was eager to bind up his wound before the next stop. I offered him one of my T-shirts to tear into strips, but he was curiously equipped with his own bandages and salves.

I surmised he had been in such trouble before.

When the time came, he clattered off into the night.

On my second journey out, I often enjoyed the company of Justin Creedy Smith, a young photographer later known as a student of exotic locales. He was a handsome, personable man; unselfconsciously gay; extremely observant; and had recently moved from England to France, where he had an apartment in Clichy-sur-Seine on the Rue de Paris. People were happy to pose for him, and he collected a large portfolio of faces on the line. With my own little camera, I took some nice shots of him.

One evening as we were talking in the aisle, an eastward bound freight train flew past us at top speed. The train was a long one, with platforms instead of cars, each heavily covered with canvas roped to the frames. Some of the tarpaulins, however, had blown free, exposing artillery and tanks. We found this odd. Later, when I returned to the States, I learned that the Soviet Union had recently promised, in a grandiose gesture, to destroy 10,000 tanks, among other military hardware, long positioned on the Western frontier.

My guess is they were sequestered in the East.

Round about this time, my journey took a dark turn. When I disembarked at Novosibirsk, on the Ob River, I was met on the platform by a policewoman flanked by two guards. She demanded to know who I was. I had scarcely begun to reply, when she snapped: "We have information you're from the Rhineland!" (The Rhineland!? How quaint!) I produced my passport. She scarcely gave it a glance. I began to explain that I was working on a book about Siberia. She cut me off, wanting to know the "real purpose" of my trip and whom I planned to meet.

This harassment continued throughout my stay. On at least a couple of occasions I was followed, rather obviously; and every night someone would ring my room at three or four in the morning and hang up. Nevertheless, I felt defiant. The morning I arrived, I went down to the lobby of my hotel (the *Centralnaya*) and asked for a city map. Told, absurdly, there was none, I strolled across the lobby to a newspaper kiosk and asked for a Metro map instead. Novosibirsk had recently opened its own subway and I knew that subway maps in Russia were superimposed on city streets.

I'm not sure why the Russians might have viewed me as a risk. If they had looked into my background, as perhaps they had, they might have noted my book on Parsons Brinckerhoff and the various defense-related facilities the firm had helped to build. From that they might have imagined I possessed some military expertise.

At Novosibirsk, I took in the sites—the Opera House, Ballet Theater, a great rail bridge, the golden-domed Alexander Nevsky Cathedral; and climbed a high embankment overlooking the Ob. One day, in front of the main train station, I came upon a man lying up against the stone steps, his body twisted, his right arm thrown over his head. The fact that he attracted any attention at all was itself notable, since the others milling about were mostly derelicts. There were also a handful of gypsies and Russian toughs in "Pravda" T-shirts. Nevertheless, he lay so still that in time he drew a small crowd. "Dead drunk," said someone, who was himself unsteady. A policeman arrived and the man, who had certainly once been drunk, was found to be dead. No sooner did the policeman depart, than I was surrounded by a family of gypsies who tried to snatch my things. Thankfully, a stationmaster showed up and dispersed them before they could.

On another occasion, I encountered a woman and her son walking a young tiger on the street. The tiger was more than a cub, and I could scarcely believe my eyes. I asked them to pose for me in a "family photo," which they did. I have the picture still.

Before leaving for Russia, a friend had asked me to locate a Shostakovich score for him that was hard to come by in the States.

It eluded my search in both Moscow and Leningrad, but, to my surprise, turned up at a music store in Novosibirsk. As it happened, I was being followed that day, so I asked the sales clerk, who was young and friendly, if there was a back way out. Without the least hesitation, she led me through the storage area to an exit at the rear of the store.

A few days later I boarded the train for Irkutsk, "the Paris of Siberia." I arrived without incident; visited the opera; the Regional Art Museum (which possessed a remarkable collection of miniature drawings by Rembrandt); the State University Library; the Spasskaya Church, with its soaring bell tower; the Decembrist Museum; and the shores of Lake Baikal. Though Irkutsk was a beautiful, well-maintained city, some odd shortages in basic items plagued it, too. One day I saw people at the entrance to a shop literally climb over each other trying to get to some new limited stock of goods. Every group, or sub-group, also seemed to have its own market share. Gypsies, for example, had evidently cornered the contraband market on perfumes and cosmetics; cab drivers, alcohol.

Toward the end of my stay, I accepted an invitation to dine at the home of a friend on the city's outskirts. I was puzzled by her directions, but at length crossed a deserted playground with broken swings to a building which looked as if it had been struck by a shell. The stone exterior was gouged and flaking; the edge of one wall sheared. The front door, with a panel of reinforced glass, hung unevenly ajar. I climbed the dark stairs to a third floor apartment and knocked. The door swung open and—Aladdin's Cave! Oriental carpets covered the floors and sofa; others hung on the walls. The dinner table, as brightly lit as an altar with candles, was richly arrayed with meat and vegetable dishes, salad, fruits, olives, caviar, vodka, and wine. In an adjoining room, my friend was playing a Chopin Sonata on a piano as her mother, with unexpected hospitality, welcomed me with open arms.

Yet the life they lived, if the truth be told, was not one of secret wealth; for they were relatively poor. The young woman was an engineering student who worked as a part-time conductress on the Trans-Siberian line. She had taste and refinement, however, and by denying herself other pleasures and amusements, had brightened her private world. As for the feast, that was an exception, in my honor; and I was moved beyond words.

*

In the course of my journey, I met a man whom I'll call M. Our paths crossed by chance, or seemed to, as one morning I emerged from my coupee to find him standing by the door. A somewhat stout Russian with a trim moustache, he was casually dressed in a sports shirt and slacks, neat in a studied way (which was unusual then among Russians), and began chatting at once. He was open and friendly; worldly, clever, versatile, amusing; liked cards, as it proved, and foreign cigarettes, and full of amiable questions about my life and work. Over poker games and vodka (mostly in my commodious coupee), we talked about everything, including politics. I was surprised by how much he knew about the West, though he claimed not to have traveled widely; and though he was discreet in talking about his own life in Russia, allowed himself odd lapses, when he seemed to drink too much. For example, he confided that, until recently, he had been a rug merchant in the Black Sea port of Sochi where, he said, he was now wanted by the police. "My dealings were all legitimate," he insisted, in heavily accented English, "but now I'm en route to Siberia to get as far from Sochi as I can."

One night (for we often talked late into the night), he suddenly remarked, "You know, sugar is a good general antidote to poison." His words came out of no where, as if he were lost in thought, and disappeared into the rush of air that swept past the open window we were by. At the time, we were five days out from Moscow, nearing Khabarovsk, the headquarters of the Russian Far Eastern Command. My mind was on what I would see there and I took in this strange bit of information with the same ephemeral surprise as I would have had he told me the tomato was a fruit.

When I disembarked, it was then mid-summer and the streets were covered in white blossoms like snow. Knots of street urchins followed me, begging; occasionally, a soldier brushed past me in fatigues. I strolled through Muravyov-Amursky Park, where the first governor of the province was commemorated by a great bronze statue; visited the Khabarovsk Regional Museum of Natural History; the Far Eastern Art museum; and the lovely Cathedral of the Assumption, with its soaring white-and-blue towers. Where the supermarket shelves in Moscow had been next to empty, here they were abundantly stocked. This was surely to keep the soldiers and their families happy, and to fuel the local industrial army that toiled on ships, gas turbines, machine tools, diesel engines, and cables in the city's vast transport junction shops.

The day before I was set to depart—by train, returning west— I began to feel ill. By the time night fell, I had a fever and a violent cough. At my hotel, I asked for a doctor, and within minutes a woman appeared at my door. I told her in Russian that I had "a stubborn cough." That brought forth a baffled "shto?" ("what?"), with a quizzical look, followed by a perfunctory exam. She gave me a prescription for a cough syrup of some kind and I at once went down to the hotel pharmacy to have it filled. When I opened the bottle, its pungent, somewhat familiar odor—masked by a licorice-like sweetness—cauterized my nose. A gulp of it seared my throat but—"Good," I thought, "I need strong stuff!"—and lay down to sleep. Some time later, I awoke, eyes wide. I was nearly delirious, had difficulty breathing, my lips were swollen, and my bladder burned. When I went to relieve myself, there was blood. I looked closely at the bottle: "Sodium hydrochloride with ammonium chloride drops." I'd seen this before, as a common Russian prescription for bronchitis. But that was not what this was.

It later proved to be ammonia at near toxic strength.

I was then over a thousand miles from anyone I knew.

The next morning, I made my way to the train. As I lay down in my coupee, I was utterly exhausted but afraid to close my eyes. Then, of a sudden, I had a saving thought. One thing every car on the Trans-Siberian has is a great samovar of steaming hot tea with stacks of sugar cubes. I remembered M.'s providential remark, which echoed through my brain— *"Sugar is a good general antidote . . ."*—and at once got up and went to the head of the car. For the next few days, I consumed great quantities of tea and sugar in the hope my system would clear. By the time the train reached Moscow, it had. My cough had also subsided, and I began to recover my strength.

When I reached Leningrad, I sought out Svetlana and recounted my ordeal. She listened gravely but, being an academic linguist, laughed when I explained how I had described my cough to the doctor in my room. "Oh, no!" she said, "You used a funny word. You meant 'persistent.' Instead, you told her your cough was 'stubborn' like a mule!"

A few days later I left my hotel for the airport in a bus. It was an overcast day and the slowly expanding bleakness of the light seemed to bleach out all living color from the brick and stone. As the bus rounded a corner, I saw of group of men beating up a man, punching and kicking him with all their might. Instead of stopping, or calling for help, the driver seemed to take it in with indifference and sped on.

*

Of all my books, *East of the Sun* was perhaps the most ambitious, conceived on an epic scale. Its largeness was fitted to the landscape, and measured itself out by epochs, from the last quarter of the sixteenth century to the end of Soviet rule. I wrote it when Mikhail Gorbachev was still in power, and when Russian society, then in seeming transition, was marked by hope. Yet already the anti-democratic forces that would raise up the oligarchs had sown their dragon's teeth.

After my book was published in December of 1992, I received a letter from Kenneth MacWilliams, a wealthy businessman who owned Woodrow Wilson's House in Princeton, New Jersey. He had a long corporate resume with top positions at the Morgan Guaranty Trust Company, Manufacturers Hanover Trust, Prudential Insurance, and Goldman Sachs. In 1988, he had been featured in

Forbes as a business titan, and now in his mid-50s, had begun a new career as a financial consultant "to assist the development of free market economies" in Russia and the former Soviet bloc. He thought my knowledge of Siberia might be of use to him and we met for lunch. We discussed the economic life of Siberia, in so far as I understood it, and shared our impressions of Russian life. He was charming and gregarious; full of zest for new projects; showed off his "White House cufflinks" (a gift from Reagan, I think); talked of his many dealings with Russian tycoons; and so on. Mistaking me for an expert, he invited me to a "Russian retreat" at his Newburyport estate. When I arrived, I found I was the only lowly figure there. Among the other participants was the founder of a huge drugstore chain; a legal consultant to the World Bank, who was then advising Eastern European countries "on the legal framework needed to promote private sector development"; and a lumber magnate who gaily told me that thousands of his saws had been ruined in the forests of Finland because so many of the trees were embedded with shrapnel from the last war.

Meanwhile, on March 27, 1994 Hugh Graham had died in Adler, Russia, near Sochi, of a stroke. At the time, he was working on an article for the *Classical Journal* that would have shown that the new Latin textbooks being produced in "post-Soviet Russia" had a pro-Soviet bias worked into their texts.

Only someone as immensely learned as Hugh could have detected that.

His body was cremated in Moscow and his ashes thrown to the wind.

CHAPTER EIGHTEEN

In Homer's *Odyssey*, there is a precise description of how Odysseus made his own bed—in rectangular form from the trunk of an olive tree, with pliant webbing made of oxhide thongs. Down through the ages the bed hasn't varied much in form. An ancient Egyptian bier was comprised of a rectangular framework of staves, mortised together and supported on four small legs; while the familiar four-poster bed was standard by medieval times. Until the end of the eighteenth century, primary attention was given to the bed-frame and its decorative embellishment; thereafter the character of the bedding—mattresses, springs, eiderdowns, pillows and the like—assumed more weight. By the 1880s, horsehair, straw, flock (residual wool), excelsior and other materials were in general use as stuffings, and mattress companies, with various patents, began to jockey for advantage in the marketplace.

These and many other curious and related facts became an unlikely interest of mine when in 1989 I was hired by the Winthrop Group, an archival consulting firm based in Cambridge, Massachusetts, to help research the story of the Ohio Mattress Company, then the largest bedding manufacturer in the world. My centennial history of Parsons Brinckerhoff had drawn Winthrop's interest; and for a handsome fee, I agreed to work in conjunction with their staff. They presented me with archival documents, the transcripts of interviews, and flew me all over the United States, from Florida to Texas to California, to tour plant facilities and factories, interview former company executives, one of whom lived on his yacht, and talk with various current and former employees. They spared no expense and I was routinely booked into fancy hotels. On one occasion, I was particularly surprised to find myself lodged in a suite of rooms at the Beverly Hills Hotel with a lavish bar, gold or brass bathroom fixtures, a living room, kitchenette, bedroom, anteroom, and so on, even though I was traveling alone. From time to time, I also spent nights in Cleveland, where the corporate headquarters were.

One morning, a principal of the Winthrop Group came round to my Brooklyn apartment to pick me up for a flight. From his remarks it was clear to me he assumed I owned the brownstone where I lived. It occurred to me afterwards that I might not have been paid so well had my modest means been known.

In the end, the research came to naught. The Ohio Mattress Company was taken over by a faction hostile to the project's core theme—that the company had thrived primarily as a family business—and the endeavor ceased. That was too bad: for the story, as a kind of cautionary tale, deserves a place in the annals of American finance. Since it may never be told rightly elsewhere, I'll tell it briefly here, in a compressed version of the summary I drafted at the time:

In 1890, a Jewish-Rumanian immigrant by the name of Moris Wuliger arrived in Cleveland, Ohio, where he went into the grocery business, delivering bread from door to door. Sometime about 1900 he opened his own outlet and in time established connections with other local entrepreneurs. One of them happened to own a furniture store, and over a friendly hand of pinochle one day he complained to Moris of the mattresses he was getting and urged him to get into the trade. He told him: "It's no big deal. All you do is take some excelsior, put cotton on the top and bottom, shove it into a bag of ticking, poke in the cotton tufts and that's a mattress." Moris took his advice, rented a barn for

$47 a month, and in 1907 founded the Ohio Mattress Company. Not long afterwards, he moved his enterprise to an abandoned stone church where he set up his factory in the nave, built a second floor out of wood from the pews, and converted the church office and part of the vestibule into his own inner sanctum.

Although mattresses are often classed as a "deferrable purchase"—since people tend not to replace them when times are hard—Moris entered the business at an opportune time. Cleveland was booming; a recent surge in population had established it as the nation's sixth largest city; and a number of major industries promised continued growth. Chief among them was Rockefeller's Standard Oil. The city also led the Great Lakes in shipbuilding, stood in the forefront of electrical technology, and was first in the nation in the manufacture of heavy forgings and tools. An outstanding network of railroads and canals also gave it access to new markets and supplies. To take advantage of such opportunities, Hungarians, Poles, Jews, Czechs, Russians, Greeks and other immigrants arrived in successive waves. Moris—more enterprising than most—built his new venture on trade credit and short-term loans; incorporated in December 1912; and steadily expanded, in tandem with Ohio's own growth. After just two decades, he was able to retire at age 61, in 1920, to Palm Springs, California, where he lived in comfort for the rest of his days.

His three sons took over, but only the eldest, Frank, persevered. Frank managed the company with acumen, manufactured and repaired mattresses of every known type and description—stuffed with shredded bamboo, dried "South American grass," horsehair, straw, excelsior (shredded wood), kapok, and cotton—and catered to customers of every class. Diversity was his hallmark. He also updated his equipment, bought two new Ford trucks to replace the big horse-drawn delivery wagon the company had used, and traded in cotton beyond his production needs.

Although his father's pinochle buddy had offered a simplistic version of the business, in those days most mattresses were, in fact, little more than a stuffed bag. The standard size was an arbitrarily symmetrical 4'6" x 6'4", and except for those utilizing excelsior or straw, could be rolled up tightly and stored. Horsehair mattresses were the most expensive; the cheapest, probably the "cotton top." The latter was made of excelsior topped by a layer of cotton felt, covered with cheap ticking, with a raw edge, and finished with cotton tufts by hand. On average, they cost about $3.75, and were delivered unwrapped directly to second-hand stores. There was also the reversible mattress which had cotton on both sides, and the all-cotton felt mattress which weighed about 50 lbs. Some cotton mattresses had a musty smell, and to eliminate it producers began to use linter cotton—the fine, silky fibers, too short to be spun into thread, that cling to the seeds after cotton is ginned. "Tufting" or threaded buttons held the mattress innards in place. Box spring foundations had recently come in, but they were crudely made out of wide wooden slats, to which heavy steel coil springs were stapled, then tied across with twine. No one had yet come up with the idea of making a whole spring unit—or had devised one for commercial sale.

Three national trade names—Stearns & Foster, Simmons, and Sealy—began to emerge as industry powers. Stearns & Foster developed a form of "cotton wadding" that would not tear or stretch; Simmons came up with the "Beautyrest," the first true innerspring mattress; Sealy developed the all-cotton tuftless mattress, with a smooth, even top. Sealy called its new tuftless mattress—without buttons that popped or pulled or hollows that caught dust and lint—a "Pillow for the Body" and implied it could cure insomnia and other neurasthenic ills. Sealy began to license local plants to make and market the bedding, and Frank Wuliger in Ohio became one of the eight original Sealy franchisees. Before long, he had cornered the Ohio market and like his father became a wealthy man.

Then came the Crash of 1929. Next to Detroit, Cleveland suffered the worst unemployment of any city in the land. Credit dried up and reduced demand, which in turn led to production cuts and layoffs. Suddenly, Frank Wuliger "owed everything and had nothing." In a telling measure of the change, that summer he had travelled with his wife, three children, their Austrian governess, a chauffeur, and their new deluxe Cadillac town car to the south of France. At the Grand Concourse car show, the Caddy had won first prize. By the following spring, the body had been taken off the chassis and replaced by a big box on the back for use in delivering mattresses.

During World War II, commercial innerspring production was curtailed since iron and steel were in such government demand. After the war, and in part because of it, Sealy developed the idea for a bedding firm enough to appeal to the five million or so Americans—many of them veterans, afflicted with lower back pain—who bought bed boards to put under their mattresses each year. Recent innovations facilitated its production, and by the Korean War, Sealy had developed its "Posturepedic," which fast became the best-selling mattress in the land.

Sealy and Simmons were now the industry's two giants. What set them apart? The Beautyrest used a barrel-shaped or circular innerspring coil, with the ends slightly bent. Instead of being tied together, or locked in tight, each coil sat loosely captive in a muslin pocket, where it was "free" to respond individually to pressure or weight. The Posturepedic coil, on the other hand, used wire of a heavier gauge for firmness; and the "coil on coil" idea—the boxspring and innerspring units having their coils in alignment—which reputedly made for more comfort and "give."

Ohio Mattress was Sealy's most dynamic franchisee. In the mid-1950s, Frank's son, Ernest, took the helm and brought to his responsibilities fresh energy and vision and a tremendous drive to succeed. Enveloping these attributes, and perhaps standing as their sum, was his "charisma." When he walked into a sales convention," one colleague told me, "it was like a king walked in." Instead of attempting to market his Ohio products more widely, he acquired new plants in already established markets within Sealy's franchising domain. Over the next decade or so, he bought the Sealy licenses for Houston, Puerto Rico, Boston, Atlanta, and Fort Worth. To prevent his takeover of the entire Sealy brand, the Sealy Board in 1971 effectively blocked him from acquiring more. He went to court to challenge their methods and so initiated a process of costly litigation that would not see its end for sixteen years.

At length, in 1986 (having converted his desire to expand by acquisition into a plaintiff's antitrust case), he prevailed, won a $77 million judgment against Sealy, and used that money to acquire Sealy itself. Meanwhile, he had also acquired Stearns & Foster in 1983.

Throughout the industry he was now known as "the Mattress King."

However, all that glitters is not gold—not even gold itself. Wuliger, by his own admission, had long been captivated by the idea of having 100 million dollars in the bank. So in November of 1988, he put his company up for sale. Though he continued to think of the business as his own, by seeking to value its assets in a public market he soon found that he could not control its fate. In the following year, Gibbons, Green van Amerongen, a Chicago-based "leveraged buyout firm," came up with $1 billion for the prize. Wuliger assumed that anyone buying the company would want to keep him at the helm. But Gibbons, Green van Amerongen had high-yield "junk" bonds to dispose of and trouble servicing their debt. They revamped the company's structure and brought in a new man as its head. Wuliger found his own judgment disparaged, threatened to leave, and three months later, did. Thereafter he tried unsuccessfully to persuade Ohio Mattress to sell him Stearns & Foster, and made a failed bid to gain control of Simmons, too.

When I first met Wuliger, he had recently had a heart attack, so I was surprised when at our lunch together—with others involved in the history-research project—he devoured a hamburger and a heap of French fries. He was an intelligent, friendly man; well groomed and fit; lived in a palatial home in Cleveland's Shaker Heights; but seemed obsessed with his former domination of the trade. During his convalescence, he had continued to call contacts from his mechanized bed. He now had far more than 100 million dollars in the bank, yet was full of regret.

The family enterprise had been his pride and joy.

Like Esau, he had sold his birthright for a mess of pottage; and three years later, he was dead.

CHAPTER NINETEEN

❦

After *East of the Sun*, I decided on a little book about stuttering, but knew my publisher would blanch. Eventually, I was able to pair the topic in a two-book contract with a history of the American Revolution, which I also wanted to write. My forebears had fought on both sides of the conflict, and I convinced my editor that I could write a fresh, dramatic account of it that also explored the subject as a civil war. That allowed me to write *Knotted Tongues*. The result was a slender book—a kind of extended essay—that looked at the clinical history of stuttering and its impact on the lives of various people, from Demosthenes to John Updike, with an account of my own ordeal.

While working on the book, in the summer and fall of 1993, I interviewed two writers, Harold Brodkey and Edward Hoagland, who had stuttered throughout their lives. At the time, Brodkey had a small office at *The New Yorker*, was known for two collections of stories, and was considered "a lion of the New York literary scene." The critic Harold Bloom (with a certain bluster) had called him "an American Proust . . . unparallelled in American prose fiction since the death of William Faulkner." When Brodkey received me, his impediment appeared mild (though that can be deceptive) and he claimed to use its forced hesitations as opportunities for gathering his thoughts. From my own experience, I doubted that was true, since consciously manipulated stuttering (for obvious reasons) is rare. Although Balzac's Pere Grandet sometimes faked a stutter to gain advantage in business negotiations, that was a novelist's conceit. In any case, Brodkey revealed little about the effect of the malady on his own life, but (a bit uncharitably) thought Updike's stutter might be an affectation, and that Hoagland's couldn't possibly be as bad as it seemed. "He uses it to dominate a conversation," he said.

Hoagland's stutter was indeed severe; marked by tenacious blocks; and though it subsided a bit with age, was a torment for much of his life. By his own description, it had led at times to a "spasmodic, garbled, gasping incoherence" and included convulsions and foaming at the mouth. In his stories he had shown himself particularly sympathetic to the down-and-out and those whom life has dealt a poor hand. His feeling for animals, which permeates his work, is bound up with the estrangement he sometimes felt from humankind. In his Foreword to *The Final Fate of the Alligators*, he observed that such a disability is almost certain to affect a writer, and alludes to Edmund Wilson's famous essay, "The Wound and the Bow," on *Philoctetes*, a play by Sophocles. "In that play," as I wrote in *Knotted Tongues*, "we find joined in the hero an invincible power with a seemingly incurable wound; and the question arises as to whether the tie between the two is inseparable—whether the power of the gift will remain if the wound is healed. First through compassion, then the physician's art, the wound is healed, in the play's resolution, and the gift retained. Some stutterers may think of themselves as having been compensated for their impediment by some special power; but most regard it as a cross. The artists among them are perhaps different in that respect, insofar as their inability to communicate in the normal way acts as a spur to creative expression. But I doubt that many, if they could awake one morning to a tongue untangled, would not count it the Day of Jubilee."

Brodkey died not long after I met him; Hoagland and I became friends. Hoagland had a substantial gift; an unlimited capacity for hard work; a fastidious determination to make everything he wrote of interest, in the way that he wrote it; and a wealth of observation and experience on which to draw. He was a naturalist; traveled widely; and acquired a great reputation as an essayist, with an eye for vivid detail. He had a knack, too, for the occasional striking phrase. His description of a stutter as "a broken field run" is just about perfect, I think.

The personal essay was his favorite form and became a way of talking in a direct and intimate fashion about anything he chose. He took infinite and exemplary pains with his writing, choosing all his words with care; but his densely written and intense descriptions occasionally devolved into brilliant inventories of a kind—of objects, situations, settings—in Africa, British Columbia, India, Alaska, accompanied now and then by a pronouncement meant to sum them up. We learn about the lives and habits of many creatures—bears, turtles, wolves, coyotes, opossums, mountain lions, moose; landscapes of every kind; their flora and fauna; and so on. Hoagland could describe anything. But not everything needs to be described—or so completely it loses the noun-like substantive being at its core.

For all his love of nature, Hoagland had no illusions about the "state of Nature" itself. One evening my wife and I were his guests at a faculty party at Bennington College but soon retired to a corner with the poet, Mary Oliver, and her partner, Molly Cook. There we discussed our pets. Afterwards, Hoagland told us that he liked Oliver's natural descriptions, but thought her understanding of Nature sentimental to a fault. One day, he said, when she was out in the woods, she came upon a young muskrat with an injured leg. Moved by its plight, she picked it up and clasped it to her breast. At once, it bit her badly. "What did she expect?" he exclaimed. "If you pick up a wild animal like that, it thinks you want to eat it, especially if it's injured or in pain."

For most of the year, Hoagland lived in a house he shared with Trudy Carter, his companion, at Bennington College where he taught. His study or retreat there had a big aquarium with a large snake in it (a kind of python, I believe) that he liked to observe. In the summer, he usually withdrew to a run-down white clapboard house—his writing cabin—with a torn shingled roof in Barton, Vermont. He had bought the house in 1969 for about $5,000 with some forty acres of land. Thousands of acres of protected state land lay behind it; and he kept his own land wild. A moose had the run of it, and used to sniff his car each morning on its way to a pond. He had a heavily-rusted propane tank for gas, no phone or electrical lines, and little plumbing. What plumbing there was worked by gravity from a cistern on a hill. Aside from a couple of small upstairs rooms, he had a kitchen, a living room, shelves of books, and two Olympia typewriters on two different stands—one for correspondence, the other for whatever novel or essay he was writing at the time. Book covers and articles were tacked up on the walls. There was a picnic table on a small lawn in front, flanked by lilies; at night the house was lit by lantern light.

Hoagland was not entirely happy at Bennington College and when he finally left abruptly, "the scene," he told me, "resembled the last act of Ionesco's *Rhinoceros*." For a decade thereafter he and Trudy lived more or less full time in a house she owned in Edgartown, Massachusetts on Cape Cod. He hated it there— "among the 1% with $98,000 dollar cars, which they take as tax-deductions, and houses lived in for only a fraction of a year." His growing blindness also made it difficult for him to get around.

In our conversations, Hoagland often relived the mortifications of his stuttering past. He recalled the appalled expressions of others, and the strategies he had to adopt to avoid being rebuffed. He told me of his horror at learning that Saul Bellow, a close friend, had once described his stutter behind his back as "repulsive." In an attempt to ease the sting of this recollection, I mentioned that I had recently come upon two or three "thoughtful and engaging" letters Bellow had written to him in a collection of the Bellow's work. He asked me which ones they were and at once recalled them clearly. Then he began to reminisce. "Alfred Kazin, Bellow, and I had been good friends," he said. "Bellow was helpful to me, and Kazin had been very helpful to Bellow early on. But when Bellow became a neo-conservative, they had a falling-out. Bellow and I met at a bar to talk about it, and I took him to task for being ungrateful. As we emerged, he said, 'Well, he'll have to make the first move.' Kazin declined to. And they never made up. As it happened, Bellow was on the MacArthur Foundation jury that year and apparently had me in mind for an award. But he so was annoyed at being taken to task that it probably cost me my chance."

Hoagland was generous in support of my work, provided a fine tribute for *Knotted Tongues*, and suggested I look into the life of William Tyndale, which led to my book *Wide As the Waters: The Story of the English Bible and the Revolution It Inspired*. After it was published, he wrote kindly: "I was so pleased to see you receiving the attention you long should have...Such stamina you have, and comprehensive thoroughness...you go way beyond Tyndale, and magisterially. A religious work." At the same time, he would occasionally upbraid me for not putting myself forward, as he saw it, or publishing in magazines.

Hoagland was a prolific writer, and took pride in how prolific he was. In a way, quantity obsessed him. More than once he noted that his first novel, *Cat Man*, had been written in 11,000 hours and was 110,000 words; that he'd written two dozen books since, as well as hundreds of essays and short stories; that on average he produced twenty words an hour for an essay, which generally took three months to complete, and about ten words an hour for a novel, which might take a decade or more. "Have you ever known anyone my age," he asked me in one conversation when he was 85, "who writes a new book every year? I've been writing for 50 hours a week for 50 years. That's 150,000 hours or a million and a half words."

Unfortunately, it irked him that I hadn't kept up with all he'd done. When I told him once that I was preoccupied with reading the Bible through in Greek, he snapped: "Why? What for? I could understand it if you were studying to be a priest!" At the end of the conversation, he enumerated, in a kind of accelerated chant, the last six or seven books of his I hadn't read. "You notice I didn't bring this up before," he said, commending his own tact. "I waited until the end." Then (as was his wont, whatever his mood), he abruptly hung up.

That annoyed me in turn; but these tensions didn't last. In later conversations, he was affectionate, humorous, enthusiastic, generous (as always), and expressed a placid satisfaction with his life. "I have no regrets," he said. His blindness seemed to make him milder and even tamed his speech. With a certain natural courage, he began to relax into the dark.

In his work, he had one great theme: that Nature needs to be preserved. Nature, in his view, was probably all there was to God. He professed himself content if after his dissolution he returned as a mote "leached out of the soil of some graveyard" or perhaps as a bit of moss. "One could do worse," he wrote.

That seems to me too meager. I hope we may hope for something more.

*

Another remarkable man I came to know while working on *Knotted Tongues* was Jock Carlisle, a naturalist like Hoagland, whose stutter had led to a more solitary life. After serving with the Royal Air Force during World War II, he had studied forestry in Scotland and North Wales; specialized in forest ecology; and in the 1950s conducted a survey of the ancient Caledonian Forest in the Scottish Highlands. For six years he traversed the mountains alone, yet in that wild, primeval setting found it "impossible to be lonely or sad." The experience had also given him time "to heal the inner wounds inflicted by the war." At times his rucksack—full of rocks, pine cones, soil samples and the like—weighed over fifty pounds, and to keep exhaustion at bay, he often relied on benzedrine. Once in an ice-storm he fell down a cliff and thought he had smashed his spine. Unable at first to move, he remembered seeing fallen deer eaten alive by foxes and in desperation began to will his limbs to stir. At length, he succeeded, started to crawl, finally got to his feet, and stumbled all night through the forest to a road. There found bleeding, he was hospitalized and revived.

During the winter of 1994–95, he wrote a good little book (still unpublished, so far as I know) about his experience called *A Highland Odyssey*. Another, called *The Wilkinsons—Men of Iron in the Industrial Revolution 1695–1808*, also failed to find a house. A third, *The Native Pinewoods of Scotland* (written with H.M Steven), took flight and in Scotland inspired "a massive conservation program," much to his credit and esteem.

In *Knotted Tongues*, I had suggested that Churchill might have growled his speech to mask a lisp or stutter. Carlisle thought not. "I met him during the war," he said. "He inspected our squadron and made the usual remarks. I listened to his speech. He had a minor impediment, a kind of slurring . . . [But] his fondness for booze affected his speech anyway, so it was hard to tell. At the time, I had other things on my mind. My uniform was soaked in high octane gas and as he stood nearby he insisted, in spite of being warned, on puffing on his cigar. I thought he might set me on fire."

On another occasion, he reminisced about London during the war. Parts of the Underground had been converted into air-raid shelters, and one day medical personnel were called to a station where they found everybody dead. Yet there was no sign of damage or of a blast of any kind. It turned out a bomb had fallen at the next station down and the force of it had been funneled up the line. "Blasts can do strange things," he added. "A huge V-2 missile once fell close to me in a field. All the people fifty yards behind me were killed. But I survived unscathed."

Carlisle eventually settled with his wife "on the edge of habitable Canada," in Deep River, Ontario, where the temperature sometimes fell to –30 C. Across the river from their house lay "rock and forest and wildlife—bears, wolves, eagles, hawks, pine marten, and mink—all the way to the Arctic except for the odd logging road." On some nights, the wolves would sing them to sleep beneath the Northern Lights.

Carlisle was remarkably good-humored and stoic about his ills. When he was 70 or so, he wrote: "I am still waiting for my gall bladder surgery. I have as many gallstones as beans in a Haitian maraca. They say it is keyhole surgery. Meanwhile, they do preliminary tests which do more harm than good. So far I have managed to survive my doctors' help." In 1996, they found a tumor in one lung. "So they whipped me on to the operating table," he wrote, "and carved me up like a rib roast. All they needed was the mustard and Yorkshire Pudding." Eight weeks later, he was back "splitting wood, shoveling snow and hauling logs."

His constant companion was a huge white tomcat named Benjamin, "lively, playful, long-haired, always hungry. A great character. He turns on our radio to wake us up in the morning, loves champagne, malty beer, crunchy grasshoppers and dragonflies, tasty moths, watercress, rich tea cookies, olives, and Ovaltine. He was a great night nurse when I was sick following the surgery, and even today is compassionate and affectionate when either of us is under the weather, returning when we recover to his rambunctious self."

Carlisle died in 2003 at the age of 79.

*

While *Knotted Tongues* was in production, I spent some time in Picton, Ontario, where I completed my research on the Loyalist branch of my family tree. *Angel in the Whirlwind: The Triumph of the American Revolution* was published in 1997, nicely-received, and even (a heady moment) optioned for a movie by the Kennedy/ Marshall Production Company of Disney Studios, which had just made *Schindler's List*. I did some theatrical casting in my mind, of course, for the fun of it, though I knew a film unlikely; and in the end the studio produced *The Patriot* instead. In doing so, I think they erred. A great movie about George Washington remains to be made. My text might have shown them how.

CHAPTER TWENTY

꙳

Reality is indivisible, however we may seek to divide its forms.

One day, when I was still adrift in my late twenties, I had decided, on a lark, to consult an astrologer about my prospects in the world. She knew nothing about me; and I expected the kind of penumbral reading one associates with psychics over a crystal ball. Instead, to my astonishment, she told me several incontrovertible, past and future things: first, that I had been born with a speech impediment (which she could not have known, since by then, in informal settings, I had learned to disguise it); second, that my mother had died when I was young; third (as proved true), that I was destined to make a living in the arts, most likely as a writer; and fourth, that I would enjoy a certain standing by middle age. These are the things I particularly remember, though I believe there was more. Looking at my own horoscope now, I can see some of what she saw, because I've learned how to read it. But at the time, of course, I was mystified.

Years later, I was intrigued to learn that my grandfather (the bishop) had once been persuaded to consult an astrologer about the whereabouts of a wallet he had lost. The wallet had all sorts of valuables in it and he had looked everywhere for it in vain. The

astrologer cast a chart for the question—"Where is my wallet?"—
and after examining the planets, told him, correctly, where it
could be found. That both pleased the bishop and annoyed him,
and into his great old age he remained somewhat abashed. He
had too honest a mind to dismiss it, but he couldn't explain it either.
And so in my own mind, too, this story curled a question mark
over the entire subject which I hoped one day to explore.

In the history of ideas, Astrology may claim an honored place.
By Astrology I do not mean the Sun-sign astrology of modern
times, which was more or less invented by a London sweets salesman
a century ago, but classical or traditional, astrology, which won
the allegiance of most of the great thinkers up through the
Renaissance. Modern astrology deserves its disrepute: it is a mish-
mash of half-baked, "New Age" notions with scant foundation in the
learned past. Classical astrology, on the other hand, is the astrology
of Plato, Ptolemy, St. Thomas Aquinas, and Duns Scotus; of
Al-Biruni, the greatest Islamic scholar of the Middle Ages;
Girolamo Cardano (the mathematician who introduced the doctrine
of cubic equations), Shakespeare, and Johannes Kepler, the greatest
mathematical astronomer who ever lived. It operates by very different principles and yields a wholly different result.

Until recently, it was almost a lost art.

Modern astrology assigns character traits to people by their
planets and signs. Those traits are often interchangeable, as broadly
conceived. Traditional astrology, on the other hand, was more
concerned with the strength or dignity of the planets in the signs
(there were five essential dignities) and the conjunction of sensitive
points of the horoscope with certain fixed stars. It is a complex
science (Kepler devoted much of his life to it), and is able to predict
as well as describe. Contrary to current opinion, it later fell into
disrepute not because it was disproven (or because the Copernican
or heliocentric model of the universe displaced the geocentric one)
but because the idea of God on which it depended went out of the
world—a world, that is, in which all things are meaningfully linked.

Astrology was once the Queen of the Sciences and Arts. At

an indeterminate time, it originated somewhere in the Chaldean East, spread to Egypt, and thence to the ancient world of Greece. From there, it swept across the Greco-Roman world, reaching all races, nations, and types and classes of men: rulers, scholars, the poor and wealthy; invaded the sciences of medicine, botany, chemistry (via alchemy), and mineralogy; occupied a central place in most religions; and convinced all but the Epicureans and Skeptics. It thrived in that learned milieu for several hundred years; but in the general decline of learning which overtook Western Europe after the fall of the Roman Empire, no science suffered a more complete eclipse. To flourish, astrology required the requisite books, instruments, astronomical tables, and relevant knowledge which only an environment sympathetic to higher learning could provide.

The Dark Ages were conspicuously lacking in those coordinates. But in the East, in the Empire of the Byzantines, it continued as an object of study; and in the Arab world it was taken up and embraced. By the 12th century astrology had openly returned to the West enriched by a number of Arab concepts, including the Solar Return, and a close examination of the fixed stars in relation to the degrees or "mansions" of the Moon. Latin translations of Arabic works (derived in part from the Greek) enthralled the learned community, and for five centuries thereafter, astrology pervaded European culture, just as it once pervaded that of imperial Rome. Many cities (such as Florence) maintained a city astrologer in much the same way that a modern community maintains a health officer, while scarcely a figure of importance— pope, general, or king—could be found without his court astrologer to advise him: Henry II and Charles IX of France; Catherine de Medici (herself proficient in the art, which she practiced at an observatory near Paris); the Holy Roman Emperors Charles IV and Charles V; and so on. When Charles V died in 1380, almost a tenth of his vast library was found to consist of astrological works. At least twelve popes were also votaries of the art—among them, Julius II, Paul III, Sixtus IV, and Urban VIII. Julius II used astrology to set the day of his coronation; Paul III, to determine the proper hour for every Consistory; Sixtus IV fixed all important dates and receptions according to the planetary hours. Beyond that, its foremost adepts included leading figures in the development of algebra, trigonometry, astronomy, and optics, as well as its adherents in the arts: the poet Dante had his own personal tutor in the subject; Chaucer was an astrologer at the court of Edward III. Shakespeare had some knowledge of it, and in his plays, it is said, every astrological prediction proves out.

All judgments were based on the horoscope, meaning "a view of the hour"—in particular, that moment of the hour when the degree of a sign rose over the horizon for a particular place on earth. In a precise way, it might be likened to a clock of heaven, giving an overall picture of the person, his life, and fate. The incidents or developments of that life were ascertained through the transits and progressions of the planets, lunar nodes, angles, and other sensitive points, together with the directions of the stars. Before any good astrologer would risk some grand pronouncement, he would consider the chart as a whole, the temperament of the person it revealed, and the manner in which that temperament was expressed. The Ascendant and its Lord (or ruling planet) was judged in those days of more general importance than the Sun or its sign, and the essential dignities of the planets (their strength by sign, exaltation, triplicity, term, and face), more important than house or aspect. The accidental strength of a planet was shown by its house placement, which in turn determined its capacity to act. Progressions and transits helped to predict the conditions of life from month to month, even day to day; and the astrologer might also consider "revolutions" or Solar Returns (charts cast for the moment the Sun returned each year to the degree it occupied at birth), or a Solar Ingress (when the Sun entered the first degree of Aries) which allowed for predictions concerning events of a wider application, affecting the political fortunes of kings and empires, the economy, pestilence and war.

Astrologers recognized that heredity, environment and education all played their part, but that the birth-time ultimately ruled. Not only did it explain human differences; it also helped to provide a useful vocabulary with which to describe them. Having one's horoscope cast in the old days was far more rewarding (and arguably more reliable) than consulting a life-counselor or therapist today. Not only could one receive a penetrating analysis of one's innermost attributes, including one's virtues and vices, but a forecast of the life that would be lived. How you lived it, if you exercised free will, was up to you.

Each reading was unique. Technically speaking, no two people except those born within four minutes of each other in the very same place could lay claim to the same fate. Even among twins such identity was rare.

Two other kinds of consultations—called "horary" and "elections"—were also common when the art was still proficient and esteemed. Horary charts gave answers to questions of any kind, from the outcome of a battle to the prospect for a trip, based on the position of the celestial bodies at the time the question was asked. Elections provided a means of selecting propitious times for any action or enterprise. All things being equal, the calculations required an expert knowledge of mathematics, spherical geometry, astronomy, trigonometry, and so on, and were a learned process, even as they possessed something of the magical aura of the acts and incantations of a priest.

Astrology never aspired to be an empirical science in the modern sense. It was (and is) a sacred and symbolic system with an empirical or "scientific" side. That system has a great deal to say about the arcane structure of Time. There is solar time, lunar time, sidereal time, atomic time, the "black hole" time of Stephen Hawking's physics, and the relativity of the space-time continuum that Einstein advanced. There is also (for lack of a better term) Pythagorean time, based in part on astronomical time, but ruled by arithmetically derived points of significance, that counts out the hours, days, weeks, months, and years by degrees along the ecliptic, in a manner which allowed for the prediction of events. In that system, the ephemeris time we go by, day to day, is actually symbolic of time on another scale. That is the Time of traditional astrology, which has endured from age to age.

In the winter of 2001, I decided to write a history of this venerable subject, and by that summer I had a contract to do so in a comprehensive form. As we all know from Lewis Carroll's *Alice in Wonderland*, nothing could be more interesting than to fall down a rabbit hole and come out somewhere into a wholly different world. It may be an implausible world, from a certain point of view; but it may also work on its own terms. It may even be more real than the world we thought we knew. If we're lucky, that happens to us at least once in our lives. For then we are given to understand something truly new.

The "implausible," of course, may also be real. Einstein discovered that Time actually stops at the speed of light; that Time becomes Space. Quantum Physics tells us that an object can in fact be in two places at the same time. That's "magic." The word comes from "magus," meaning one wise in occult or "hidden" things. So high magic (as opposed to hocus-pocus) has to do with the secret and invisible structure of our world.

It took me a long time to understand what that might mean.

I spent several years immersed in astrological lore, the ancient Babylonian, classical Greek and Roman, and medieval Arabic texts; the writings of Renaissance adepts; as well as most of the modern handbooks that have crowded popular bookshelves from the latter part of the 19th century on. Once the writing was behind me, I titled my book (after a phrase in Shakespeare's *All's Well That Ends Well*) *The Fated Sky*. However, knowledge of a subject is not the same as competence in it, and though I was content enough with the story I had told, I was keenly aware that I was still an outsider looking in. I therefore decided to apprentice myself to a traditional astrologer, to begin an in-depth study of the correct practice of the art. It was my great good fortune that I chose John Frawley, an Englishman, who was just then trying to ease himself out of teaching so he could get on with his own writing tasks. Nevertheless, he kindly took me on.

In every field, there are usually only a handful of reliable guides. In astrology, Frawley is foremost among them—witty, entertaining, deeply learned, and wise. He seems to know everything of value about his subject, and by his own substantial contributions, has enlarged its contemporary scope. His inner knowledge of the Tradition, moreover, has led him to formidable insights into the meaning of Biblical and literary texts as well as the sacred structure of some classics of religious art. To my mind, few if any scholars are more worth reading (or hearing, since much is now on disk) on the planetary cycles of Homer's *Odyssey*, fate in Shakespeare's *Macbeth*, the astrology of Milton's *Paradise Lost*, the operation of the stars on works by Keats and Hopkins, and divine allusions in paintings by Botticelli and Vermeer. In such work, he has shown a learned exactitude that Irwin Panofsky and E.H. Gombrich would surely have admired.

For Frawley, a converted Catholic, astrology is a religious discipline, to be approached with humility and reverence, enshrining a knowledge "above human station, imparted to man as a grace." His two-year course in its horary practice was a rigorous one and required the student to get things right.

On March 20, 2005, at 1 p.m., I enrolled. In a fledgling attempt at auspicious timing, I did so with my progressed Mercury conjunct my natal Ascendant, which seemed apt. There were other things I might have considered. Yet I cannot say I erred.

*

On the morning of October 8, 2005, the sound of a utility truck, with its engine churning, woke me as it backed down the steep dirt road that runs past our house. The truck's revolving lights were flashing. "A power line down," I thought. Only then did I become fully aware of the torrential rain splattering on the skylights and drumming like thunder on the roof. The next morning my wife and I learned that lines were down all over New England, that neighboring towns were flooded, the mighty Connecticut River perilously rising, dams in danger of breaking, and that nearby streams in Walpole, Greenfield, and Bellows Falls had begun to crest. This was unwelcome news on several fronts. Friends and colleagues were coming to visit—it was Columbus Day weekend— to celebrate the publication of a book of poems by my brother, Jim.

As the deluge continued and the day wore on, one by one, or two by two, the guests arrived, muddy and drenched, amazed they had made it to our covenanted ark. About 4 o'clock, the phone rang. Two other guests—Marvin and Evelyn Farbman, my brother's oldest friends—called to say their car had been rear-ended in the downpour while passing through Hartford, Connecticut on their way from Middletown. They were waiting for the police to show up and would be late. Hartford, however, is not that far, and our dinner plans still held. Forty-nine minutes later I looked at my watch and thought, Ok, When will they arrive? I posed this question to myself aloud and briefly retired to my book-battlemented study, where I clicked on my computer and called up a chart.

*

It was only some time after I began my studies with Frawley that I ventured to interpret a chart. It seemed to me a big thing to try, and out of a kind of humility—or diffidence—delayed the day. I had come to think of myself (pretentiously perhaps) almost as a priest in training who must first go through a series of ritual ablutions before performing a sacred rite. Frawley himself had emphasized the divinity of what I was acquiring, and I decided early on that however skeptical I might be of some of its aspects, I could hardly come to it in the right spirit unless I engaged it on its own terms. That involved not just "a willing suspension of disbelief," as befits poetic understanding, but "standing under" and receiving something directly to "understand" it, as Travers once explained.

Before long, the chastity of my approach became untenable, since astrology is not only a theoretical subject but a hands-on craft, and Frawley wanted to get me into work clothes as soon as he could. I was bound to make all kinds of mistakes, of course, some of them egregious; but so must I learn. In subsequent months, my practical knowledge grew enormously, and despite many blunders, my apparent facility with prediction even began to go to my head. During the end of the baseball season and throughout the playoffs, I regularly predicted the outcome of the games. (This, in fact, would continue through the World Series and into the football season where one of the few contests that failed me turned out to be the closest game in college football history: between USC and Notre Dame. I thought the chart gave it to the Irish, but USC won in the last second after a dubious call. Later, that win would be technically reversed.) Meanwhile, my confidence in Frawley's methods had exponentially increased. Eventually, I found that I could divine the outcome of many political contests, determine if a house for sale was overpriced, find a lost animal (as I did on a couple of occasions for friends), foretell the outcome of a trial, and so on. Sometimes the answer was obvious; often subtle; occasionally, extremely complex.

*

We can think of the process of time in many ways—as a blind unfolding of chance events; as an evolution of things partly directed by our will; or (as viewed from above, so to speak) as a known or foreknown sequence or pattern, mapped out by the relationship between the planets and stars. That relationship is both symbolic and mathematically precise. The idea of seeing time all at once is like a snapshot of a process, a freeze-frame of something in motion that also shows the end toward which it tends. In history (and life) we sometimes encounter images of such things where the extremities of Nature rivet a moment in place, or preserve a physical motion intact. One may think of the recovered bodies, encased like fossils in lava, from the eruption of Vesuvius, which were captured by the sudden catastrophe in the acts of everyday life. Two thousand years later, they were unearthed in those life-like postures, as if time stood still. People struck by lightning have also been found in states of petrified motion—as in the celebrated case of some Italian reapers, who happened to be dining under an oak tree when they were all struck by the same flash. Some passers-by approached and found them seemingly still engaged in their repast. One man had his hand in a dish, another was in the act of putting a piece of bread into his mouth. Their end had been so swift that their faces had not even had time to register pain. Only the blackened, charred tincture of their skin betrayed their searing fate.

Astrological time dissolves partitions between familiar realms. If a freeze-frame gives us the still-life of a process, the horoscope also shows us where that process will go. It may be compared to a seed (Kepler was fond of the seed analogy) as a coded image in little of how life will unfold. But the correct, functional image is the universe itself. In traditional astrology, Time is eternally inscribed as a circle on the ecliptic, where it can be seen as proceeding or unfolding by degrees—literally so: for by counting the degrees between planets and the aspects they make, the "time" of an event can be known. The "where" of that aspect is the "when" of the event. Time and space—as Einstein glimpsed, but grasped in another way—are in fact two different faces of the same thing.

There is an amusing moment in Martin Scorcese's otherwise misbegotten film, *The Last Temptation of Christ*, when an out-of-breath Christ, hurrying to keep an appointment, asks one of his disciples: "What time is it?" And of course the knowledgeable viewer knows that Christ is on God's Clock, not just ours, inexorably moving toward the fullness of Time in fulfilling His fate. At that moment, Christ is living through two different kinds of time—the kind we keep by our ephemeris (and so ephemeral) and the time according to the divine scheme. In a sense, astrological time is a version of the latter. Everyday time in our world is counted out by seconds, minutes, hours, and so on; astrological time, by degrees along the ecliptic, which symbolize the seconds, minutes, and hours in which the events of our lives unfold.

The "time zero" of a horary chart—and therefore all timing figured within it—is fixed by the moment the question is asked. The question can be a straightforward look into the future ("When will I get my raise?") or pertain to a follow-up event based on something past—as, "When will she see him again?" To make the right judgment, one must consult an ephemeris (an astronomical guide to planetary longitude and declination) which tells you what the planets are up to in their daily round—i.e., whether fast or slow, direct, retrograde, or in station—since these variants are in constant flux.

In timing, one must first look at the sign and house the relevant planets are in. The nature of each question tells you which houses are involved, and therefore which planets—namely, those that rule the signs on their cusps. If the question concerns a sibling, you look to the sign on the cusp of the third (which governs siblings) and the planet that rules that sign; if a friend, the eleventh; if your pet, the sixth. The person asking the question (if a figure in the drama) always gets the first. Indeed, one can think of the chart as a theatrical stage. Planets show the characters in the drama; aspects between them show events. Once you've figured out which planets are involved (there are usually no more than two or three), you need to determine if they connect. There are usually only a handful of ways they can. One is by angular aspect (conjunction, sextile, square, trine, or opposition—at, respectively, 0, 60, 90, 120, and 180 degrees). Another is by "translation of light." That happens when one planet aspects a second and "translates" its light by aspect to a third. If another planet gets in the way, it prevents the event from taking place. No aspect, no event. But if an aspect occurs, its time, or timing, can be fixed.

Every question also has its own practical time frame or scale. If you want to know when you might meet the person you will marry, you are probably talking about weeks, months, or years; but if you're expecting a friend to call, probably minutes, hours, or days. There is a long, a medium, and a short unit of time to be determined in each case. Once you've established that unit (based on the strength of the relative houses and the quality of their signs) timing is found by converting it to the number of degrees required for the aspect between two planets to perfect.

That, it would seem, is how God tells time.

*

My studies with Frawley had not always kept strictly to the order of lessons, as opportunities arose to pose questions that future lessons would address. However, once I started casting charts, I practiced on as many as I could. Some were beyond my competence, of course; most, despite my fumbling, taught me something new. From time to time, I ran my fledgling efforts past him, and he usually responded promptly with illuminating corrections in detail. I had worked hard all summer to grasp the fundamentals—the meanings of the signs and houses, accidental and essential planetary dignity and strength, the quadruplicities and triplicities, subtle concepts of "reception," "derived Ascendants," and so on—according to the esoteric tradition in which I was being schooled. But to date at least I'd had relatively little practice with "timing," and none beyond such everyday events as "When will the carpenter call?" However, as I began to apply my skill to more sober questions, the efficiency of the charts gave me pause. I was stunned at their precision (which I might otherwise have admired) and somewhat troubled by their power. Where did the line between power and wisdom lie? Here, potentially, was a fearful instrument—like the enchanted, mischief-making broomstick of the cautionary tale— that once unleashed might not be unspelled.

*

Although the Catechism of the Catholic Church, set forth in 1992, condemned astrology, Church tradition had long accepted the view of St. Albert the Great, St. Thomas Aquinas, Duns Scotus, and others that astrology was viable as long as certainty was not presumed in matters involving free will. St. Albert, whose disciple Aquinas was, considered astrology "the 'middle' science' between metaphysics and natural philosophy." In his view, its wonders "more intensely provoke men to love God' for "no human science attains this ordering of the universe as perfectly as does the science of the judgment of the stars." Most popes had agreed, two popes had not, but the venerable trdition had been generally affirmed by the Council of Trent convened. Therefore, when Cardinal

Joseph Ratzinger (a "strict constructionist," by most standards) in his pre-papal role as Cardinal-Prefect for the Doctrine of the Faith declared that the Catechism was not teaching "new doctrine" but "the ordinary theological tradition," many within the Church, including some Jesuit doctors, took that to mean that nothing had changed. Indeed, although the Franciscan friar, Duns Scotus, was a convinced astrologer, "no errors" were officially found in his work; and in 1993 he was beatified. In his *Opus Oxoniense*, Scotus had written: "The stars incline the will but in no wise necessitate it. [Yet] frequently it comes to pass that . . . he who knows the virtues of the Signs and the Planets therein placed, may foretell, if he knows when any creature is born, the whole life of it." Astrology, it would seem, was therefore accepted within "the ordinary theological tradition" of the Church.

*

As our growing company of guests warmed and dried themselves by our two woodstoves, we began to have a high time of it (as we always did) despite our absent friends. Cinnamon apple cider spiked with rum helped get things going, and I was soon asked what the chart for Marvin and Evelyn Farbman showed. On my computer, I had entered the vital statistics (4:49 p.m. EDT, Brattleboro) which placed 7 degrees Pisces on the Ascendant or 1st house cusp. The Ascendant signified our home, and Pisces, a double-bodied sign, aptly showed my wife and self as one. Our planet was therefore Jupiter, which in classical (not modern) astrology rules that sign; and in this question, in accord with tradition, we were also co-signified by the Moon. For our friends, we looked to the 11th house, where Capricorn, ruled by Saturn, lay on the cusp. So the cast of the play was assembled. I had now to determine if Saturn would make an aspect with Jupiter, the Ascendant, or the Moon. If it did, we were in luck, and I could figure out when the Farbmans would arrive. I examined the chart. No aspect between Saturn and Jupiter was shown, or between Saturn and the Ascendant. Could that be? Then I saw that as the Moon advanced into the next sign, it would exactly oppose

Saturn after proceeding 18 degrees. That meant (given the practical time-scale of the question) our friends would arrive only after great difficulty (aspect by opposition) in about 18 hours—or between 10:30 and 11 o'clock the following morning. However, the Moon was angular (in the 10th house) and its mean daily motion, as the ephemeris told me, fast. That might shave an hour or so off the clock. About 9:30 then, which still seemed a long way off.

I thought I must be wrong.

Not surprisingly, everyone else did, too. The Farbmans were usually as reliable and punctual as an atomic clock. Like the ideal postman, whom neither rain, snow, sleet, nor gloom of night can stay, we all knew they would make their way to us any way they could. Various bets were placed on how soon they would arrive.

An hour or two later, the phone rang again. "We had to wait a long time for the police to come," Marvin told me. "I think it best if we not try to get there tonight. Besides, our Subaru is damaged. We have to change cars. But we'll come as early tomorrow morning as we can."

Despite a late night, most of us were up by eight the following morning to feast on lox, eggs, bagels, and great mugs of Green Mountain hazelnut coffee as we talked on and on. Jim played miniature soccer with our Shiba-Inu (a tawny-colored, fox-like dog who proved a matchless goalie for his little rubber ball), while our 97-year-old stepmother fed cream cheese covertly to our Chow. My wife, Hilary, read some items from the *Brattleboro Reformer* (the local paper) aloud: Elian Gonzales, the Cuban castaway found clinging to an inner tube off the coast of south Florida six years before, was back in the news and had granted an interview to "60 Minutes"; the U.S. Senate was preparing to give Bush $50 billion more for his war in Iraq. President Bush himself was confidently "predicting" that Harriet Miers would be confirmed to the Supreme Court. We all had much to say about these matters. Outside, the storm continued unabated. In the distance, beyond our gray-weathered tool shed, I could see red sumac leaves glistening in the rain.

Though my brother's book had not been published quite in

time for the party, the rest of us asked him to recite something from it as we waited for the Farbmans to arrive. At length he agreed and recited with metrical perfection an incantatory sonnet translated and adapted from Luis Vaz de Camoes:

> Times change, hearts change,
> trustlessness, trust;
> what's craved now must
> seem new and strange.
>
> Memories stain,
> hopes go bust;
> of joys (joys?)—just
> longings remain.
>
> Time turns the year's
> dead white to green,
> my words to tears—
>
> change, each day seen,
> itself appears
> a changed routine.

Everything about the weekend had something to do with Time.

After the reading, Jim held forth about Camoes. He was, he explained, Portugal's national poet, and the leading figure of the Portuguese Renaissance. His famed epic, the *Lusiads*, based on the voyage of Vasco da Gama around the Cape of Good Hope, "may not be the greatest epic after the Odyssey," he told us, "but it's the most hypaethral in the Homeric sense, for Camoes himself voyaged to the Far East. As a soldier of fortune and explorer he spent time in India, Macao, and the Mekong delta, the Moluccas, and Mozambique. According to one story, he saved his unfinished manuscript during a shipwreck by swimming to safety with it between his teeth." Jim had just regaled us with that congruent anecdote when at 9:30 sharp I heard the crunch and slosh of mud and dirt as the Farbmans in their provision-laden Prius wheeled into our drive.

*

Astrology has nothing to do with the absolute distance of planetary bodies, gravity, force fields, or relative light. All the scientific objections to it are to a system that doesn't exist. Its sacred character is based on divine light—the very essence of light, from which all lesser lights proceed. As Frawley explains in his fundamental text, *The Real Astrology*—by far the most important book on the subject since William Lilly's *Christian Astrology* was published in 1647—we must think of the stars and planets as akin to Platonic Ideas. The Fiat of Light that existed as essence of light for three days—before the Sun, Moon and Stars were created on the fourth—thereafter shone upon the world, and in our being, in its various refracted forms. As the celestial bodies move—for example, as Venus moves, lives, and has its being—all things Venusian are affected by its light: not by the visible light it shines with, but with the essence of the light it represents: like the imprint of a Platonic Idea.

"Light from light," as in the Nicene Creed.

At the end of the *Republic* (in the Myth of Er, son of Armenius), Plato compares the life of man to a wheel spun round a spindle. As Frawley points out, this is an astrological conceit. The axis of that spindle is formed by the lunar nodes—points on the ecliptic known as the Dragon's Head (the North Node) and the Dragon's Tail (the South). We come into this world through the first and, it may be, go out by the second. So one Tradition holds. Another, expounded by the 3rd century Neoplatonic philosopher, Porphyry, in "The Cave of the Nymphs in Homer"—which also describes the descent of the soul into matter through the spheres—assigns the gates to the solstice points.

"The birth-chart," writes Frawley, "deals with the Lesser Mysteries—the art of becoming human, recovering the lost dignity and integrity that are necessary before embarking on the Greater Mysteries of the life of the spirit. Thus in it we see the possibilities for the formation and nurture of the soul." Some planets are dignified or strong, others weak and impaired. The first are more apt to act correctly, for lesser or greater good; the second, otherwise. The seven classical planets (those framed to the naked eye) incarnate the Seven Capital Virtues and the Seven Deadly Sins, to a greater or lesser extent, depending on their strength. The four temperaments— choleric, sanguine, melancholic, and phlegmatic—are the ground of their being and color all their acts. In rather bold terms, Frawley describes their moral force:

> Saturn offers wisdom and discrimination, abstention from evil; its sin is avarice. Jupiter gives faith and right judgment; its sin is gluttony, which, as with all the sins, should be understood in its widest sense: the greed for experience is gluttony too, needing the discrimination of Saturn as a curb. Mars, perhaps the most unfashionable of the planets, gives greatness of soul, the ardour for both the lesser and greater jihad—the outer and the inner holy war—the power to do good; its sin, of course, is wrath. The Sun gives life, dignity and clarity—literally elucidating—and thence prophecy; its sin is pride. Venus offers love and the urge for conciliation; its sin, lust, loses this right desire in the flesh. Mercury gives articulation and mental understanding, its sin being envy, which is misunderstanding, and thus its product is lies. The Moon gives procreation—again, in its widest sense; as the fastest of the planets, its failing, as with the hare in the fable of the hare and the tortoise, is sloth.

The celestial lights show us, by description, who we are; and by prediction, how essence works in our lives. By consideration of our planetary dignities, aspects, and receptions, we find our weaknesses and strengths. That portrait is objective, and possibly discouraging; yet it points to a redemptive path—which, explains Frawley, is described by finding the "Internal King": not the ostensible chart ruler (which rules the Ascendant), but the "Lord of the Geniture," the strongest (most dignified) planet in our chart. This is the planet that can help tame the rest, bring order out of chaos, and begin to prepare us for that inner harmony that transcends all planetary strife. "Rather than the life we are given," he writes, "we choose the life we want." In his view, "Shakespeare's Henry IV is a study of this process, as Hal escapes from his Ascendant ruler" (the fleshly self that Falstaff represents) "and becomes king; that is, he becomes truly a human being and is then fit to enter on the crusade that is the spiritual life." To put it another way, in his repudiation of Falstaff, who is all appetite, Hal escapes from the tyranny of desire. Astrology is, and can do, many things: but its ultimate purpose is the purpose of all true knowledge: to orient us correctly, with humility and reverence, toward God.

This Teaching proved of inestimable value to my life.

In many respects, my chart was a troubled one. A "modern" reading would embellish it with a Venus-Uranus-Neptune trine. But once that is scrapped (as it must be, since these planets have no real place in the scheme), the cold, phlegmatic facts were: 1) that I had no planets in their own signs or exaltations; three planets (the Moon, Saturn, and Mercury) in detriment; and 3) three (Saturn, Mercury, and Jupiter) retrograde. Worse, Jupiter was actually stationary, in the process of turning back—about to flop on its "sick bed," as Frawley would say. Finally, Jupiter and Saturn were exactly opposed by "antiscion" (their shadow placement across the solstice axis) which described the secret duel in which they were engaged.

Yet, seek and ye shall find. Mars had strength by triplicity; Saturn, though impaired, dignity by term and face. There were also three helpful aspects: Jupiter trine Sun (so, potentially, faith and good judgment linked to clarity and dignity of life); the Moon sextile Mars (the urge to create linked to a determination to do the right thing); and Mercury conjunct Mars (which joined that determination to articulate understanding). Saturn, Jupiter, and Venus enjoyed great accidental dignity by being in angular houses (respectively, the 4th, 7th, and 10th); Mars and Jupiter were in mutual reception (that is, in each other's signs, in mutual support); while the Sun, Mercury, and Mars were all in the 11th House of Good Fortune, where (if we are wise) we count our blessings up. Moreover, the 11th is often said to have angular power. So: here embedded in my beleaguered chart was indeed an array of weapons for the "holy war" within. Moreover, various fixed stars, by their alignment, favored high purpose, fruitful exertion, refinement, and gain. Chief among them was Markab in Pegasus, sacred to the Muses, but, born of Medusa's blood, holding the "full power of the desire nature" in thrall. That held a warning.

I looked to Mars as my Internal King.

*

The Signs have their Rulerships and Exaltations; the Houses, according to an equally ancient tradition, their Joys. The whole redemptive story, as Frawley explains in a brief, gem-like essay, may be found in the Joys of the Planets and why they occupy the Houses they do.

There is a structure to reality that Astrology describes. Astrology, in turn, reflects the structure that is. In the end, I was more interested in the fact that it worked than what it could do. For the great Truth it pointed to—the reality of intelligible meaning in the structure of Creation—was yet another proof for me that God exists. In a sense, it also confirmed the doctrine of original sin. For everyone's chart has some errant feature. As Herman Melville put it, "The Devil always slips in his card."

*

Art is long; Life short; but Truth abides. According to rabbinical tradition, as I noted in *The Fated Sky*, each of the twelve tribes of Israel represented a zodiac sign, and the symbols for the four fixed signs—a man, a lion, a bull, and an eagle—were carried as totems in the Egyptian desert by the Hebrew host. These same symbols make up the composite creature we call the Egyptian Sphinx, and in accordance with Ezekiel's vision came to stand for the four great Christian evangelists—Matthew, Mark, Luke, and John. They also stood for the four basic temperaments, which (some say) the evangelists exemplified.

It is all one. The seven tribes to be vanquished by the Israelites in Canaan in order to gain the Promised Land, are the seven contending planets within us, which are (Josephus tells us) signified by the seven-branched candlestick of the Menorah, which are the seven circuits of the Tabernacle at the end of the Jewish feast, which are linked to the seven cardinal virtues, which (in the round of Truth), are one with the planets in their perfect strength.

The Twelve Labors of Hercules are also a figurative description of the Sun's passage through the twelve signs and are akin to the stories the Babylonians told about their own solar hero, Gilgamesh, "whose life unfolded in twelve epic songs." It is said that each of the twelve disciples of Christ likewise stood for (or embodied) a sign—an idea that was carried over into medieval romance, where the twelve knights of King Arthur's Round Table (a symbol of the zodiac) also stood for the twelve astrological types. The idea that those types together constitute a complete circle of humanity is also carried over into our jury system, which is supposed to ensure that a man is properly tried by a representative assessment (or complete cross-section) of his peers.

The names of the days of the Western week, of course, are those of the star-gods, as derived from Roman and Norse mythology. Our seven-day week itself derives from a convergence around the 2nd century B.C. of the Sabbath cycle of the Jews, in which the seventh day was held to be holy, and an astrological week based upon the planets (which included the Sun and Moon) according to which each day was ruled by one of the seven planetary gods. Each hour of each day was also so ruled, hence the cycle of planetary hours. Following Egyptian practice, there were twenty-four hours in a day, but before clock time they were not all of equal length: the twelve daytime hours were equally divided from sunrise to sunset, the twelve nighttime hours from sunset to dawn. In sequence, the hours belonged to Saturn, Jupiter, Mars, the Sun, Venus, Mercury, and the Moon, in an endless circle, with each one in turn serving as regent or ruler for that day.

From the beginning, the sacred scheme was imaged in Creation and recounted in story, myth, and types. We can never trace anything "all the way back" to Nature, because *created* Nature can never be the back of the mirror for what we know. The greatest stories describe the reality of which Story is a part. We are *in* those stories, as well as in the one, all-encompassing Story of Creation itself. Like the life of the Solar Hero, our virtuous days follow the path of the ecliptic, the one true and unerring pattern of our round. When errant, we wander like planets back and forth across that line.

It is all One.

The *structure* of Creation and its redemptive story is *above* chronology, as we understand it, in the same way that the Zodiac of Signs and Celestial Houses is above the constellations which bear their names. The invisible blueprint or sequential pattern has nothing to do with Evolution, or the "Big Bang" theory, or any other such notion as to how things came to be. Such concepts may intrigue our speculations. But they will always end in the same blank place: in the self-referent phenomena of that which was created, not in the meaning, which is the pattern, or blueprint, itself.

Astronomical time is a figure of prophetic time. And both describe events. One reality figures the other. The first belongs to the present, the second to the future, that is, to the eternal present, in which all time is one. Fate and free will in this sense are not at odds, for God knows in advance not only all things "fated," but all the free choices we will make. By that foreknowledge, the future exists already, and has happened, in His mind.

Yet, mortal as we are, though we may eventually know what everything is, we will never know what everything means. Ludwig

Wittgenstein once touchingly glanced at this idea in one of his mournful moods when he wrote, "We feel that when all possible scientific questions have been answered, the problems of life remain completely untouched." Religion occupies the sacred heart of all those questions to which the problems of life give rise, and astrology is the most venerable branch of that inner knowledge from which religion springs.

Its merits hardly stand or fall by my fledgling practice of it, or the level of competence I achieved. I came to it late; abided in its world for a time; and went on with my life—because a life is to be lived. Unless you happen to be a professional astrologer, its constant practice is too much. Like everything else, it has its time and place. I have described my experience in applying it, under capable guidance. Readers can draw their own conclusions as they may.

CHAPTER TWENTY-ONE

❦

Over the years, to relieve the difficult solitude of writing, I occasionally sought part-time work of an extroverted kind. In the summer of 1991, for just that reason, I became the House Manager of the Prospect Park Picnic House in Brooklyn, New York. My office was located in the Litchfield Villa, an Italianate mansion with round turrets, columned porches, and a square central tower modeled on a ducal palace in Urbino. The Picnic House itself had scenic views of the park's ninety-acre Long Meadow, with floor-to-ceiling windows, hardwood floors, a raised stage, and a recessed entrance with a Palladian Arch. On the whole, it was an elegant venue, with room for up to 240 people for weddings, parties, concerts and other events.

One summer day in July, I was overseeing a jazz concert there when a lovely, intelligent woman, a bit younger than myself, took up her seat next to mine on the patio outside. We struck up a conversation and I asked her how she happened to know of the event. She explained that her friend was the agent for the musicians on stage. Over the course of the next hour or so I also learned that she lived not far from me in Park Slope; worked as the private secretary for a writer; had grown up in Chicago; and had two dogs and a number of cats. Our family backgrounds were somewhat alike—with a Slavic, Jewish, Christian mix; and where my grandfather had been a Methodist Bishop, her uncle had been a Monsignor in the Catholic Church. For both of us, recent romantic attachments had also made Spanish Harlem a second home. I liked her at once and asked if I could see her again. She wanted to know how early I got up in the morning, since she rose at dawn to walk her dogs. Later, on our first official date, as we got to know each other better, she observed, smiling: "You process everything as tragic; I process it as absurd."

That seemed a good match.

We didn't really begin to see each other, however, till well into the following year. I explained to her at the time (which must have seemed incredibly evasive) that I had a monumental manuscript deadline to meet and wouldn't be free to socialize till spring. I was then working on *East of the Sun*, and since I had already secured one deadline extension, knew if I missed another it might cost me my advance. My livelihood depended on it; and for the next six months I worked on the book night and day, often till dawn. When I finally called her the following May, I was astonished to find that she hadn't been swept up by someone else. Before long, we began living together, and married when we moved to Vermont in 1996.

For part of each week, Hilary would commute to New York, where she worked as the private secretary to Francine Pascal, an extremely popular writer of books for young adults. Francine had a luxurious apartment in mid-town Manhattan just south of Carnegie Hall and a villa on the Riviera in the south of France. The villa had been acquired from her brother, Michael Stewart, the prolific Broadway librettist, who had written *Bye Bye Birdie*; *Hello, Dolly!*; *Mack & Mabel*; *George M!*; *42nd Street*, and other abiding hits. Upon his death, Francine had taken charge of his estate, and as his work was constantly revived, she was often called upon to make practical adjustments to the texts.

Hilary found all this engaging, having studied theater and dance.

Francine was always warm and generous towards me and I enjoyed the occasions when we socialized. Through her I also met the playwright James Lee. Lee was a handsome, entertaining, quick-witted man, best known for his play, *Career*, that debuted off-Broadway in 1957 and was later made into a film. In the late 1970s, he had also worked on scripts for the TV series *Roots*. On March 17, 1995, my wife and I were invited to a private reading at Lincoln Center of his new play, *The Bastard of Bermondsey*, about James Boswell and Samuel Johnson. Johnson was read by Philip Bosco, Boswell by Campbell Scott. I thought the play was terrific. Lee could only see its flaws and later revised it, repeatedly, changing the title to *Boswell's Johnson*. He placed it with the William Morris Agency but, so far as I know, it was never produced.

Lee once told me, after he read *Angel in the Whirlwind* on a trans-Atlantic flight, that "the funniest thing" in the book was when Martha Washington said, "George is always right." He added, "And how about Big Ben Arnold, trying to score with a sixteen year old. That should have had everybody guessing he'd be a bad boy some day." In an interesting letter he also recalled an afternoon he had once spent with David O. Selznick, the Hollywood tycoon. Their conversation turned to *Gone With the Wind*, which Selznick had produced. Selznick remarked that Margaret Mitchell had explained to him that "except for Scarlett and Rhett, all the other characters in the book were people of their time. But Scarlett and Rhett were 'Twentieth Century people.'" Perhaps that explains why the book, and movie, did so well.

*

Though my concert management days were long behind me, George Rochberg and I remained close. In 1995, he had sold his papers to the Paul Sacher Foundation in Switzerland, which had begun to establish a formidable archive of music-related material that included the papers of Anton Webern and the Stravinsky estate. On June 11, George wrote with triumphant satisfaction to say that all of his "scores, journals, correspondence & other accumulated" items would now be "in safe-keeping for 'study' by scholars 'til the end of time.'" He added: "I always worried about my 'posterity' & there it will be" housed in "a neat, Swiss, orderly, efficient, squeaky clean, probably very anti-septic looking carpeted place of library-silence, people tiptoeing about, talking in whispers, 'moving to & fro, talking of Michelangelo . . . .'"

George was an energetic correspondent and the many letters I received (now also with the Sacher Foundation) were always revealing. One, pointedly dated "May 18, 1996, 3:30 a.m.", after he had just returned from a trip to Rome, touchingly reminisced about the momentous Italian journey he had taken a half-century before. Unable to sleep, "and therefore I might as well do something useful," he said, he recalled his first meeting with Luigi Dallapiccola; his embrace of the new, in twelve-tone music; and the tender companionship of his devoted wife and son.

We enjoyed the synchronicities of Fate. The same year my wife and I moved into our house in Vermont, George and Gene moved into the retirement community of Dunwoody Village out-side Philadelphia in Newtown Square. Not long after I'd written some pages on Benedict Arnold, George happened to introduce me to Todd Cook, the treasurer of the Marlboro Music Festival, and his wife, Peggy Shippen, a direct descendant of Benedict Arnold's infamous paramour. Peggy, like her eponymous forebear, lived in Philadelphia where she belonged, as Arnold's Peggy had, to the social elite. Through her, my wife and I met the composer Richard Wernick, who had been Rochberg's sometime colleague at the University of Pennsylvania. They had once been friends; shared the same family tragedy in the early loss of a son; but as composers (in Wernick's mind at least) had become rivals, with a pronounced animus on Wernick's part. In other respects, he was outgoing and friendly, as was his wife, Bea. Bea played the trombone and was the daughter of an astrologer whose clients had once included Katherine Anne Porter and the psychologist Erich Fromm. Her mother in turn had learned her craft from Marc Edmond Jones. According to Bea, Jones had once been quietly consulted in the 1940s by nuclear physicists at Columbia University about their work on the atomic bomb.

Meanwhile, on May 15, 1997, knowing that *Angel in the Whirlwind* was about to be published, George wrote (with synchronicity in mind) that he had "only a few days before put the finishing touches to *Circles of Fire* for 2-pianos, . . . my 'Art of the Fugue.'" Though he declined to compare his piece to Beethoven's *Grosse Fuge* (a difficult and enigmatic work), "[mine] rises I hope—certainly I've worked very had to achieve it—to the level of music where it must be judged as such. But naturally these are strange times in which to practice such ancient austerities." Two months later, in mid-July, he and Gene came to Vermont to visit, and we had an outing on the Connecticut River followed by a garden tour. He was now working on a chamber guitar concerto (*Eden out of time and out of space*) for the virtuoso guitarist, Eliot Fisk. "I'm afraid Eliot is going to be very disappointed," he wrote to me on September 5. "He wants a kind of public piece, a crowd-pleaser which shows him off to advantage. This moves in the diametrically opposite direction."

But Fisk was thrilled.

Among his own works, he especially valued *Slow Fires of Autumn*, which he felt had been touched by something like grace. For a sainted figure like Mozart, he wrote, the mystical "Being of Music . . . trailing clouds of glory" was a "constant companion, though it paid a lot of attention to Beethoven, too." For others, its "mere presence" was something to be grateful for. More deeply, George believed that one had to open oneself up to such Entities or Spirits and serve them for "we are not an end in ourselves. [True artists] must strive to free themselves from the pull of matter by releasing the energy in matter which is consciousness."

George had a general distaste for orthodox belief; abhorred, as he put it, the "narrow-chested, nationalistic legalisms, rituals, and tribal echoes" of Judaism as a faith; thought the ancient Jews had conceived their punitive God "as an outward expression of their own stern, austere, hammered out . . . collective psyche"; and had filled the frightening cosmic silence of the void "by talking out loud [to Him] in prayer, ritual, and song." At the same time, with his ancient Jewish soul, he thundered against corrupt idolatries in life and art. Though he yearned to find his way to a "merciful, tender, or loving" God, he feared no such God was there. Like the orchestral horns in his 5th Symphony—which is one varied movement, that "unfolds as a spiraling form in ever widening turns"— we, in calling to God, are like the mortally wounded Roland in the medieval chanson, "blowing his horn with his last ounce of strength to call back Charlemagne, his king, ...who is too far away to hear our desperate cries for help."

Even so, George had an intuitive conviction of a higher power. He believed that music—for him, the paradigmatic art— had been given to man (by whom? one might ask) so he could express the best that was in him, which "had to do with his deepest feelings, rooted in a moral order in the universe." The truth is, for George, God was never really out of sight. In his remarkable essay, "Fiddlers and Fribbles," written in 1986 to sort out his own obsession with duality, many of the great questions of being, knowing, and doing are posed, probed, and ultimately joined together in a unified field theory of cosmic intent. Since, he concluded, the SuperForce, or Big Bang, that created sounds, sights, smells, and things to be tasted, must have also intended the capacity to hear, see, smell, and taste, which we possess, Man himself, far from being some accidental, evolutionary offshoot or fortuitous creation must have been part of the intention of the Big Bang from the start. World Consciousness, as belonging to this Force, was "built into us," and our physical selves were made to support its knowing light. The drive or urge of World Consciousness to become more self-aware was in turn reflected in art. For George, that was the moral of Blake's striking statement in The Marriage of Heaven and Hell that "Eternity is in love with the productions of Time."

All this could not have been the result of some blindly expanding phenomenon, but implied (to me at least) Mind—our mind; the Divine Mind; God. By extension, the existence in Nature of intelligible laws—however paradoxical—imply (in my view) a mind able to grasp them. We were, then, fully intended by the Divine Mind of God. Moreover, just as a blindly expanding, or contracting, universe could scarcely produce of itself "Purpose" (even in the organic sense of a seed), even less could it create such a subtle thing as free will. For free will is choosing *on purpose*—at any given moment, to follow through on something—*or not*.

Our experience implies that for everything there is a cause. From a world marked by incredible beauty, pattern, and design, inhabited by intelligent beings—who can not only appreciate these things, but reflect on their own capacity to do so—we can (if we wish) posit a mindless cause (like the Big Bang) or an intelligent cause, like God. "Consider the lilies of the field, how they grow": not in some blind green groping, but with geometry, purpose, shape. "There is," wrote Chesterton, "the finality of the flower." It has often been said that "if there were no god, it would be necessary to invent him," to satisfy our need. But as Anthony Burgess once noted, a need presupposes that which can meet it—as hunger implies food and thirst drink. "The higher the intelligence," wrote Herman Melville in his novel *Mardi*, "the greater the faith, the less the credulity." It is simply incredible—that is, one would have to be incredibly credulous—to believe that the creation, in all its intelligible wonder, was self-created, and that meaning itself had no meaning—which is the dead end of that surmise.

*

Though a mystic of a kind and a passionate artist, George was a very balanced man: wholesome, "normal," loyal, honest, true. He rejected the quest for pleasure for its own sake—"Don Juanism," as he called it—and wrote (as one steeped in opera might): "No matter how many sweet moments of conquest there may be, no matter how many Donna Annas and Donna Elviras, the stone guest eventually arrives for supper. We must all bear the consequences of our acts." He had few if any artistic neuroses (aside from heavy smoking) and was a dedicated family man. The loss of his son, who was an aspiring

writer, was always with him and George found ways to set his words
to music in several cherished works. His pride in his daughter, a
prominent Assyriologist, was foremost in his talk. His preoccupation
with suffering also did not distort him; and his healthy, good-
humored, but deeply serious nature, was nicely reflected in his
bold and beautifully flowing hand.

As he worked on his Memoir, George sent me chapters—
and "interchapters"—to read. We also talked politics. When
George W. Bush was elected President, he remarked: "All my adult
life I have dreaded the coming to America of a kind of smiling,
Christianized Fascism, but couldn't have imagined it in this form."
A few months later, he wrote that he had "given up almost entirely
on the news." By then, his desire to write music had also waned. He
had begun a 7th Symphony, but it remained, as he put it, "a series of
disconnected sketches" which his physical exhaustion would not
let him "connect up."

He fell ill in the fall of 2003 and died on May 29, 2005. The
end came with averted eyes. "If we talked of death," his wife Gene
told me later, "it was only in passing—after all, at a Retirement
Village where the average age is 85, the subject is prominent
enough to ignore . . . .There were no deathbed scenes, only tender
words of encouragement for returning health. So you can see the
levels on which we lived—knowing, not admitting, keeping up a sur-
face that all would still be well, so the end was a shock and a descent
into an unknown world without him & the overwhelming desire to
follow him wherever he had gone."

At his funeral—held at Valley Forge, Pennsylvania on June 3,
2005—the pianist Marcantonio Barone gave George this fine salute:

> As I got to know George, I came to recognize that a con-
> versation with him could take as many twists and turns as a
> story by his beloved Borges. I also began to see that I would
> never be able to understand either George or his music if
> I weren't prepared to set aside a dualistic view of certain things
> in life, to recognize that, to a mind and a spirit like his, things

or concepts that might seem to the rest of us to be locked in a state of mutual opposition are actually one and the same, or are, at the very least, different facets of a whole . . . He saw no conflict (because, in reality, there was none) between his distaste for religious convention and his profound faith in the sublime. And, again, there was no inherent distinction between the ferocity with which he stood up for the artistic principles he cherished and his almost childlike devotion to the people—and the music—he loved. After all, only a man as tender-hearted as George could have written the music that one early listener described as 'radiantly violent.'

I kept in contact with Gene, to whom I was also close; and in 2007 she wrote that she had just rediscovered *The Works of Sir Thomas Browne*, which I had sent them as a Christmas gift in 1979. "This treasure has pulled me out of a terrible apathy & lethargy," she remarked kindly, "that came over me once I no longer had George . . . . I am alert enough now to carry out and carry on with all I can muster, all the things important to George & his work . . . . So you & Browne became lifelong friends of ours & the wonderful thing is how our feelings remain strong despite distances of space & time. . . . For now, just these few words of the many that race through my mind to say how meaningful your talks with George were for him & how proud he would have been (& is?) for the beautiful dedication you wrote for him in *The Fated Sky*."

In addition to overseeing the publication his last works—*Eagle Minds* (a selection of letters exchanged between George and the Canadian composer Istvan Anhalt); his memoir *Four Lines, Five Spaces*; and *Chromaticism: Symmetry in Atonal and Tonal Music*—Gene took charge, with her usual energy and dedication, of the establishment of the "George Rochberg Music Room" at Montclair State University in New Jersey. It was there, she wrote, that "George & I met and never parted till 2005 & if *The Fated Sky* is read correctly we shall meet again in the forever—

wherever that is. Those were George's words. And your words, too, give me courage and loving friendship."

Gene had long wanted to give me some tender momento of our bond, and on January 6, 2013, when she was in her 94th year, she wrote to say that "a most special package was coming" my way. She then explained that "many years ago" they had traveled to Bethlehem for the reopening of the Church of the Nativity, which had evidently been closed to visitors for some time. The next day they "roamed around the town and stopped in at an antique store. There we saw this marvelous cross, which the owner sold to us as 'the Great Cross of the Crusades.' We bought that cross and treasured it till now, when I happily give it to you, in thanks for the splendor of a wonderful friendship."

The next day, the package arrived. Inside was a large, 8"x10", hand-forged metal cross of indeterminate age, with brazen serpents twined on each of its four, symmetrical arms, with a smaller Jerusalem cross set between each arm. In the center was an oval moonstone with metal rays shooting forth in a sun-burst. Attached to the top, by little metal rings or links, was an image of St. Peter clutching the keys to the Kingdom of God. I replied at once (January 12, 2013) that I would cherish the gift "as a talisman for my best efforts and an emblem of our abiding love."

It occupies a place of honor in my study, facing Albrecht Durer's woodcut of St. Jerome; and when it draws my gaze, I think of our exalted friendship, our connected lives in art, and the Rochbergs together in Bethlehem long ago.

CHAPTER TWENTY-TWO

$\text{\tiny ❦}$

During all my years as a writer—perhaps to my practical detriment—I seldom went to literary parties, or talked much about my work, which seemed to me idle when I had writing to do. And there was always the risk I might talk my work away. "The less said about some things, the better," Travers remarked to me once. She was thinking, I believe, of faith and love. I would add creative endeavor to these two, to complete the trinity of things best cherished by silence in our lives. There is a wise little poem by Anna Akhmatova that speaks to an aspect of this, which I wish I had discovered in time to share with Travers before she died:

> There are some words that one cannot renew,
> And he who says them wastes away a hoard.
> Two things alone are infinite—the blue
> Of Heaven and the mercy of the Lord.
> (Translated by Sergei Roy)

Whatever my reserve, I was glad as a writer to be read, hoped for recognition, and was particularly grateful to receive an award from the American Academy of Arts and Letters in 2002. On that occasion, I found myself seated on stage between the playwright Horton Foote (whose work I loved and admired) and the Socialist Realist painter Jack Levine. Foote was frail, spoke softly, and had to steady himself in his chair; but the tender expression of his face reflected the sweetness of his soul. Levine made a number of wry comments about the pretensions of the day, but was otherwise in a doleful mood for, he said, photography would soon make his work obsolete. Edna O'Brien spoke, as did Robert Giroux; the poet John Hollander was honored, along with William Bolcom and Ned Rorem (both composers), and Frank Gehry, the architect.

Hollander, whom I'd never met before, strode across the stage to greet me. The painter Wolf Kahn (introduced to me by Hoagland) turned out to be a neighbor, with a house a few miles away. He told me that he often played poker in town with "big wigs, like judges, who like me in the game because they clean me out. But," he added, "the losses hardly count. That's why they call me 'One sketch, Wolf,' because I can always recoup my losses with a sketch." He had recently written a little book that Updike had agreed to write the preface for. "I'm poaching on your territory," he said.

Afterwards, my wife and I found ourselves seated for lunch at a table with Horton Foote and several other playwrights, including Romulus Linney, Christopher Durang, and John Guare. I was puzzled by this until I learned that Foote had supported my award. As we were being ushered to our chairs, he told me kindly that *Wide As the Waters* had meant a great deal to him, which meant a great deal to me. I also spoke with Guare, with whom I corresponded in the following year. Few things are more heartening to a writer than the approbation of his peers. One particularly nice letter from Guare will ever remain among those I most prize.

After the Academy event, Hilary showered me with tulips and roses, a few select gifts, the perfect card, and two cases of Cabernet Sauvignon and Merlot wine from Windsor Vineyards, each bottle bearing a special label with my name.

Aside from assorted readings, I was otherwise involved in

a public arts event perhaps two other times—most notably, as co-chair of the Poetry division of the Brattleboro Literary Festival (a large, annual regional extravaganza) in 2012. At the time, I hoped to invite poets of more traditional taste and achievement than usually attend, and proposed Rachel Hadas, Richard Wilbur, and John Hollander, along with Mary Oliver and Donald Hall. I wanted Hall not only to read from his own work but talk about other poets, since his life, as recounted in his book of recollections, *Their Ancient Glittering Eyes*, had been richly entwined with theirs. Richard Wilbur, I learned, had been invited the year before, but the Festival had neglected to offer to chauffeur him about, even though he was then ninety and lived in Northampton nearby. Hollander and Oliver were both ill. Hall's infirmities also stood in the way. "I wish I could take part," he wrote me, "but I can't do it. I have a great deal of difficulty getting around. My balance is gone and my knees buckle. I agreed some time ago to do readings in the Upper Peninsula of Michigan, and I dread it . . . I don't know as I can do any more . . . ."

Rachel Hadas came, read well, and by the sheer quality of her work, proved a "star." One board member had objected to her appearing on the grounds that not all her books had been published by "major houses"; another wanted to know (as a hurdle for inclusion) if she'd be willing to participate in a "poetry slam."

When I told my great teacher, Edward Tayler, about it, he laughed. In time, Ted and I had forged a deep and affectionate friendship that grew in number, weight, and measure through the years. In 1990, he had asked me, as a former student, to write a letter on his behalf to Michael Sovern, then University President, in support of his appointment as Lionel Trilling Professor in the Humanities. I was glad to oblige.

"Dear Dr. Sovern," I wrote,

> During my decade at Columbia, I had several fine teach-
> ers, both in the College and in the Graduate School of Arts
> and Sciences. But Professor Tayler was quite beyond compare.

Although he certainly stood out as a scholar, he also made it his high purpose to help students understand that the search for literary meaning was involved with the search for truth. That, combined with his earnest concern for their individual development, created an atmosphere that gave the utmost meaning to learning and humane discourse. I doubt that any other teacher asked quite as much from his students—or inspired greater esteem. As a measure of my own, when I graduated from the College in 1971, I declined a Kellett Fellowship to Oxford in order to remain within the orbit of his supremely literate world.

It gave me tremendous satisfaction to write this, in part because I wanted him to know how I felt. In turn, he was grateful and asked me to send copies to the University Provost, Vice President, and Dean. Others of course rallied behind him too and his appointment was announced on July 6, 1990.

Two weeks later, he wrote to thank me for my "working words." From then on, he became a fairly regular correspondent, shared information about his family, a China trip, a visit to Vinalhaven Island in Pensobscot Bay, a scathing review he wrote of a new book on Donne; and so on—and cheered on my writing life. His wife, Christina, also became a friend. As always, I sent him copies of my books. He generally closed his letters with "Yours in the ranks" (after Edmund's dark valediction in *Lear*) or Kurt Vonnegut's "So it goes." Many of his notes were written from the country cabin (or "camps," as they called it), that Ted and Christina kept at Lower Beech Pond in Tuftonboro, N.H. "Dear Barry," he wrote in characteristic fashion on September 9, 1997. "Much activity here . . . . Coyotes, working together, snatching cats off porches in Concord. Black bear, seen regularly nearby, opened the outdoor refrigerator of the lady who bakes pies for one of the restaurants, ate thirteen (berry) pies but left two (meringue). I am a hold out here, the one inhabitant on the shores of the pond—but the air has the feel of autumn."

We discussed many things, from everyday matters to esoteric ideas; yet I can't say for sure what his own convictions were—though I know he was greatly devoted to St. Augustine. He once told me he had "begun as a Methodist," like myself. As to where he ended up, I thought it impertinent to ask.

It meant much to me that he thought well of my work. In one particularly nice letter he told me how much he enjoyed my handling of "even very difficult subjects," and recalled that once when John Millington Synge had gone to hear John McCormack, the great tenor, sing at the Abbey Theater, he couldn't contain himself and exclaimed: 'There he is again, so bloody *clear!*'" I cherished that, since I saw it as part of my task to make difficult material accessible to others in good narrative prose. In the course of that clarifying process, I found that in order to make something intelligible to others, I first had to make it intelligible to myself.

Yet I doubted at times I could sustain a writing life. An independent scholar makes at best a precarious living and I wondered if there might be a teaching post somewhere I could fill. In January of 1995 I sought his advice. "On the one hand," I said, "I can readily see why a college or university might be reluctant to hire me, even as a writer-in-residence—since I've never taught, do not have a doctorate, and (as the very diversity of my writing indicates) failed to specialize. On the other hand (to put forward my own case), there is the depth of my academic training (for which I am daily grateful), my continuing (if unaffiliated) scholarship, and (according to its merits) my literary work. Perhaps it is far-fetched of me to expect to find a niche." Even so, I asked him to write a general letter of recommendation for me, which of course he did. He also suggested I apply for my doctorate *extra muros*, with a defense of my published work. Technically, my application to do so was a decade late, but (due to Ted's intervention) that condition was waived and on February 27, 1996, before an eclectic panel of Columbia professors, I successfully defended my work. When my degree was awarded on May 15th, I had a valued new credential, but no practical opportunities arose.

As Ted entered his 70s, his health faltered. "I see doctors, suffer tests," he wrote, though "nothing yet worries me much or threatens to extinguish my cheerful flame." He was not always fortunate in the doctors he saw. In 2010, he developed "foot drop" (a gait abnormality where the forefoot drags due to local muscle paralysis or damaged nerves), and consulted the head of sports medicine at Columbia. The doctor prescribed Robaxin, an anticholinergic muscle relaxant, and assured him of no marked interactions or side effects. "So," Ted told me, "I overdosed for ten months, whacked out my acetylcholine transmitters, destroyed some memory, and interrupted neural pathways to the 'organizational' areas of my brain." The result was "mild dementia, getting worse" before he chanced upon an article that exposed the medication's risks. Though he stopped taking Robaxin at once, for a time its ill-effects remained. "You can see that I am even having trouble pushing the pen, much less being able to think my way in and out of a syntactical unit," he wrote to me on May 31, 2012, as his writing wandered a little on the page. In time, however, he rebounded remarkably, and his mind remained keen.

In subsequent letters we exchanged views on modern poets. Louise Bogan held up well for him, along with one or two poems by E.E. Cummings and Hart Crane. "Early Stevens, late Eliot and Yeats—there's the tune . . . . But I can do without 90% of Berryman and Pound." I knew he also esteemed Frost, Hardy, Tate, among others, some of Yvor Winters too, and once inserted into my copy of Winters' *Collected Poems* a list of the pieces he particularly admired—including "Sir Gawaine and the Green Knight," "On a View of Pasadena from the Hills," "Time and the Garden," and "Midas" (which he said was about Ezra Pound).

In April of 2012, Ted came upon a review of a new book on Ivan the Terrible and thought mine should have been referenced. I replied on the 16th: "It's good of you to be miffed on my behalf, but . . . .My history-writing days are done. My last two books will appear (and appear to disappear, no doubt) this summer: one on the ancient and early modern Olympic Games (for "young adults");

the other on Islam (late 8th-early 9th c.) at its height. Then I pivot at last into my venerable years, to work, I hope, on poems. When the time comes, I will do my best to elect an astrologically propitious time to start —when Mercury is strong, Saturn exalted, neither squared by other planets and the Moon not Void of Course. If I abide by the strictures of Elias Ashmole (who was good at such things), Mercury should also rule the hour."

I was half in jest, of course, as he knew; but he enjoyed the construct of my plan.

In the Spring of 2016, I re-read Ted's four books along with a handful of his essays, and wondered if there was anything I'd missed. He replied: "Yes, I have essays but also want to ask your help, even some kind of collaboration. I begin to realize that I have a lot of stuff that maybe deserves a wider audience." We hoped to consult early that summer, but "many small illnesses" set him back.

The United States was then in the throes of its Presidential election, which ended (against all expectation) with the elevation of Donald Trump. Hillary Clinton, of course, had been favored, though the Press in general did everything it could to equate her use of a private email server as Secretary of State with the contemplated atrocities of her opponent, whose overall incapacity, degenerate nature, and gross deportment had made him a national disgrace. I had foreseen the outcome from his horoscope, and wrote Ted about it early in the fall. One had only to note the exact conjunction of Regulus with Mars on his Ascendant and Algol on his Mid-heaven cusp to predict a reign of criminal mischief, violence, and probably war.

On the day of Trump's inauguration (which I couldn't bear to watch, and which I trust will one day be set aside as a Day of National Atonement), I decided to spend my time more usefully by improving my Greek and reading the Old Testament apocryphal Book of Sirach, which is rich in wise proverbs, including many about power. It contains a verse about "kings sitting on the ground," (11:5) which I thought must have inspired Shakespeare's great lines in Richard II: "For God's sake, let us sit upon the

ground/And tell sad stories of the death of kings." The Geneva
Bible of 1560 would have been his likely source, though (as we
know from Ben Jonson) he also knew some Greek. I wrote Ted
that I had been delighted to discover on my own what must be
common knowledge among Shakespeare scholars; he replied,
with pedagogical pride (for I would forever be his student) that
scholarship had overlooked it. So instead of wasting my time
watching the coronation of a fool, I had made a small contribution
to Shakespearean scholarship.

At 86, Ted finally "discovered the meaning of cutting back," was
unable to manage the physical demands of his New Hampshire camp,
and gave up teaching because "one cold will keep me down, and
I mean like man very down for six weeks. I cannot live with that,
as you know." When I mentioned I had recently joined the local
Episcopal Church, he teased me (quoting Milton), "So you have fled
to the bishops 'where the hungry sheep look up and are not fed?' No
matter. This closet Thomist may go there yet." Mindful of the sufferings
of King Lear, he also wrote to me about a former student (and mutual
friend) who had fallen on hard times: "He was a foolish and fatally
fond man at the peak of all his successes, now a feeble old man more
sinned against than sinning. A terrible punishment." Yet in the face
of his suffering, we both agreed, he had shown incredible fortitude.

On May 15th, 2018, I came down to New York to see him
(as we had arranged at the end of March); spent the afternoon
with our ailing friend, then in near-hospice care; and that evening
went by Ted's apartment—only to learn that he had died of heart
failure three weeks before. I had known this visit might be my last,
yet . . . . I had so much still to tell him, which I can only do now in
the quiet converse of my heart.

Subsequently, Christina sent me a computer file containing
his Shakespeare teaching notes, which I hold dear.

Tayler taught at Columbia full time for forty years, then on
an ad-hoc basis for another seventeen, through 2016. From 1985
to 2003, he also oversaw the writing component of the Core
Curriculum. That meant managing sixty Teaching Assistants as well

as two thousand students—without additional pay. As demanding as that was, it gave him a chance at last to emulate his beloved teacher Theodore Baird, as he had done years before as a graduate assistant at Stanford, where (with the poet, Thom Gunn, his friend and classmate) he had gained a reputation and a following among the students for a composition class he taught. Tayler's Columbia course was called "Rhetoric and Logic" (writing and thinking) and was widely revered. Paul Auster, Ric Burns, Tony Kushner, and other writers were among his students, along with dozens of outstanding scholars in universities throughout the States.

Ted once shared with me a long letter he had written about Baird to William Pritchard, a friend and fellow-scholar at Amherst whom Baird had also taught. For my benefit, he wrote at the top, "The closest I get to a memoir."

That increased my resolve to preserve something of this wondrous man in mine.

CHAPTER TWENTY-THREE

In February 1998, I received a notice from Pomfret School that its Wrestling Room was to be named in honor of Hagop Merjian, who was about to retire. We hadn't seen each other in thirty-two years. I decided to attend—and there he was, the grizzled old warhorse of the school, aged but ageless, vibrant, massive, quick. At our reunion, we could hardly say enough. So it has been for twenty years now since. As I begin to grow old, he is one of my dearest friends.

Typically, our visits to his home occasion bold etymological excursions embellished with a Middle Eastern feast—bulghur pilaf spiced with cumin, shish kabob, prasa (leeks), sumpug (eggplant dishes), boureg, spanakopita, and so on—often accompanied by a little discourse on the history of each dish and the meaning of its name. I have stood with him in his kitchen as he talked non-stop about something or other while he simultaneously cooked, steamed, or grilled xema, imam-bayeldi, shish-kebab, and fish.

He is full of good stories. I once sent him a recording of early Christian Syrian chants. He replied with a short, dramatic tale of a detour he and his beloved wife, Haiganoush (or "Aggie," as we called her), once took by car through the mountains between Bulgaria and Greece. The usual road had been blocked by a farmer's strike, so his driver careened up the side of the mountain onto a narrow path used by sheep and goats. The path, winding along a precipice, was slick with manure. "I looked out the window on my side," he recalled, "and saw that the tires of the mini-Renault were inches from the edge. One tiny mistake would send us to our deaths. We were almost a quarter of a mile up that mountain, and in the intensity of that moment, in the silence of those fears, I heard behind me in the back seat, where Haiganoush had dropped her head into her lap—unable to endure the sight of our demise— a whispered moaning, Armenian liturgical chant, the soft litany of the Song of the Dead. That melody stays with me even now."

In recalling some of his Columbia professors, he remarked that Jacob Taubes was "a flamboyant brilliantly multi-lingual, very European *privatdozent*, who wore his jacket like a cape and used to hold his cigarette upright between his forefinger and thumb. His lectures were packed with eager students, and in his walks about campus often followed by acolytes who hung upon every word. But he was also 'a satyr' and went 'the way of all flesh,' doomed by those urges and lusts which often accompany brilliant men who abuse authority and adulation. His father was perhaps the most famous Rabbi of Western Europe. His wife, a suicide. I met his two children just before she walked into the Atlantic Ocean in 1969." Of Mark Van Doren: "A remarkable teacher and a truly gentle, honorable man, who spoke in a lilting, incisive voice. His Shakespeare course was always oversubscribed." Of Louis Simpson: "His favorite poet was Milton. If he could find a way to talk about Milton instead of Byron, for example, he would. One day he came into class when the assigned work was Byron's *Don Juan*. He asked us whether anyone cared to discuss it. No one raised their hand. Simpson said, 'Well, I don't either. Let's go to a movie.' So we all trouped off to the Thalia to see a foreign film." Of Lionel Trilling: "He avoided talking to undergraduates when he could. He kept his eye on the clock, and a moment before the bell sounded would snap his book (or folder of notes) shut, and go straight out the door."

Many of Hagop's letters are marvels of length and animation, with wide-ranging commentary on art, politics, wrestling, pets, history, and other preferred topics, with a diagnosis (always introduced by an ellipsis) of the weather at the top—". . . lambent, frutescent showers," ". . . first snow. . . good air to split splits in," ". . . early evening, the barn shimmering in the mushroom light, the sweet gloom of dusk." In all, they reflect the bountiful energy and interests of his capacious life. When typed haphazardly, they are often scrawled over with Armenian, Turkish, Greek, and Arabic words. His ethnic salutations—"Affandim, Magnoon, Barry-Jan, Ya Benson Philimou, Ya Benson Kyrie, Ya Sidi Benson, Khadifa"—are an ever-affectionate reminder to me of the world from which he came. Almost always, too, there is some surprising word—"diaskeuasis," "zetetic," "paraleipsis," "thurible," "ensorcelled," "anagnoresis," "chatoyant," "nacreous," "glaucous," "marcesent," "tabescense." "chrestomathy"—naturally spawned by his love of unorthodox terms. Then out of the sometimes obscure thicket of his coinage will emerge a time-honored, exquisitely simple Armenian phrase. And so, of a dear friend who died, he wrote: "She was the wild jasmine of our lives."

He has fought to find time to do his own writing and in April 2001, told me: "I share with you the anchorite's deepest hunger for the cloister and the privileges of the adytum." His dedication as a teacher long made that hard to indulge. At his retirement dinner in 1999 (attended by hundreds, where I spoke briefly), he declared in an unusually spare speech that the foundation of all good teaching was "love." For emphasis, he repeated the word several times.

Poetry has been the work of his old age. Like his letters, his poems are crowded with unusual, often foreign words, coined or reminted, neologisms and the like, verbalized nouns—"mausered," "coriandered," "ruddled," "creviced," "dervished," "gargoyled," and so on. At times, they are reminiscent of the word-play of Gerard Manley Hopkins. Also, as in the work of Cavafy (one of his favorites), past and present mingle with equal familiarity in the memory of place. When an uncle learned that Hagop's mother didn't know the day of her birth, he exclaimed: "She was born a few days before the full moon/ After the New Year of the big fire that/ Burned the city of Harpoot!" ("Birth Days") And here is the opening stanza of "Syntagma Square: Athens," which commemorates the massacre, at Churchill's behest, of Greek civilians on December 3, 1944. On that day, Athenian police, allied with Nazi sympathizers, were allowed (for political reasons) to kill left-wing, patriotic demonstrators who had fought with the British for the liberation of Greece:

1985

> I am standing on the Square, on Syntagma,
> Where she told me that if I kneeled and listened
> To the spilth of blood between the stones
> I would hear the hallowed voices of the martyred,
> That in the imbrued flume of the innocent ones
> I might, if I sought, see their faces, too,
> Locked in a timeless, accusing stare.
> Voices, even now, weeping the "J'accuse" to the
> Wide cyanotic Hellenic sky: cries unredeemed."

In "Mnemdji: Baba," about his own father, who "fled from the massacres of Hamid," he wrote:

> Near death, he took me aside that late summer
> Evening, his stentor voice still resonant, and
> In the Anatolian Turkish which was his true
> Tongue, said: "All our actions weighed against
> The sufferings of this world, are lewd...."

> He died a few days after telling me that.
> September came, strange, sweet, penitential.
> The earth seemed jeweled, heavy, and fecund
> And it seemed as if I could see gargoyle Memory,
> Hovering around the white gates, climbing

Our stone gateposts, sitting and waiting
For me, clinging, leering, jubilant even.
Ancient Baba, my effendi, our gerontos—gone.
And with him the "scandalon" of loving another,
Whether he loves you or not.

For Hagop, the past is never quite past, but a ripe, ambiguous taste upon his tongue:

Now I know why the melons from Kaiseri had
Flesh treacled in the skin of golden saffron, and
Pastes made from the mulberries in Malatyia—
Dragon's blood fruit "like fists" from trees Osman
Himself planted a thousand years ago to feed the
Fibrous serpentine larvae he brought from the East . . .
("Keeping Home")

Even rural Connecticut cannot escape its ominous link to the plight of far-off lands. In "Pomfret, 1994" (one of a series of poems about "Hunger"), want and starvation find their way to his door:

The cat leaps on to the table. Any sun will do.
Icicles do not melt in direct sunlight.
The wind barked and moaned at the house all night.
Catabatic, inconsolable, consuming bone-wind.
In the barn even the heated watercock freezes tight.
And the rimey breath of the sheep seeps in the
Keep of the cote, tinfoily dew in silvery flight.
Outside, my footsteps in the snowy dunes
Fill swiftly (like the *scloop, scloop* of the
Jackass hooves outside my window in Cairo,
Erased in the gusts of the morning simoom:
Cut deep, sand-filled and double-duned.)
A month ago, in the barm of the harvest, the
Sheep barely nibbled the fresh, winey bristle.

Now, in the quick of their stalls they bruit,
Cold-hungry, they fight even for the coarse
Brogs and spiles of vetch and thistle.
Hunger and cold. Everything eaten. Gone.

Hagop once asked me to make a list of "publishable" favorites, concerned that some of his poems might seem too "ethnic" for much appeal. I replied:

12 April, 2009, Easter Sunday.
Dear Hagop,
Your poems have everything. They are prodigies of bounty—ambitious, broad, full of life, ferocity, light, tenderness— forces of Nature, like the verses cast up by the sea in 'Walking Carpenter's Beach.' Out of your own tidal mix of Greek, Armenian, Turkish, Arabic, English, and German words you seem to have created your own compact poetic diction, in which nothing is trite, and no horror of the past is sullied by platitude.

The might of them grows with each reading, and their 'ethnicity' (to address your concern) is—as any authentic, strong sense of place is, or provenance—a singular virtue, not a flaw. No one with any true poetic sense would say these poems are 'parochial' or 'Armenian,' but come out of the Book of the World in which the Armenian holocaust is a Rubric, writ large.

I tried to make a list of my 'publishable favorites' but the list grew absurdly long. Here and there, of course there is some overlap ('Memory'/'Mnemdje Baba') ('Grimoire'/'Bones'); and now and then my ear tells me some might be trimmed. But there isn't one I don't think well of, with their knowing embrace of far-flung lands; the architecture of flowers; the sensate, wholly original details of New England winters; poetic tradition; History; and the sacred obligation of poetry to keep Memory alive."

Of his own, occasional excess, he once said: "I too have found passages . . . . meta-fluxed and overfilled," but "ahh, when I luxuriate in the loveliness, the lovingness of the language—it is so hard to extricate one's self . . . who wishes to end loving???)" Over the years, moreover, he has "labored, loved, and luxuriated" in translations from other tongues. Drawn naturally to the poets of the besieged, exiled, downtrodden, torn—Hikmet, Lorca, Mandelstam, Cavafy, Paz, Celan—he also identifies strongly with the Palestinians, Yazidis, and others "whom the world wants to forget." He has always observed April 24 as a holy day for Armenians, the day commemorated as the beginning of the genocide. He told me: "I have never worked on that day."

Not much divides us. Now and then we argue gently about Gurdjieff—whom he somewhat resembled in his youth, with his black Armenian eyes and handlebar moustache; or the "madness in religion," as he sees it, in looking to an imaginary God. I may be Anglo-Catholic, for the most part, by faith and conviction; he, by his own description, a kind of Pelagian heretic. Yet he is also a "vir sanctus"— as Augustine said of Pelagius himself.

Nothing else counts.

*

I had long lost touch with my Pomfret classmate, Miguel de Torres, but over the years his older sister, Ines, and I sometimes crossed paths. She had married the poet Galway Kinnell in 1965, and kept an apartment in Greenwich Village, where I also lived for over a decade, from 1976 to 1988. She once offered to show my poems to him, but I was too shy to accept. Moreover, it seemed to me that I hadn't written enough. On another occasion, Ines invited me to stay with her at her apartment in Madrid; but I was too caught up then in the struggle to sustain a living to risk a break from my routine.

As often in my life, I failed to grasp Opportunity by the forelock as it swept on by.

The Village apartment they kept was strewn with books and papers, and when I came by once with Miguel in 1966, during my freshman year in college, Kinnell had recently published his one novel, *Black Light*. I remember that the title, along with several other possibilities, was underlined on a piece of paper on his desk. He was scarcely, if at all, aware of my existence, and the only time I spoke to him directly, if briefly, was a couple of years later at the uptown apartment where Miguel's parents lived. This was around 1968. I was visiting Miguel at the time, and Kinnell came in with the poet Paul Zweig. They had just given a reading together, I believe at the 92nd Street Y. As it happened, I was also acquainted with Zweig, who had been my English teacher at Columbia in my sophomore year. As a teacher, he had been neither good nor bad. I remembered three things from his class. The first is that he thought one of John Donne's poems was about "the aristocracy of love"; the second, that he found it incredible that Daniel Defoe's profligate heroine, Moll Flanders, had never contracted venereal disease; and the third, that he realized he was capable of murder when one day in a rage he had hurled his cat, who had soiled his couch, across the room. There's a fourth memory I have, too—prophetic and odd. One morning after class we encountered each other in the lobby of Hamilton Hall. I wasn't feeling well and the subject of illness came up. He told me that whenever he felt even slightly sick, he expected to die. A decade later, he was diagnosed with lymphatic cancer, from which he died at the young age of 49.

One afternoon in 1980 I chanced upon Ines in Washington Square Park. The poet James Wright, a close friend of Kinnell's, had just died of throat cancer, and she told me that her husband had managed to reproduce in himself, in a psychosomatic frenzy, all the symptoms of his friend's disease. From other remarks she made afterwards at their apartment on Hudson Street, I realized her marriage was frayed.

On later occasions, she confided much to me about the dissolution of her marriage; her romance with Joseph Brodsky (now widely known); her family life; and the secret journals she had kept about it all for many years. In May of 2001, I spent two days with her at her home in Sag Harbor. She was then in the process of transcribing and editing a portion of this material for possible publication, but was deeply worried about betraying Brodsky's confidence and trust. At the same time, she said: "He was a public figure. Wouldn't a biographer benefit from knowing what Brodsky did or said on such and such a day?" She asked my advice, but I was reluctant to give it. At length I told her to let her conscience be her guide.

As we sat together on the beach and talked, she had a sweet way of holding my hand. It was lover-like, though we were never such, and implied a closeness I would not have assumed. I'm not sure why she confided in me as she did, except that by then we had known each other for almost forty years. I slept in an upstairs bedroom, but awoke that first night to the terrified cries of a rabbit that had been cornered near my bed by her cat. Ines helped me rescue the creature, but (to my annoyance) thought my concern for it sentimental, noting that it had happened before.

Some fourteen years later, I attended the 50th anniversary reunion of my Pomfret class. That put me in mind of Miguel; and in turn, of Ines. I wrote to her and she invited me to visit when I could. That proved difficult (as I was often home-bound by aging and disabled pets); but on May 23, 2015 we spoke at length on the phone. She had taken up painting again (having painted before); was about to leave for Portland, Oregon, to spend three months with her son, Fergus; but told me in passing, to my dismay, that she and Miguel had been estranged for many years. In the meantime, both Brodsky and Kinnell had died. She had recently attended a memorial for Kinnell with her son at New York University, where his praises were sung. "They made him out to be some kind of god," she said, "but of course I didn't see him that way."

TWENTY-FOUR

For the soul to dispute its own existence is perhaps a feature of its fallen state. Once you cease to believe in the soul, as Chesterton observed, you begin to disbelieve in the mind. Because the mind has no basis for itself. In time (believing only in the now), you come to believe in mindless things—in money, brute force, self-interest, advantage, power; in pride, lust, sloth, anger, envy, gluttony, greed—all the cardinal sins which men bowed down to in the idols they raised. It is a culture of death, in which death is stronger than life, because there is no belief in a life beyond it. And it makes for a religion of despair.

There are legions of fine people who profess not to believe in the soul. But their lives are balanced on the head of a pin. They may be governed by their upbringing, which heped them to develop positive habits, or by the example of others they admire. Often, deep down, they are restrained by their conscience, which they can't explain. But released from such constraints (for this is the true banality of evil), the nicest person can become a heartless savage, indifferent to all the things to which the soul aspires. This commonly happens in extreme circumstances, like war.

The inner judgment of the human race tells us that we have always known that this life is not all there is, that there is an "after" to it, for in all the great myths (which are archaic tales of true meaning), there is a reckoning for how we live. No one truly believes—or has ever believed, I suspect—in justification by faith alone: that it doesn't matter what kind of life you live, or what you do in the world. What would that mean—that we believed in a Teacher whose Teaching we could ignore? Or that we are saved by a faith in something in which we don't truly believe? We all know in our bones that "good works" count—not as "credits" but for Good.

We may think of the great myths and storied tales, like Homer's epics, as wonderfully imagined fictions in which reality is artfully rendered. But they are parables, more truly, of the world of essence, which— though unimaginable to some—is as real as the world we know. All stories, in one way or another, are about the virtues and vices. They have to do with the consequences of our thoughts and actions, and could be called morality tales.

We are suffused with meaning. Where does it come from? Can meaning mean nothing? If it could, it would not be what it is. It comes from some Intelligence, vaster than ours, in which ours is subsumed. As for Nothingness: we aren't Nothing. We can't even imagine what that is. We can only feel it as a pang of fear, a loss of that which we know, as the opposite of what we are. We have no reason to believe in it, really. We only think we see its "remains" as the spirit of life departs from the body we have.

From the moment I understood what an unearned gift life was, I began to appreciate the least thing, which seemed to me as great as the greatest; and that helped allay my fear of death. I found deliverance in the fact that although I deserved nothing, I had been given everything. What more could I ask? My feeling must be akin to what Auden came to when he wrote: "I have always felt that to be walking this earth is a miracle I must do my best to deserve."

We would be wise to exhort ourselves (as Moses exhorted the Israelites in the desert) to remember the wonders they had seen. For it applies with equal justice to the wonders we know. The earth spinning on its axis at over 1,000 mph, as it revolves at a speed of some 67,000 mph around the Sun, as we—held by the miracle of gravity in place—sense no motion. How unimaginable would that be in itself, without laws to explain it? such laws being miracles themselves. Everywhere you look: a miracle—a wonder—an angel with a flaming sword! No thought of the ordinariness of things makes sense. Life itself is a miracle. How would any other miracle, or some new one, more clearly confirm the existence of God? "All the miracles done in the world," as St. Augustine so wisely put it, "are less than the world itself."

It takes no great leap of faith for me to believe that the wisdom of the ages exceeds the range of my own understanding, or the poor power of my doubts. Knowledge begins with reverence for the divine. Once you deny the divine, you are left only with the vanity of your own opinion, in the maze of your own presumption, which can teach you nothing of itself. It can only end in the uneasy feeling that your life is somehow "wrong." For we know (as we must) deep down that we are a part of something larger, with a meaning (however much beyond our grasp), to be acknowledged and served. Otherwise, our fate is like that of the fallen angels in Milton's *Paradise Lost*, who "reasoned high

> Of Providence, Foreknowledge, Will, and Fate—
> Fixed fate, free will, foreknowledge absolute—
> And found no end, in wandering mazes lost.
> Of good and evil much they argued then,
> Of happiness and final misery,
> Passion and apathy, and glory and shame:
> Vain wisdom all, and false philosophy!

Ranier Maria Rilke once observed that our capacity to comprehend experiences like visions and the spirit-world "have by daily parrying been so crowded out of life that the senses with which we could have grasped them have atrophied. To say nothing of God." Are there angels? I can't say. But people in our lives may play angelic roles. Is Providence working through them? Perhaps. Why not? For even the most hapless among us may be chosen, on some occasion, to transmit a message of bright worth. William Blake claimed to have encountered angels now and then on his London walks. "Be not forgetful to entertain strangers," we are told, "for thereby some have entertained angels unawares."

The world is luminous with the presence of contained, incarnate forces, which pertain to both the living and the dead. A good poem incorporates the power of the time of its conception and brings that power down into it. We call it inspiration or a lightning strike. But it has "staying power." In that sense, a good poet is like the priest of the sacraments—an intermediary between the world of matter and celestial powers.

If a poem does not arise from some real place in oneself, it is worthless, no matter how artful. But if it does, it will often preserve, as in a vial, the quality or tone of the state from which it arose. The occasional poems I wrote when young, however imperfect, still capture states of being for me that I might otherwise have lost. Many, I realize now (somewhat to my surprise), were implicitly devout, whether their themes were love or desire or (as often) the art of poetry itself.

*

George Rochberg once told me, "Never let publishers tell you what to write. If you do, they'll take your soul." Commercial publishing is a business, largely driven by "big" books. I happen to like big ideas, and on the whole they served me well in obtaining good advances; but the subjects I chose were my own.

I am grateful my editors allowed me to write the books I did.

In one of her more revealing letters, P.L. Travers remarked, "Everything I write is, in a way, a means of clarifying things for myself, teaching myself and also it is a message to everybody I know." As I look back on my own work now, that seems to me an apt description of it, too. One evening in 1967, when I was still an undergraduate at Columbia living in the East Village, I dropped by the carpentry workshop of my friend, Peter Murkett (my Pomfret/Columbia classmate) who was beginning to establish his trade.

We decided to ask the I-Ching about our careers. I don't recall what his casting showed; mine indicated teaching; and I have often thought about this since. There are many ways to teach, and it seems to me now that my books were largely written as private tutorials for whoever might read them; and in that way I have managed, in aggregate, to reach over half a million people, which is quite a large classroom to address.

My work was sometimes praised as original, but that was not my aim. I brought my own unknowing to my subjects, to preserve my sense of wonder, and an unconventional mix of story, fact, anecdote, and legend, to the writing for layered depth. Our minds may compartmentalize things; but reality is a dense and interconnected weave. It is the weave of the life we live.

Only two of my books were controversial: *The Fated Sky*, on the history of Astrology; and *Master of War*, my biography of General George H. Thomas, the great Union general of the Civil War. My biography of Thomas predictably incurred the wrath of those who idolize Grant. It is always safe, of course, to write a book in praise of a presumptive hero, though in Grant's case his biographers have had to do a lot of special pleading, while unable to explain away his battlefield negligence, with its needless carnage, which foreshadowed the shabby nature of his corrupt (and corruptly negligent) presidential terms. For a long time after he died, "Grantism" stood for "shady politics, bribery, and corruption," as the great historian Catherine Drinker Bowen chose to remind us in *Yankee From Olympus*, her biography of Oliver Wendell Holmes. That is glossed over now. Even so, about a third of the Civil War community agreed with my assessment; the other two-thirds would have liked to boil me in oil.

The Fated Sky was an easier target, since anything esoteric is viewed askance.

I have said all I care to on that score.

Some of my book ideas were rejected over the years, perhaps justly, including one on superconductivity; an account of the fall of the House of Rurik (Russia between 1584–1613); a book about the St. Louis Bridge; a biography of Robert Louis Stevenson; and a series I wanted to title, *The Lives of Writers Who Have Enchanted the Young: A Young People's Non-Fiction Book Series*, the first volume of which was to feature Robert Louis Stevenson, P.L. Travers, and Rachel Field. I also proposed a book about the Field family as an American epic, since the family included a Supreme Court Justice appointed by Lincoln; Cyrus Field, who laid the Atlantic cable; a relative in France involved in royal scandal; and Rachel Field. But my agent and my editor at Simon & Schuster both assured me it wasn't commercial because the Fields weren't well-enough known. Both told me, "If their family name had been Ford or Rockefeller, that would have been something."

Yet it seemed to me the Fields were prominent enough.

I also had it in mind to write three astrology-related books. First, an account of my studies under Frawley (playfully titled *The Sorcerer's Apprentice*); second, *Astro-Sleuth: A Young Person's Fiction Series featuring the Use of Classical Astrology in Solving Crime*. It imagined a high school student who writes a Sun-sign astrology column by day for her school paper, but at night uses her in-depth knowledge of traditional ("real") astrology to solve perplexing crimes. Her collaborator is a hard-boiled, maverick police detective. They team up first by accident. Then he starts to bring her the cases he can't solve. My third, related idea was *The Lords of Time: A Primer on Classical Astrology* for the young.

*

When my wife and I bought our house in Vermont in 1996, we noticed an old woodstove in the garage. It was rusted over so we had it sand-blasted and painted with stove-black. It proved to be a handsome hand-crafted Norwegian "Lange" stove, decoratively embossed. On either side was a relief casting of St. Eustace, the patron-saint of huntsmen, kneeling in prayer before a stag whose legs are entwined with the Tree of Life, a Cross between his horns. In the iconography of the Christian tradition, the image symbolized piety and religious aspiration supported by the refuge of mountain heights. That appealed to me greatly and for a decade or so the stove, though old, kept our home warm.

I have always had a fondness for animals, but from my wife I acquired a wonderful appreciation of the animal kingdom in all its aspects and our inescapable obligation to cherish all creatures in our care. Over the years we have cared for many, in a house overrun. Their spirited company, and unconditional love, exemplified that irrepressible zest for life we all long for. I have worked the names of our pets into some of my book dedications and acknowledgement pages. Perhaps one day I'll get to write about them, too.

In Vermont, I also took up the study of T'ai Chi Ch'uan, which had intrigued me since my college days. As a sophomore, I had been introduced to Sophia Delza, a master of the Wu Form, which my stepmother had practiced for many years. Sophia had trained as a dancer; lived for a time in post-war Shanghai, where her husband was involved in relief work; studied under Ma Yueh-Liang (a famous teacher); and upon her return founded the Delza School of T'ai Chi at Carnegie Hall in 1954. She wrote several books on her practice, and it is fair to say that she introduced T'ai Chi to the United States.

She came from a dynamic family. One sister, Elizabeth, was a celebrated dancer; another, Marie Briehl a psychoanalyst who had studied with Anna Freud. Her brother, Leo Hurwitz (whose son was my Columbia classmate) was a documentary filmmaker of note who had made "Native Land" in 1942 narrated by Paul Robeson, about labor struggles in the 1930s, and a film about the Dust Bowl called "The Plow That Broke the Plains."

When I met Sophia, she lived with her husband, Cook Glassgold, a painter, in the Chelsea Hotel. She had an exotic, colorful way of dressing; held peremptory views; corrected her students firmly, in keeping with her own strict standards; and had a heart of gold. My stepmother had studied with her for over a decade and Sophia used to visit us now and then in our Chelsea apartment a few blocks from the Hotel. In the early 1980's, when I was working on my first book, she was looking for a publisher to reissue her classic, *T'ai Chi Ch'uan: Body and Mind in Harmony*, which had long been out of print. I had few contacts then, but through my graphic design work had become acquainted with Leon King, an editor at Schocken Books. Schocken mainly published Judaica, but Leon had some referrals, and in 1985 her book was reissued by the State University of New York at Stony Brook.

In her last years, her classes were sought out by those in the Gurdjieff Work as an adjunct to the movement exercises Gurdjieff had taught.

Sophia's husband, A. Cook Glassgold, was just as remarkable—an accomplished, versatile, civilized man. Over the course of his long life, he had been an artist, editor, labor organizer, musician, Curator of Painting at the Whitney Museum of American Art, and played a leading role in overseas relief efforts after World War II.

A small, spry man of unhurried energy and tremendous will, he was highly knowledgeable without being condescending, and had a precise, friendly manner touched with aristocratic reserve. When he died on his 86th birthday of a heart attack in 1985, his funeral was attended by mourners from all walks of life. All who spoke testified to the depth of his decency and the humanity of his soul. One recalled that when he was attending to his duties in Shanghai, a shipment arrived on the Jewish Sabbath with urgently needed supplies. When his co-workers, in deference to the Sabbath, declined to unload the trucks, he took a crowbar and broke the locks. "Man is not made for the Sabbath, but the Sabbath for Man," as he well understood. Another speaker recalled sharing a room with Cook at a music camp. One afternoon, as they were strolling through the woods, they came upon an old snare set for birds in a tree. They were both eating ice-cream cones and, his friend recalled, "I thoughtlessly left mine in the snare." The next morning before dawn, Cook got up suddenly and said, "We have to go!" They struck out into the woods, came to the tree and, just as Cook had feared, found a bird helplessly flailing in the snare. He gently reached in and freed it. "Now we can go to breakfast," he said.

After he died, Sophia found hidden in a desk—"in a place,"

she told me, "where, according to an old Chinese custom, he knew I would find it"—a letter he had written telling her how much he had loved her, and how much she had meant to him in his life. She told me this story the last time I saw her, when she was about 90, as we were strolling along West 23rd Street near the Chelsea Hotel, her hand still warm and firm, gently clasped in mine.

*

After my last book was published, I put commercial publishing behind me and embraced a frugal retirement enriched by the study of Biblical Greek, the practice of T'ai Chi, a devotion to poetry, religious worship, and contemplation of the stars. It was time. I had written fourteen books, compact with whatever knowledge and understanding I possessed, as I possessed it; and carefully fashioned, with all that my tact and hard work could do. Practically speaking, as a writer, there was no end to the subjects that might have engaged me, but that would have left no room for introspection and repose. The literal weight of past "learning" also wore upon me, as my bones, like the timbers of our house itself, groaned under its sheer poundage. So I donated or dispersed some seven thousand books to libraries and second-hand stores.

And so as this Memoir arose and took shape it my mind, it gave me a chance to make sense of my Self—how I had come to be the way I was, and why I had lived the life I had. I wanted to pay tribute, too, to those who had tried to guide me, or had furnished a good example, whether I had followed it or not. Above all, whenever my time should come, I wanted to depart this world with understanding, not in a dissociated state.

Our house lies five miles outside of town, encompassed by forest, and picturesquely perched on a ridge with terraced gardens that lead down to a valley below. The ridge is made of slate, of an adamantine hardness, and when we put on an addition some years back, it took 100 sticks of dynamite to blast out the cavity where the cement foundation was poured. To prevent rock-fly, huge tarpaulins made of used tires laced together with steel cables were draped across the ground.

My rustic setting suits me. On most mornings I awake to count my blessings and am suffused with that sense of simple good fortune that the Roman poet, Horace, once so nicely described:

> Hoc erat in votis: modus agri non ita magnus,
> hortus ubi et tecto vicinus iugis aquae fons
> et paulum silvae super his foret. auctius atque
> Di melius fecere. bene est. nil amplius oro,
> Maia nate, nisi ut propria haec mihi munera faxis.

In my slightly free translation:

> This is what I prayed for: a modest piece of land,
> with a garden near the house, and a never-failing spring,
> some woodlands too—this much and more
> the gods have granted. I ask for nothing else,
> O son of Maia,* but that these blessings last.

Amen.

---

*Mercury, the god of Fortune

EPILOGUE

THE ARCHER

He bent his bow till both ends met
Just in a circle at his ear,
Then shot: the arrow sang: it set
Its course aloft into the black
And million starry spangled sphere.
Up, up it sang, its perfect track
Was straight, toward what fixed star it flew
Or falling star, its head appeared
(Though who could follow it were few)
A star itself to our rapt view.

But he, soon as that shaft came clear,
New branches into arrows cut,
And fitted them against his ear,
And hitched his bristling quiver up.

—Benson Bobrick,
March 15, 2019

ENDNOTES

Most of the quotations in this book are taken from personal and family papers and correspondence. The Papers of my maternal grandfather, James Chamberlain Baker, are in two main collections: at the Claremont School of Theology in Claremont, California, and the Boston University School of Theology in Boston, Massachusetts. Correspondence between my father and my grandfather, quoted in the book, is at the Boston University School of Theology, as part of my grandfather's archive. My correspondence with George Rochberg is in the Paul Sacher Archives in Basel, Switzerland; my correspondence with Edward W. Tayler in the archives of Columbia University. My correspondence with P.L. Travers remains, for the time being, in my own possession and that of Danielle Woerner. All other material pertaining to my great uncle Charles G. Howard, my father, mother, brother, and all others named form part of my own unplaced Papers, which (I trust) will one day find a home.

Most of the citations below are from published articles and books, with the exception of a few on–line sources. Here and there a letter is specified that is not dated in the text.

CHAPTER ONE

"What use is the right fact": P.L. Travers, *Friend Monkey*, New York: Harcourt, 1971, p. 267.

"some had been in America...Tappan": Benson Bobrick, *Angel in the Whirlwind: The Triumph of the American Revolution*. New York: Simon and Schuster, 1997, p. 12.

"Matthew Benson...floor": Ibid., p. 12–13.

"every third or fourth": Ibid., p. 12.

"in the mechanics of it": Benson Bobrick, *Testament: A Soldier's Story of the Civil War*. New York: Simon and Schuster, 2003, p. 6.

"lived the life...eyes": Ibid., p. 8.

"I ask forgiveness": Quoted in ibid., p. 36.

"I almost feel anxious": Quoted in ibid., p. 44.

"I have seen": Quoted in ibid, p. 46–47.

"It is true": Quoted in ibid., p. 48.

"Though wearied": Ibid., p. 179.

"The tendency": Quoted in ibid., p. 179.

"he was intellectually hungry": Ibid., p. 182.

"With Protestant pride": Ibid., p. 182–183.

"You can more easily": Quoted in ibid., p. 183.

"There was a natural": Ibid., p. 183.

"same love of": Ibid., p. 183.

"the university consisted": Ibid., p. 184.

"the ministry...otherwise": Ibid., P. 184–185.

"disabled from": Quoted in ibid., p. 185.

"He had come a long way": Ibid., p. 185.

"he was often called upon...sacrifice": Ibid., p. 185.

"Dr. Baker impressed himself": Quoted in ibid., p. 186.

"when he first began...epitaph": Ibid., p. 186–187.

CHAPTER THREE

"colorful and stimulating": *Oregon Law Review*, June 1957, Volume 36, No. 4. Article by Orlando John Hollis, p. 336.

"pepper his lectures" and "private understanding": *Eugene Register-Guard*, March 21, 1971, p. 10A

"sweated under": Ibid.

"put into day to day": *Oregon Law Review*, June 1957, Volume 36, No. 4. Article by Orlando John Hollis, p. 336.

"that a member": Ibid.

"push other people": *Eugene Register-Guard*, March 21, 1971, p. 10A

"Son, there is nothing": Quoted in James Stanley Barlow, *Appalachia and Beyond*, "Vignettes from Academe," p. 33.

"Nobody could dislike him": Quoted in Eugene-Register-Guard, March 21, 1971, p. 10A.

"In all its forms": Ibid.

CHAPTER TEN

"You are here to build": Quoted in David Denby, *Great Books*. New York: Simon & Schuster, 1996, p. 31.

CHAPTER ELEVEN

"These are the only lines": Benson Bobrick, *Knotted Tongues: Stuttering in History and the Quest for a Cure*. New York: Simon & Schuster, 1995, p. 17.

"mine was that": Ibid., p. 159.

"I tried to say": Ibid., p. 160.

"Each day": Ibid.

"By the time": Ibid., p. 160-161.

"began to look down": Ibid., p. 161.

CHAPTER THIRTEEN

"part of that remarkable": Linton, Michael. "George Rochberg's Revolution," in *First Things*, June 1998, www.firstthings.com.

"at the very edge": "Rochberg, George." *Contemporary Musicians*. 2006. www.encyclopedia.com.

"America's first and greatest": Liner Notes, "Violin Concerto," *American Classics* CD.

"didn't have to be defended": Linton, "George Rochberg's Revolution," in *First Things*, June 1998, www.firstthings.com.

"Any musician who has not felt": Ibid.

"the cutting, dark": Istvan Anhalt and George Rochberg *Eagle Minds: Selected Correspondence, 1961-2005*. Edited by Alan M. Gillmor. Waterloo, Ontario, Canada: Wilfrid Laurier University Press, 2007, p. 80.

"there could be no justification": Neil W. Levin, "George Rochberg, 1918-2005," *Milken Archive of Jewish Music*, mikenarchive.org.

"Twelve-tone composition": "Tradition and Twelve-Tone Music," Rochberg, *The Aesthetics of Survival. A Composer's View of Twentieth Century Music*. Ann Arbor: The University of Michigan Press, 1984, 2004, p. 30.

"a completely rationalized": Anhalt and Rochberg, *Eagle Minds*, ed. Alan Gillmor, p.xx.

"open, always en route": Rochberg, *Five Lines, Four Spaces: The World of My Music*. Urbana and Chicago: University of Illinois Press, 2009, p. 73.

"energy of pulse": Anhalt and Rochberg, *Eagle Minds*, p. 96.

"Mr. Rochberg's quartet": Donal Henahan, "A Rare New Work Played by Quartet," *The New York Times*, May 17, 1972.

"there is a fire," etc.: Rochberg, "Envoi," *The Aesthetics of Survival*, p. 253.

"with passages of warm": Daniel Webster, "Rochberg's *Concord Quartets*, *The Philadelphia Inquirer*, January 22, 1979.

"gorgeously harmonized," etc. Raymond Erickson, "The *Concord Quartets*," *The New York Times*, January 23, 1979.

"hard to think of": Herbert Kupferberg, "A King of Quartets to Crown a Jubilee, *The Detroit News*, January 28, 1979.

"The serialists really should": Joan DeVee Dixon, *George Rochberg: A Bio-Bibliographical Guide To His Life and Works*. Stuyvesant, New York: Pendragon Press, 1992, p. xxvi.

"demonstrations or illustrations": Rochberg, *Five Lines, Four Spaces*, p. 106.

"stylistic efforts": Anhalt and Rochberg, *Eagle Minds*, p. 6.

"rested on thinly": Rochberg, *Five Lines, Four Spaces*, p. 261.

"incapable of expressing": Dixon, op. cit., p. xxv.

"opened the way": "George Rochberg," Theodore Presser Company, www.presser.com (July 6, 2005).

"had a soft spot": Composer's Notes to *American Bouquet*, CD, Arabesque Recordings, 2000.

"Ideas had gone": Robinson Jeffers, quoted in Melba Berry Bennett, *The Stone Mason of Tor House: The Life and Work of Robinson Jeffers*. Los Angeles: Ward Ritchie, 1966, p. 76. Also: *Robinson Jeffers and a Galaxy of Writers: Essays in Honor of William H. Nolte*, p. 58, n. 4.

"Modernism ended up": Dixon, *George Rochberg*, p. xxvi; Martin Anderson, "George Rochberg, Powerful composer," obituary, The Independent, July 1, 2005.

"leaving the mind": Anhalt and Rochberg, *Eagle Minds*, p. 147.

CHAPTER FOURTEEN

"It was as if . . . extra distance": Franz Kafka, *Diaries*, p. 404.

"Once more in Aries": James Bobrick, *Throwbacks: Selected Poems*, New Bedford, MA: Spinner Publications, Inc., 2005, p. 21.

"Scared sick": Ibid., p. 42.

"Shivering in her hues": Ibid., p. 41.

CHAPTER FIFTEEN

"Every position on any issue": The United States vs. The National Committee for Impeachment, 469 F. 2d 1135, Docket No. 309, CourtListener.com. Court of Appeals for the Second Circuit. Argued September 26, 1972, before Paul Raymond Hays, James Lowell Oakes, and William Homer Timbers, Circuit Judges. Decided October 30, 1972. Oakes delivered the ruling.

"I had seen": *Knotted Tongues*, p. 163.

"a series of": Quoted in ibid., p. 173.

"For a stutterer": Ibid.

"loci of efffects": Quoted in ibid., p.172.

"There are many": Ibid., p. 176.

CHAPTER SIXTEEN

"The cauldron of plenty": "Zen Moments: Sunt Lachrymae Rerum," in P.L. Travers, *What The Bee Knows*. New Paltz, NY: Codhill Press Reprint, 2010, p. 202.

"cheerfully licked": "Only Connect," in ibid., p. 290.

"gallivanting around": Ibid., p. 291.

"The Dark Fortnight": *The Irish Statesman*, January 29, 1927.

"Coming Toward Meadows": "*The Irish Statesman*," November 17, 1928.

"poetic merit": "From the Brothers Grimm Newsletter," Vol. Four, Issue Two, p. 2.

"his housekeeper": Quoted by Griswold, "Remembrances: Revealing Herself to Herself," *LA Times*, June 16, 1966.

"Child in the manger laid": "A Christmas Song For a Child," in *What The Bee Knows*, p. 260.

"a colorful entertainment": Quoted in *A Lively Oracle*, edited by Ellen Dooling Draper and Jenny Koralek. New York: Larson Publications, 1999, p. 51.

"What wand": Quoted in ibid., p. 53.

"By indirections find directions out": *Hamlet*, Act 2, Scene 1, line 65.

"If it is literature indeed": "On Not Writing For Children," *Children's Literature*, Vol. 4. Philadelphia: Temple University Press, 1975, p. 15–22.

"the automatically growing": "The Fairy-Tale and Teacher," *A Lively Oracle*, p. 201.

"If one was willing": Letter to the author, July 6, 1985.

"There are times": Edwin Muir, *Autobiography*. St. Paul, Minnesota: Graywolf Press, 1990, p. 105.

"For the life of every": Ibid., p. 49.

"to work *with*": Letter of February 21, 1984.

"climb up through": *What The Bee Knows*, p. 193.

"I must live over again": Quoted in Robert Richman, "Edwin Muir's Journey," *The New Criterion*, April 1997.

"Good . . . . in life as in story": "The Black Sheep," in *What The Bee Knows*," p. 230.

"there are no rights": "Letter to a Learned Astrologer," in ibid., p. 54.

"puts his foot": "The World of the Hero," in ibid., p. 16.

"Accept everything": Interview with Jonathan Cott, *A Lively Oracle*, p.158.

"moral virtue": "The Unsleeping Eye," in *What The Bee Knows*, p. 191.

"Dear Danielle and Barry": Letter to the author, September 21, 1976.

"Let ideas just": Letter to the author, July 26, 1977.

"to remember the Labyrinth": Ibid.

"descending into the Underworld": Letter to the author, January 13, 1982.

"gentle" and "so terrible after all": Letter to the author, July 6, 1987.

"It will make the bread," etc.: Letter to the author, March 18, 1982.

"good": Letter to the author, July 21, 1981.

"wanting to rest," etc.: Ibid.

"It was a very moving," etc.: Letter to the author, March 18, 1982.

"It has been a difficult": Letter to the author, July 6, 1985.

"limb by limb": John Milton, *Areopagitica*, paragraph 26.

"None of us can help": Eugene O'Neill, *Long Day's Journey Into Night*. New Haven: Yale University Press, 1962, Act Two, Scene One, p. 61

CHAPTER SEVENTEEN

"to a degree . . . merciles": Benson Bobrick, *Fearful Majesty: The Life and Reign of Ivan the Terrible*. New York: G.P. Putnam's Sons, 1987; reissued by Russian Life Books, Monpelier, Vermont, 2014, p. 15–17.

CHAPTER EIGHTEEN

"In 1890, a Jewish-Hungarian immigrant, etc.": Based in part on the archival hisory document I drafed as a narrative summary in 1989. Others involved in the research were Kathleen McDermott, George Smith, and David Dyer.

CHAPTER TWENTY

"the 'middle science'": Alan J. Ouimet, O.F.S., The Condemnation of Astrology and the Secret Vatican Archives and Pope Sixtus V. www.Academia.edu

"the birth-chart deals": John Frawley, *The Real Astrology Applied*. London, ENG: Apprentice Books, 2002, p. 139.

"Saturn offers wisdom: John Frawley, *The Real Astrology*. London, ENG: Apprentice Books, 2000, p. 123–124.

"Rather than the life": Frawley, *The Real Astrology Applied*, p. 142.

CHAPTER TWENTY-ONE

"scores, journals": Letter to the author, June 11, 1996.

"indefinable and ineffable," etc.: Letter to the author, September 29, 1997.

"general distaste," "narrow–chested," and "talking outloud": Anhalt and Rochberg, *Eagle Minds*, p.212.

"unfolds as a spiraling" and "blowing his horn": Composer's Notes to Symphony No. 5.

"built into us": "Rochberg, *The Aesthetics of Survival*, p. 160.

"There is the finality": G.K. Chesterton, *The Everlasting Man*. San Francisco: Ignatius Press, 1993 Reprint, p. 264.

"The higher the intelligence": Herman Melville, *Mardi*. New York: Signet Classics, p. 251.

"a series of disconnected": Anhalt and Rochberg, *Eagle Minds*, p.235, fn.8.

"As I got to know George": Tribute provided to the author by Marcantonio Barone. Reproduced by permission.

CHAPTER TWENTY-FOUR

"I have always felt": *The Complete Works of W.H. Auden: 1969–1973*, Vol. 6, Princeton, NJ: Princeton University Press, p. 514.

"All the miracles": St. Augustine, *The City of God*. New York: Penguin Classics, Book X, Chapter 12, p. 1043.

ABOUT THE TYPE

The text is set in Minion. Designed by
Robert Slimbach in 1990, it was inspired
by late Renaissance-era type and is intended
for body text and extended reading.

Part pages are set in Perpetua. Designed by
English sculptor and stonemason Eric Gill in 1925,
it is often used in dedications and memorials.

Made in the USA
Middletown, DE
26 August 2019